Learn Polish

A Comprehensive Guide to Learning Polish for Beginners, Including Grammar, Short Stories and 1000 Popular Phrases

Contents

Part 1: Polish

Learn Polish for Beginners: A Simple Guide that Will Help You on Your Language Learning Journey

Introduction

Congratulations on making the life-changing decision to learn a foreign language. Knowing another language has recently become one of the most valuable skills to have, and not only in the job market. Due to the globalization and the fast development of technology, the whole world has become an interconnected web. Today, we work in multinational companies, take part in international webinars, and travel to the most beautiful places in the world. No one can imagine going abroad without knowing a tiny bit of English or the local language. Thus, the decision to learn a foreign language, especially an "exotic one", seems to be one of the best investments you can make. Plus, the investment can be made without huge sums of money—as long as you stick to affordable yet reliable and informative sources (like this book!).

Your decision to learn a foreign language is a bit more specific—as you decided to learn Polish. However, whatever your motivation for doing so, you won't be disappointed. Before you immerse yourself in learning, let's get familiarized with some basic information about both the country of Poland and the Polish language.

The country of Poland has existed since 966 AD—the year of declaring Christianity as a national religion by the first Polish king.

Poland is located in Central Europe and shares its borders with Germany on the west, the Czech Republic and Slovakia in the south and Ukraine, Belarus, Lithuania and a bit of Russia on the east. In the north, it has access to the Baltic Sea (around 400 km of the coastline).

Polish is certainly not one of the most spoken languages in the world—since it is the official language of Poland exclusively. It has around 38 million speakers in Poland, but many immigrants in countries such as the USA, UK, Germany, Norway, and Ireland are Polish. The Polish Community Abroad includes, for example, more than one million Poles in the UK and nearly one million in the States. What is also interesting is that many Americans are of Polish origin—due to the mass emigration caused by the difficult political situation in Poland in the 18th and 19th centuries.

Many native speakers of English consider Polish (along with Chinese, Arabic and Japanese) as one of the hardest languages to learn due to its heavy inflectional system and, probably, pronunciation. It may be partially true; however, the beginning is always the toughest part of any language journey, yet speaking one of the hardest languages in the world is quite an achievement.

Polish is a Slavic language, yet its written form is not based on the Cyrillic alphabet but the Latin script. Therefore, the Polish sounds can be tough to learn, especially some unusual consonant clusters like *szcz* or *dźdż*. However, the more you practice the pronunciation, the more automatic it becomes. Furthermore, the beginning is always the hardest part of any language journey since your first language data interferes with the new data that comes into your mind.

This book will teach you the vocabulary and grammar basics, along with some cultural background. With just fifteen-twenty minutes of practice a day, you will be able to have a decent conversation in the target language, and your use of Polish will improve.

Now let's take a look at some features of Polish that English speakers might find unusual and are not familiar with:

• The Polish language contains seven cases (nominative, genitive, dative, accusative, ablative, locative, and vocative). The cases might make the process of learning a little overwhelming at the beginning, but there's nothing to be afraid of.

• The Polish gender system is very different from the English one—since gender in Polish is grammatical, whereas it is biological in English. For instance, the Polish word *stół* [table] is masculine, *książka* [book] is feminine, and *jajko* [egg] is neutral.

• Polish is a highly inflectional language— it means that nouns, verbs and other parts of speech can have different endings or prefixes, depending on the case, gender, number, tense, and other features.

• Due to the abundance of inflections, Polish sentences can be created in multiple ways. Unlike English, Polish does not require a fixed order (such as subject + verb + object). Although there are more popular patterns, you can place each word in a sentence randomly, and it will be grammatically correct (of course, there are some minor exceptions).

• All Polish women's first names end with the vowel "a", except for the ones with foreign origin.

• Polish shares many grammatical and lexical features with the other Slavic languages, such as Czech or Slovak.

• Because of the influence of the inflectional system, Polish people add inflections to foreign names. For instance, you can notice different suffixes added to Harry Potter or Spiderman in different cases (like Harrego Pottera, Spidermana, Harremu Potterowi, Spidermanowi, etc.).

• There are only three grammatical tenses in Polish—past, future, and present. The rules of forming tenses are quite different too—since tenses are created by adding a suffix or a prefix in most cases.

- Polish people put a lot of stress on formal forms of address. It is highly advisable to address a person you don't know or your boss/teacher with a word *Pan/Pani* instead of just *you*. Addressing someone by using the *you* form in situations like a job interview or a formal meeting is considered rude.

Before getting into the actual learning, you need to know that this book is not a grammatical textbook. It is meant to teach you the basics of Polish to give you the foundations, and at the same time, make your learning fun, straightforward, easy, and enjoyable. Long and boring foreign language classes at school are probably things of the past—and you don't want to go back to the textbooks full of tough exercises and lists of words to memorize for a test. This book will provide you not only with the knowledge about the language but also with some cultural background based on real-life experiences.

The book consists of several chapters divided into subchapters that explain some grammatical rules, teach vocabulary, and provide you with some exercises based on repetition and using logical thinking and creativity. You can expect some exercises that will make you recall knowledge that you have already acquired while learning from the previous chapters. Thus, it is advisable to start from the beginning in order to make the most of the learning program included. Without further ado, let's get straight into the learning.

Good luck!

Chapter 1 – The Very Basics

To make the process of learning fast, fun and enjoyable, let's equip you with some general information about the Polish language—several basic rules of creating a sentence, some essential vocabulary, and a handful of useful expressions. Learning can run smoothly, provided that the process is ordered in some way. In other words, it is better to learn the basic units at the beginning, and then go to the advanced structures. Thus, let's introduce the Polish pronouns.

Pronouns

English appears to contain only a few personal pronouns when compared to Polish. Why? The answer is pretty simple: Polish personal pronouns are inflected by case, gender, and number. Think for a moment about the English personal pronouns. What are they? You probably know that there are only three ways of using an English pronoun; for example, *me, my* and *mine* or *you, your* and *yours*.

Polish pronouns are quite different since each pronoun has not three but seven different forms. Why? Each pronoun looks different in each case (as mentioned earlier, there are seven cases in the Polish language). Pronouns look different not only in different cases but also in different genders and numbers. For now, let's stop theoretical explanations and see how Polish pronouns work in practice. You are about to learn the basic Polish pronouns:

Ja – I

Ty – you

On – he

Ona – she

Ono – it

My – we

Wy – you

Oni/one – they

These pronouns are in the so-called nominative case. It means that they are in primary form. To be more precise, they are just equivalents of the English ones—they have the same meaning. Now, let's repeat the Polish pronouns. Try to focus on pronunciation.

Ja – I

Ty – you

On – he

Ona – she

Ono – it

My – we

Wy – you

Oni/one – they

You have probably noticed that the last pronoun, *they,* has two different forms in Polish. *Oni* is for masculine, and *one* is for the feminine. You can use *oni* when you refer to a group of men and *one* when you refer to a group of women. When the group consists of men and women, you always use *oni.* To sum up, *oni* is a more general pronoun—it can refer to a group of men or mixed groups—but *one* can refer only to a group of women.

Exercise: Try to guess the Polish pronouns based on the English equivalents:

I

You

He

She

It

We

You

They

Now let's try to do the same exercise once again but in a random order:

You

She

They

I

He

You

It

We

Congratulations! You have just learned the basic set of Polish pronouns. The last thing to remember is the distinction between the masculine and feminine pronoun *they*. It is vital to know the difference from the beginning—since the pronoun *they* is a classic example of interference between languages, so it can be harder to acquire.

Let's try another exercise:

How do you refer to the group of men?

How do you refer to the group of women?

How do you refer to the group of men and women?

Having learned the Polish pronouns, let's move on to the next step.

Być - to be

Knowing only some pronouns will not take you far. In order to make a first proper sentence, we need two ingredients—a subject (that can be a pronoun that you've already learned) and a verb. Thus, let's teach you one of the most important verbs: *być* [to be]. Before we start, let's brush up on the Polish pronouns. Try to guess the Polish pronoun based on the English one:

I

You

He

She

It

We

You

They

The Polish verb być [to be] will be a piece of cake. Let's see how it works:

Ja jestem - I am

Ty jesteś - you are

On jest - he is

Ona jest - she is

Ono jest - it is

My jesteśmy - we are

Wy jesteście - you are

Oni/one są – they are

The Polish verb *być* [to be] is not that irregular as the English one. It looks totally different in the last option—with the pronoun *oni/one* [they]. Although *być* is not that difficult, it requires some exercise to make itself comfortable in your mind. Let's repeat everything and try some exercises:

Ja jestem – I am

Ty jesteś – you are

On jest – he is

Ona jest – she is

Ono jest – it is

My jesteśmy – we are

Wy jesteście – you are

Oni/one są – they are

Exercise: Try to guess the verb *być* based on the English equivalents.

I am

you are

he is

she is

it is

we are

you are

Oni/one – są

Let's randomize the order a little:

You are

She is

They are

I am

He is

You are

It is

We are

Before we move on to the next level and try to add another ingredient to our sentence, let's explore something interesting. Polish verbs don't require the pronoun in a sentence. In other words, you don't have to say *ja jestem* [I am] to be fully understood. Instead, you can say *jestem* [I am], and it will be perfectly fine. You can omit the pronoun because the ending in *być* carries all the necessary information about the person or the doer of the activity. As mentioned, this rule applies to all Polish verbs, but now let's focus on *być*.

Let's see how the process works in practice:

jestem – I am

jesteś – you are

jest – he is

jest – she is

jest – it is

jesteśmy – we are

jesteście – you are

są – they are

Exercise: Try to guess the English equivalent based on the Polish form of *być*:

jestem

jesteś

jest

jest

jest

jesteśmy

jesteście

są

Congratulations! You have just learned the essential ingredient of the Polish language that will make your learning go smooth and easy. As promised, let's move on to the next level.

Formal pronouns

Before you are introduced to the formal pronouns, you need to know that formality and keeping the distance is a thing in Poland. Polish people use polite forms a lot in formal situations. For example, it is impossible to imagine a Polish student addressing their teacher using *ty* [you]. There is a general Polish rule that says, "If you don't know a person, it is advisable to use a formal form of address." Otherwise, your behavior might be considered rude. If you know a person, yet he/she is not a member of your family, a co-worker or a friend, use formal forms of address too. If you have known someone for a while in Poland, you can suggest "*przejście na ty*", which literally means "*switching to you [form]*".

So what are the formal pronouns that you should definitely know and use daily in Poland? Here they are:

You (singular) – Pan/Pani

You (plural) – Panowie/Panie/Państwo

Let's look at the distinction between feminine and masculine in the singular form of *you*. You can use *Pan* if you want to address a man, and *Pani* if you want to address a woman. Now, let's focus on the distinction in the plural form of *you*. You can use *Panowie* if you address a group of men, *Panie* when you address a group of women and *Państwo* when you address a mixed group or a couple (for example a married couple). To sum up, we have a set of formal forms of address, and they have their own distinctions based on gender. Since they are not only quite a mess but also absent in the English language, let's do some exercises.

Exercise: Try to come up with the correct answer.

How do you address one woman?

How do you address one man?

How do you address a group of men?

How do you address a married couple?

How do you address a group of women?

How do you address your teacher (female)?

How do you address your boss (male)?

How do you address an old lady?

How do you address your friend's parents?

How do you address a female shop assistant?

How do you address a policeman?

It was a demanding exercise since it required you to imagine a real situation, yet, as previously mentioned, a pronoun is not the whole story. We need at least a verb to produce something meaningful and functional. When we use the *you* form, we treat it as a second person singular or a second person plural. However, formal forms of address act like a third person singular. First, let's look at the *you* form (informal):

You are (singular) – ty jesteś

You are (plural) – wy jesteście

Now, let's focus on the formal forms of address. They look like this:

You are (singular) – Pan/Pani jest

You are (plural) – Panowie/Panie/Państwo są

To sum up, if you decide to use a formal form of address, you no longer use a verb that corresponds with a second person. Instead, you switch to a form of a third person. Since this phenomenon is quite challenging, let's do some exercises.

Exercise: Try to guess the Polish forms of address and their corresponding *to be* verb based on the English equivalents and the context provided. Remember that you have to switch to the third person in Polish! Take your time, and don't get discouraged. This is a tough exercise since it is based on an element that doesn't exist in English. Try to imagine the situation.

You are – a woman

You are – a group of men

You are – a married couple

You are – a man

You are – your boss (male)

You are – your teacher (female)

You are – an old man

You are – your friend's parents

You are – a policeman

You are – a waitress

You are – two men

You are – two women

It was a hard exercise! Now, you have gained more opportunities just by learning a handful of very basic language items. Let's take you a level higher!

Questions

It is time to ask some questions using the newly acquired verb *być* [to be]. As far as English is concerned, a question is formed in the process of inversion. You just make a subject (for example a pronoun) and a verb switch their places, and that's it. In Polish, a question can be formed in various ways. The first way of forming a question is based on using a special word *czy*–something that acts like the English *do* in questions, such as *do you like*? etc. Let's look at the examples:

Am I? – Czy (ja) jestem?

Are you? – Czy (ty) jesteś?

Is he? – Czy (on) jest?

Is she? – Czy (ona) jest?

Is it? – Czy (ono) jest?

Are we? – Czy (my) jesteśmy?

Are you? – Czy (wy) jesteście?

Are they? – Czy (oni/one) są?

So the Polish pattern is as follows. Firstly, we have to say *czy*, then we say a person (a pronoun in this case), and at the end, we say the verb *być*. The good news is that the form of *być* remains unchanged in questions. What is more, saying a person is totally optional–sometimes it is better to avoid mentioning a subject since it may sound unnatural. Let's try some exercises. For the exercise you are about to do, let's use the pronoun in questions.

Exercise: Try to build a question using *czy*, *być,* and a pronoun based on the English questions.

Am I? –

Are you? –

Is he? –

Is she? –

Is it? –

Are we? –

Are you? –

Are they? –

Now, let's randomize the order a little.

Are we? –

Am I? –

Is he? –

Are they? –

Is she? –

Are you? –

Is it? –

Are you? –

Remember what was previously mentioned about the questions at the beginning? There are different ways of forming a question in Polish. The second way doesn't require using the special word *czy* that acts like an interrogative word. It requires only the verb and nothing else, yet if you want to use this form, you have to change your intonation. When asking a question with only a verb, you must use rising intonation. Let's see the examples to make everything clear:

Am I? – jestem?

Are you? – jesteś?

Is he? – jest?

Is she? – jest?

Is it? – jest?

Are we? – jesteśmy?

Are you? – jesteście?

Are they? – są?

Now you are familiar with the most common way of asking questions in spoken Polish. Yes, Polish people usually don't use the first way when they speak. To make a conversation smooth and efficient, they prefer the second way based on changing the intonation. It is time you practiced your intonation too.

Exercise: Try to form a question using a rising intonation based on the English equivalents.

Am I? –

Are you? –

Is he? –

Is she? –

Is it? –

Are we? –

Are you? –

Are they? –

Let's try in a random order:

Are we? –

Am I? –

Is he? –

Are they? –

Is she? –

Are you? –

Is it? –

Are you? –

You have just learned how to ask a question in Polish. However, remember that most of the time, you will be faced with strangers; thus, it is advisable to ask a question with some formal forms of address. Remember that the formal forms switch from the second person to the third person. Here you can use only the first way—the one with the special interrogative word *czy*. Let's analyze the examples:

Are you (singular)? – Czy Pan/Pan jest?

Are you (plural)? – Czy Panowie/Panie/Państwo są?

It is time to practice the formal ways of asking a question. Again, imagine a situation and choose one suitable option. Focus on proper pronunciation.

Exercise: Try to form formal questions based on the English equivalents and the context provided. Remember that you have to switch to the third person in Polish!

Are you? – a woman that you've just met in a park

Are you? – a man that is sitting next to you on a train

Are you? – a female shop assistant

Are you? – your friend's parents

Are you? – your host family

Are you? – your IT teacher

Are you? – your boss

Are you? – a woman that works in a tourist information center

Are you? – a doctor

Are you? – two men that are talking

Are you? – two women that you are talking with

Are you? – a couple that you are talking with

With some essential vocabulary that you are going to learn in the following chapters, you will be confident enough to get creative with the questions you have learned here. Let's go to another level!

Negatives

Stop for a moment and summarize what you have already learned. If you've got to this stage, you probably know Polish pronouns with their formal equivalents, the most important verb—*być* [to be]—and how to ask a question. Congratulations! Let's take you to another step—expressing negatives in Polish. To learn how to create negative forms of *być*, let's go back to the positive forms. Try to do this quick and easy introductory exercise.

Exercise: Try to guess the Polish form *być* based on the English equivalents. If you are confident enough, you don't have to use pronouns.

I am –

You are –

He is –

She is –

It is –

We are –

You are –

They are –

This quick exercise should have shown you how easy the process of forming negatives is. If you want to create a negative form, you just add the word *nie* to the verb, and that is it! Polish *nie* means *no* and is used also as a negative word in a sentence. Let's look at some examples.

TIP: Remember that the pronoun is optional.

I am not – (ja) nie jestem

You aren't – (ty) nie jesteś

He isn't – (on) nie jest

She isn't – (ona) nie jest

It isn't – (ono) nie jest

We aren't – (my) nie jesteśmy

You aren't – (wy) nie jesteście

They aren't – (oni) nie są

Now it is time to practice a little. Let's do some quick and easy exercises.

Exercise: Try to guess negative forms of *być* (you should be confident enough to do it in a randomized order now):

You aren't -

She isn't -

They aren't -

I am not -

You aren't -

It isn't -

He isn't -

We aren't -

Before we move on to the next level, let's explore how to express negatives with formal pronouns. Remember what was previously mentioned at the beginning about the formal forms of address and their form? They act like a third person, not the second person. Let's take a look at some formal pronouns accompanied by a negative form of *być*:

You (singular) aren't - Pan/Pani nie <u>jest</u>

You (plural) aren't - Panowie/Panie/Państwo nie są

To sum up, formal forms of address in negative expressions are based on the same rule—you just add the word *nie* before the verb. Nevertheless, you have to remember that it is no longer the second person singular. Let's try a short exercise.

Exercise: Try to come up with 'formal negatives' based on the English equivalents and the context provided:

You aren't - a male shop assistant

You aren't - a couple you've just met on the train

You aren't - a woman that is sitting next to you on the bus

You aren't - a group of people that have just come to your company to see your boss

You aren't - your boss (female)

Well done! You know Polish pronouns, one of the most essential verbs and formal forms of address that you will be using a lot in Poland. Before we move on to some real context, let's look at some challenging exercises that summarize everything you have acquired.

A short Revision

Exercise 1: Try to form Polish expressions based on the English equivalents. You can use long or short forms.

She is -

It isn't -

Are they? -

He isn't -

I am -

Are you? -

They aren't -

You are -

She isn't -

We aren't -

It is -

I am not -

Are they? -

We are -

He is -

Is it? -

Exercise 2: Based on what you have learned in this chapter, try to guess whether the person requires a formal form of address.

Your close friend that you've known a lifetime

Your new boss

Your friend's parents you're seeing for the first time

Your parents

Your teacher

A shop assistant

Your brother

A stranger that you want to ask for directions

Your grandma

A policeman

A waiter

Your boyfriend/girlfriend

Exercise 3: Try to use the Polish *pronoun + to be* expression based on the English equivalents and the context provided. It is your task to decide whether a particular person requires a formal form of address. Take your time and focus on the task as this requires using your imagination!

You are – Your close friend that you've known a lifetime

Are you? – Your new boss

You aren't – Your friend's parents you're seeing for the first time

Are you? – Your parents

You aren't – Your teacher

You are – A shop assistant

Are you? – Your brother

You aren't – A stranger that you want to ask for directions

You are – Your grandma

Are you? – A policeman

You are – A waiter

You aren't – Your boyfriend/girlfriend

Now let's go up another level!

Introducing Oneself

As you go through the learning in this book, do all the exercises, and focus on each task, you will notice some positive effects. Think for a moment about all the stuff that you have already learned and take your time.

Now it is time to teach you how to introduce yourself and begin a simple conversation. We won't be covering detailed questions and answers—as you will learn more in the other chapters. For now, let's just see how you can say your name.

The most common pattern of introducing yourself in Polish is as follows: You say, *"Jestem* [I am]*"* and add your name. You have already learned the verb *być* [to be], so introducing yourself won't be a problem.

Exercise: Try to introduce yourself in Polish.

The second way of introducing yourself is saying, *"Mam na imię"* and adding your name. *Mam na imię* can be translated as *My name is.*

Exercise: Try to introduce yourself in Polish using *mam na imię.*

You can, of course, say your full name—your first name + last name. To do that, you cannot use *mam na imię*; you have to use *nazywam się* and add your name.

Exercise: Try to introduce yourself in Polish using *nazywam się.*

Now you have learned how to introduce yourself. When it comes to informal situations, use *jestem* or *mam na imię* phrases. It is better to use *nazywam się* and say your full name in formal situations.

Saying your name is a good start, yet it is better to know the question too. You need to understand at least that someone is asking you to introduce yourself! Actually, there are two ways of asking someone. You can use *jak masz na imię?* to know someone's first name or you can use *jak się nazywasz?* to know someone's full name.

When you hear *jak masz na imię?* you can say *jestem* + your name or *mam na imię* + your name. When you hear *jak się nazywasz?* you usually say *nazywam się* + your full name. Let's make these phrases work in practice.

Exercise: Try to answer in Polish these questions.

Jak masz na imię?

Jak się nazywasz?

Jak masz na imię?

Jak się nazywasz?

You can now introduce yourself in Polish or ask someone about his/her name! It is good to know that you don't have to use *jestem/mam na imię or nazywam się* all the time. You can just say your name or full name, and it will be fine! Sometimes it is even better to say only a name without a phrase because it makes your language use less artificial.

Let's summarize your conversation skills. Someone has just asked you to introduce yourself, and you successfully replied. What is the next step? You have to ask the person about his/her name. You can do it using the phrase *a ty?* which literally means *and you?* Let's try to do it!

Exercise: Try to introduce yourself and ask someone to introduce himself/herself.

We are not done with introductory questions. We need to learn some formal stuff that will be even more useful since it is Poland, remember? As previously mentioned, it is better to use *nazywam się* in a more serious conversation—since Polish people almost always say the full name in formal situations.

To ask someone to introduce himself/herself formally, you need to use patterns:

Jak się Pan/Pani nazywa? – What is your name?

Now imagine a situation and try to ask someone about his/her name. Let's provide some context, yet you will have to decide whether it is formal or not and use the most suitable way of asking this question.

Exercise: Try to ask about a person's name based on the provided context.

A new person in your class

Your father's friend from school

Your new teacher

Your new boss

A random person you've just met in a restaurant

A new member of your sports team

A new coworker

A policeman

Great! You are making your first steps towards having a decent conversation in Polish!

Chapter 2 – Numbers

Numbers in Polish may seem a little tricky at the beginning, but don't worry. We'll show you how to hack your way through this complex numeric system so that you will conclude that it wasn't as black as it was painted.

Numbers 0–10

Let's start with something fairly easy—how to count from 0 to 10. Your task is to say all the numbers out loud.

TIP: Focus on proper pronunciation.

zero – zero

one – jeden

two – dwa

three – trzy

four – cztery

five – pięć

six – sześć

seven – siedem

eight – osiem

nine - dziewięć

ten - dziesięć

Now, let's do that again, a little slower this time. Repeat all the numbers twice.

zero - zero, zero

one - jeden, jeden

two - dwa, dwa

three - trzy, trzy

four - cztery, cztery

five - pięć, pięć

six - sześć, sześć

seven - siedem, siedem

eight - osiem, osiem

nine - dziewięć, dziewięć

ten - dziesięć, dziesięć

TIP: The more times you say all the words out loud, the faster you will learn.

Next, try to repeat all the numbers one by one.

zero

zero, jeden

zero, jeden, dwa

zero, jeden, dwa, trzy

zero, jeden, dwa, trzy, cztery

zero, jeden, dwa, trzy, cztery, pięć

Stop here for a moment. Take a deep breath and repeat all those numbers once more. From 0 to 5.

zero, jeden, dwa, trzy, cztery, pięć

Let's continue counting.

zero, jeden, dwa, trzy, cztery, pięć, sześć

zero, jeden, dwa, trzy, cztery, pięć, sześć, siedem

zero, jeden, dwa, trzy, cztery, pięć, sześć, siedem, osiem

zero, jeden, dwa, trzy, cztery, pięć, sześć, siedem, osiem, dziewięć

zero, jeden, dwa, trzy, cztery, pięć, sześć, siedem, osiem, dziewięć, dziesięć

Repeat the numbers several times if you need to.

At this point, you may have noticed that Polish is full of hissing sounds—impossible to pronounce when you are a beginner. However, they represent the pure essence of this language. Okay, are you ready for some practice? Let's use the numbers!

Exercise 1: What is your telephone number? – Jaki jest Twój numer telefonu?

One of the primary uses of numbers from 0 to 10 is when you are talking about phone numbers.

In Poland, the format of a mobile phone number is nine digits divided into three parts. Therefore, when somebody asks a Polish person for their phone number, they usually reply with three 3-digit numbers, e.g., 609-345-812 (six hundred and nine, three hundred and forty-five, eight hundred and twelve).

For this practice, we'll show you the easy way, which is also commonly used in Poland. When you learn bigger numbers, we will go back to this subject again.

If you want to ask someone what their phone number is, you simply say:

Jaki jest Twój numer telefonu?

Take a moment to repeat this phrase several times.

Jaki jest Twój numer telefonu?

A person may reply:

Mój numer telefonu to...

Or simply start dictating their phone number.

Let's try it now. You shall be asked a question, and you will answer with *"mój numer telefonu to..."* and give your number:

Jaki jest Twój numer telefonu?
Mój numer telefonu to...

Let's do it again.

Jaki jest Twój numer telefonu?
Mój numer telefonu to...

Easy, isn't it? Do you want to spice it up a little? You shall be provided with three different phone numbers in English. You simply have to translate them into Polish:

509-432-611
812-790-665
608-419-723

Exercise 2 – Plus and minus – Plus i minus

We will continue our practice with some simple calculations. The purpose of this exercise is for your brain to be able to name random numbers without thinking about them too much. You want to skip the whole in-head translation, and this will definitely help.

Let's start with a couple of phrases.

When you want to ask how much a number *plus* another number is, you say:

Ile jest 2 plus 3? – How much is 2 plus 3?

To reply, you say:

2 plus 3 to jest 5. – 2 plus 3 is 5.

When you want to ask how much a number *minus* another number is, you say:

Ile jest 7 minus 1? - How much is 7 minus 1?

To reply, you say:

7 minus 1 to jest 6. - 7 minus 1 is 6.

Here are ten simple examples, and your task is to calculate the result and answer with a full sentence.

Ile jest 10 - 4?
Ile jest 1 + 1?
Ile jest 4 + 3?
Ile jest 9 - 6?
Ile jest 5 + 5?
Ile jest 4 - 2?
Ile jest 8 - 3?
Ile jest 1 + 8?
Ile jest 9 - 5?
Ile jest 2 + 6?

Feel free to practice more if you need to.

Next, you will learn the numbers from 11 to 20.

Numbers 11–20

It is about time to fill your number vocabulary with some "big fish"— expect even more hissing sounds.

eleven - jedenaście

twelve - dwanaście

thirteen - trzynaście

fourteen - czternaście

fifteen - piętnaście

sixteen - szesnaście

seventeen - siedemnaście

eighteen - osiemnaście

nineteen - dziewiętnaście

twenty - dwadzieścia

Have you noticed that all numbers from 11 to 19 end with *naście*? It means more or less *teen* in English. Makes sense, huh?

The majority of them are also constructed in a very simple way— that is a number from 1 to 9 + *naście*.

Now, repeat those numbers again, a little slower this time.

eleven - jedenaście

twelve - dwanaście

thirteen - trzynaście

fourteen - czternaście

fifteen - piętnaście

sixteen - szesnaście

seventeen - siedemnaście

eighteen - osiemnaście

nineteen - dziewiętnaście

twenty - dwadzieścia

How about you repeat all the numbers now from 0 to 20? Repeat all of them at least twice.

zero - zero

one - jeden

two - dwa

three - trzy

four - cztery

five - pięć

six - sześć

seven - siedem

eight – osiem

nine – dziewięć

ten – dziesięć

eleven – jedenaście

twelve – dwanaście

thirteen – trzynaście

fourteen – czternaście

fifteen – piętnaście

sixteen – szesnaście

seventeen – siedemnaście

eighteen – osiemnaście

nineteen – dziewiętnaście

twenty – dwadzieścia

Let's put it into practice now.

Exercise 1

This exercise is divided into two parts. In the first, you will be asked to translate the numbers into Polish. In the second, you will continue with simple calculations to keep your brain at top speed. Here we go!

Translate the following numbers into Polish:

seventeen

eleven

thirteen

twenty

eighteen

twelve

fifteen

nineteen

sixteen

fourteen

Finish the following sentences. Calculate the result.

10 + 9 to jest...
3 + 10 to jest...
20 - 3 to jest...
8 + 8 to jest...
19 - 7 to jest...
12 - 1 to jest...
15 + 5 to jest...
10 + 8 to jest...
18 - 4 to jest...
9 + 6 to jest...

Exercise 2

You are officially about to level up with some more complex sentence structures with the use of numbers.

A perfect example to practice is by learning how to talk about your address. Most people in Poland live in flats, not houses; therefore, you have to know how to address both the number of the building and the apartment. Let's say that this is your address:

Nowa Street 13, flat number 4, which should look like this: **ul. Nowa 13/4**

You can be asked the following question:

Jaki jest Twój adres? – What is your address?

You will reply:

ul. Nowa 13/4 (read 'ulica Nowa trzynaście przez cztery)

The '/' symbol is read as *przez* and separates the building number from the flat number.

Now how would you say *Sokola Street 2, flat number 11* in Polish?

If you said, "*Ul. Sokola 2 przez 11*," you're on fire! Let's practice more.

Woronicza Street 8, flat number 20

Spacerowa Street 5, flat number 1

Hoża Street 12, flat number 19

This is only to show you the correct format of an address in Poland, so next time you see it, you will be able to say it properly!

Big numbers (21-100)

So far, you have learned numbers from 0 to 20. Great job! The good news is... from this point it is going to be a little less complicated. All the donkey work is done, so you should enjoy this part. Let's start with some big guys... numbers from 21 to 100!

Don't worry; you won't have to repeat 100 numbers. Instead, you will be provided with some guidelines, and your job is to follow them to name the numbers yourself successfully. A little theory is crucial though.

Say these words out loud, one after another:

twenty – dwadzieścia

thirty – trzydzieści

forty – czterdzieści

fifty – pięćdziesiąt

sixty – sześćdziesiąt

seventy – siedemdziesiąt

eighty – osiemdziesiąt

ninety – dziewięćdziesiąt

one hundred – sto

Similar to the numbers from 11 to 20, these have something in common. They all start with a single digit number (from 1 to 9) and have a particular ending. Now, most of them end with *dziesiąt*, which simply translates to *ty* as in *forty*. But... the first three numbers are quite different. Let's repeat them twice this time.

TIP: Remember that the ending changes from the number 50.

twenty - dwadzieścia, dwadzieścia

thirty - trzydzieści, trzydzieści

forty - czterdzieści, czterdzieści

fifty - pięćdziesiąt, pięćdziesiąt

sixty - sześćdziesiąt, sześćdziesiąt

seventy - siedemdziesiąt, siedemdziesiąt

eighty - osiemdziesiąt, osiemdziesiąt

ninety - dziewięćdziesiąt, dziewięćdziesiąt

one hundred - sto, sto

Repeat all the numbers several times so that you can move on to the next challenge.

Once you have learned all of the above, you can practically name every single number from 0 to 100. Simply add a number from 1 to 9 at the end, and you are all set. Do you want to try? Here are a couple of examples first.

Repeat:

Twenty-three - dwadzieścia trzy

Thirty-nine - trzydzieści dziewięć

Sixty-six - sześćdziesiąt sześć

Eighty-two - osiemdziesiąt dwa

Are you getting the idea of how easy it is? Now, you try. Here are ten examples in English, and your task is to translate them into Polish. Ready? Let's begin!

78

51

60

100

83

47

62

34

29

95

How about we use these numbers and learn something useful at the same time? It is time for some more exercises.

Exercise 1 - Ile masz lat? - How old are you?

You are going to learn how to ask somebody their age, and how to reply.

There is a significant difference when it comes to talking about your age in English and Polish. In Polish, we say, "*I have x year*," not "*I am x years old.*"

The word for *I have* is *mam* (and it has nothing to do with a mother). You also need a word for *years*, which is *lat*. So, how would you say *I am 31 years old* in Polish?

Mam trzydzieści jeden lat.

Here are a couple more examples before things get complicated. Your task is to translate the following sentences into Polish:

I am 25 years old.
I am 68 years old.
I am 41 years old.
I am 15 years old.
I am 9 years old.

Now, let's add a little complication to this. You are already familiar with the fact that Polish words like to change their endings depending on several factors. Same goes for 'years' in Polish. In most cases, you are going to use *lat* as in the examples above. But... this word has two other forms, *lata* and *rok*. Let's start with the latter.

We use *rok* in one case only, when something is 1 year old. That person might say:

"Mam rok."

Let's skip the fact that a one-year-old person wouldn't be able to talk about their age, so use your imagination here. Now, repeat it, "*Mam rok.*" Repeat it as many times as you want until it is stuck in your head.

Let's move on to *lata*. There are only three cases in which you will use this ending. When a number (no matter how big) ends with 2, 3 or 4, you will use *lata*, e.g.:

Mam dwa lata.

Mam pięćdziesiąt trzy lata.

Mam dwadzieścia cztery lata.

There are three exceptions. If you want to say that you are 12, 13, or 14 years old, you will use *lat*, not *lata* (even though these numbers end with 2, 3, and 4). So let's practice these numbers only. Say these sentences out loud:

Mam dwanaście lat.

Mam trzynaście lat.

Mam czternaście lat.

Let's sum up all the information so that you are not confused. Repeat all the phrases.

We use *rok* only if we want to say:

I am one year old. – Mam rok.

We use *lata* with numbers that end with 2, 3 or 4 (except 12, 13 and 14), e.g.:

I am 4 years old. – Mam cztery lata.

I am 32 years old. – Mam trzydzieści dwa lata.

I am 63 years old. - Mam sześćdziesiąt trzy lata.

We use *lat* with all the other numbers, e.g.:

I am 5 years old. - Mam pięć lat.

I am 12 years old. - Mam dwanaście lat.

I am 48 years old. - Mam czterdzieści osiem lat.

I am 91 years old. - Mam dziewięćdziesiąt jeden lat.

I am 70 years old. - Mam siedemdziesiąt lat.

Okay, let's practice. You will be asked to translate the English sentences into Polish, keeping in mind the correct form of the word 'years'. But first, here is one more thing to learn. If you want to ask someone their age, you will say:

"Ile masz lat?"

Say it several times, and let's start the exercise.

Ile masz lat? (45)

Ile masz lat? (12)

Ile masz lat? (1)

Ile masz lat? (99)

Ile masz lat? (62)

Ile masz lat? (24)

Ile masz lat? (100)

Ile masz lat? (38)

Ile masz lat? (13)

Ile masz lat? (53)

Exercise 2 - Ile to kosztuje? - How much is it?

Now let's learn how to use numbers when asking for a price. The currency in Poland is called *złoty*. You should know that the word *złoty* changes too. We'll explain it to you, but you may find it a lot easier as you have already learned different forms of *years* in the previous exercise. Here, the rule is pretty much the same. Let's have a look.

Złoty can have three different endings and everything depends on the last digit of the number we are using it with. Therefore, there is:

złoty

złote

złotych

We use *złoty* with only one number in Polish, which is *jeden*. So, if anything costs 1 zł, you are going to say:

jeden złoty

Easy. Now repeat *jeden złoty* several times.

We use *złote* with numbers *dwa, trzy, cztery* and all the other numbers where the last digit is '2', '3' or '4' except '12', '13', and '14'. So, we can say that something costs:

siedemdziesiąt dwa złote

dwadzieścia trzy złote

pięćdziesiąt cztery złote

The only exceptions are the three numbers mentioned above (12, 13, and 14). All the other numbers, no matter how big they are, will go with *złote*–as long as they end with *dwa, trzy* or *cztery*. Now let's practice a little. Here are several examples and you simply add either *złoty* or *złote*:

sześćdziesiąt trzy...

trzydzieści dwa...

jeden...

osiemdziesiąt cztery...

trzy...

The last form is *złotych,* and you will use it with all the other numbers. Here are some examples. Say them out loud, one after another:

pięć złotych

dziesięć złotych

dwadzieścia osiem złotych
pięćdziesiąt jeden złotych
sto złotych

You should understand how the word changes now, but just in case you are still a little confused, let's sum it up.

We use *złoty* when we are talking about something that only costs '1 zł'; therefore, you say:

To kosztuje jeden złoty.

One more time. *To kosztuje jeden złoty* means *It costs 1 zł*. Say it several times *To kosztuje jeden złoty*.

Let's move on.

We use *złote* with numbers that end with 2, 3 or 4 (except 12, 13 and 14). How would you say *It costs 42 zł*?

To kosztuje czterdzieści dwa złote.

And *It costs 24 zł*?

To kosztuje dwadzieścia cztery złote.

Perfect. One more case to go.

We use *złotych* with all the remaining numbers. How would you say *It costs 12 zł*?

To kosztuje dwanaście złotych.

And *It costs 95 zł*?

To kosztuje dziewięćdziesiąt pięć złotych.

Let's do some serious exercises now.

Exercise 3

In this exercise, you will answer one question. In each case, you will have to use the correct form of the word *złoty*. Feel free to repeat the question out loud too. You will need it when communicating in Polish. Ready? Let's begin.

Ile to kosztuje? (3 zł)

Ile to kosztuje? (45 zł)

Ile to kosztuje? (12 zł)

Ile to kosztuje? (100 zł)

Ile to kosztuje? (62 zł)

Ile to kosztuje? (1 zł)

Ile to kosztuje? (23 zł)

Ile to kosztuje? (89 zł)

Ile to kosztuje? (51 zł)

Ile to kosztuje? (34 zł)

Ordinal numbers

You may be wondering why you need to learn ordinal numbers too. Well, you will need them to be able to talk about time. Before we get into more detail, you have to know the difference between the Polish way of measuring time and the American one.

In Poland, people use a 24-hour clock, which means that the words *am* and *pm* don't exist. If you want to say it is 1 pm, you will actually have to say *it's 13 o'clock*. Let's have a quick look at the Polish time format. From 1 am till noon, there is no difference; therefore, we have:

1 am – 1

2 am – 2

3 am – 3

4 am – 4

5 am – 5

6 am – 6

7 am – 7

8 am – 8

9 am – 9

10 am – 10

11 am – 11

12 am – 12

Easy, isn't it? Now, here is where the big difference is present:

1 pm – 13

2 pm – 14

3 pm – 15

4 pm – 16

5 pm – 17

6 pm – 18

7 pm – 19

8 pm – 20

9 pm – 21

10 pm – 22

11 pm – 23

12 pm – 24 or 00

Converting into the 24-hour format is fairly easy—you just have to add 12 to each hour after the clock strikes noon. But that is not even the point here. Our goal is to learn how to talk about time, so here it goes.

Ordinal numbers are crucial if you want to be able to talk about time. For this lesson, we will only focus on the first 24 numbers and the feminine form. Oh, and all adjectives change depending on the gender of the noun. Here, the word *hour*, in Polish *godzina,* has a feminine form; therefore, you will have to use a feminine form of the adjective that appears before it.

If you want to ask someone what time it is, you will say:

"Która jest godzina?"

To answer, you will simply start with:

"Jest..."

And you will add the time.

Let's start with ordinal numbers. Try to say all the words out loud and repeat them as many times as you need.

It's 1 am. – Jest pierwsza.
It's 2 am. – Jest druga.
It's 3 am. – Jest trzecia.
It's 4 am. – Jest czwarta.
It's 5 am. – Jest piąta.
It's 6 am. – Jest szósta.
It's 7 am. – Jest siódma.
It's 8 am. – Jest ósma.
It's 9 am. – Jest dziewiąta.
It's 10 am. – Jest dziesiąta.

It may be a little too much; therefore, repeat all the numbers again.

pierwsza
pierwsza, druga
pierwsza, druga, trzecia
pierwsza, druga, trzecia, czwarta
pierwsza, druga, trzecia, czwarta, piąta
pierwsza, druga, trzecia, czwarta, piąta, szósta
pierwsza, druga, trzecia, czwarta, piąta, szósta, siódma
pierwsza, druga, trzecia, czwarta, piąta, szósta, siódma, ósma
pierwsza, druga, trzecia, czwarta, piąta, szósta, siódma, ósma, dziewiąta
pierwsza, druga, trzecia, czwarta, piąta, szósta, siódma, ósma, dziewiąta, dziesiąta

Feel free to revise all of them until you have memorized the first batch of ordinal numbers. Once you have learned them and are comfortable, move on to the next part: ordinal numbers from 11 to 24.

One more time, how do you say *What's the time?* in Polish? If you said *Która jest godzina?* you can be proud of yourself. We haven't mentioned that question for a while now, so good job if you still remembered it.

All right, say all the sentences out loud:

It's 1 pm. - Jest trzynasta.
It's 2 pm. - Jest czternasta.
It's 3 pm. - Jest piętnasta.
It's 4 pm. - Jest szesnasta.
It's 5 pm. - Jest siedemnasta.
It's 6 pm. - Jest osiemnasta.
It's 7 pm. - Jest dziewiętnasta.
It's 8 pm. - Jest dwudziesta.
It's 9 pm. - Jest dwudziesta pierwsza.
It's 10 pm. - Jest dwudziesta druga.
It's 11 pm. - Jest dwudziesta trzecia.
It's 12 pm. - Jest dwudziesta czwarta.

The last four hours are pretty easy as you only add the digits you have already learned. Now, let's repeat the above numbers once again, but slower:

trzynasta
trzynasta, czternasta
trzynasta, czternasta, piętnasta
rzynasta, czternasta, piętnasta, szesnasta
trzynasta, czternasta, piętnasta, szesnasta, siedemnasta
trzynasta, czternasta, piętnasta, szesnasta, siedemnasta, osiemnasta
trzynasta, czternasta, piętnasta, szesnasta, siedemnasta, osiemnasta, dziewiętnasta
trzynasta, czternasta, piętnasta, szesnasta, siedemnasta, osiemnasta, dziewiętnasta, dwudziesta

trzynasta, czternasta, piętnasta, szesnasta, siedemnasta, osiemnasta, dziewiętnasta, dwudziesta, dwudziesta pierwsza

trzynasta, czternasta, piętnasta, szesnasta, siedemnasta, osiemnasta, dziewiętnasta, dwudziesta, dwudziesta pierwsza, dwudziesta druga

trzynasta, czternasta, piętnasta, szesnasta, siedemnasta, osiemnasta, dziewiętnasta, dwudziesta, dwudziesta pierwsza, dwudziesta druga, dwudziesta trzecia

trzynasta, czternasta, piętnasta, szesnasta, siedemnasta, osiemnasta, dziewiętnasta, dwudziesta, dwudziesta pierwsza, dwudziesta druga, dwudziesta trzecia, dwudziesta czwarta

Now, instead of repeating all the numbers one by one, let's mix them up. You will have to say what the time is based on the given example in English:

Która jest godzina?
(It's 2 am.)
Która jest godzina?
(It's 6 am.)
Która jest godzina?
(It's 12 am.)
Która jest godzina?
(It's 9 pm.)
Która jest godzina?
(It's 12 pm.)
Która jest godzina?
(It's 4 pm.)

Of course, we can go on and on, but that is not the point. Why? Because we have only learned round hours. To be able to talk about time, you will have to know how to say minutes as well. We will show you the easiest way possible so that you literally don't have to memorize anything new.

As previously mentioned, to talk about the time you have to know ordinal numbers. You should, however, be aware of one crucial thing:

you will use them only to name the first part of the time, i.e., when referring to hours. For the second part—minutes—you will use regular numbers, which you already know. Here is an example:

If you want to say that *It's 10:15 am*, you simply say

Jest dziesiąta piętnaście.

See? The first part (hour) is an ordinal number, while the second one (minutes) is a regular number. No philosophy here. Here are some more examples. Let's start with an English version and give you time to think of the Polish equivalent. Make sure you say them out loud as many times as you need:

It's 2:15 pm. – Jest czternasta piętnaście.

It's 1:20 pm. – Jest trzynasta dwadzieścia.

It's 5:30 am. – Jest piąta trzydzieści.

It's 4 pm. – Jest szesnasta.

It's 9:30 pm. – Jest dwudziesta pierwsza trzydzieści.

It's 9:15 am. – Jest dziewiąta piętnaście.

It's 2:24 am. – Jest druga dwadzieścia cztery.

It's 8:25 pm. – Jest dwudziesta dwadzieścia pięć.

It's 1:05 pm. – Jest trzynasta pięć.

It's 3:30 am. – Jest trzecia trzydzieści.

It's 11:35 pm. – Jest dwudziesta trzecia trzydzieści pięć.

It's 5:40 pm. – Jest siedemnasta czterdzieści.

It's 6 am. – Jest szósta.

It's 8:45 am. – Jest ósma czterdzieści pięć.

It's 7:40 pm. – Jest dziewiętnasta czterdzieści.

It's 8:10 pm. – Jest dwudziesta dziesięć.

Exercise 1 – What's the time? – Która jest godzina?

This short exercise is your follow-up. Its main goal is to give you some extra practice so that you can revise what you have learned. In the first part, you are going to name ten different hours based on English examples. In the second part, you are going to do the opposite thing: you will be given ten various hours in Polish, and your task will be to change them into English versions, using *am* or *pm*. Ready?

Part 1 - Give Polish equivalents:

It's 10:12 am.

It's 5:16 pm.

It's 11:05 am.

It's 6:20 pm.

It's 12:55 pm.

It's 7:29 am.

It's 1:03 am.

It's 9:17 pm.

It's 11:10 am.

It's 4:40 pm.

Part 2 - Give the English equivalents:

Jest pierwsza czternaście.

Jest dziesiąta czterdzieści pięć.

Jest dwunasta osiem.

Jest dwudziesta pięćdziesiąt.

Jest osiemnasta trzydzieści.

Jest czternasta dziesięć.

Jest druga trzydzieści siedem.

Jest piąta pięć.

Jest dziewiętnasta dwadzieścia.

Jest dwudziesta trzecia pięćdziesiąt dziewięć.

Excellent! You have learned how to say how old you are, your telephone number, and other useful things.

Chapter 3 – Deconstructing Polish

Before we move on to the next level, let's summarize what you have already learned:

- how to conjugate a pronoun
- how to use "to be"
- how to introduce yourself
- how to address someone formally
- how to say how old you are
- how to count up to 100
- how to say your address
- how to use the Polish currency
- how to tell the time

Every time you forget about something you learned in a previous chapter, go back and check it. You don't need to hurry—this book doesn't require any deadline. Sometimes you might forget some rules, vocabulary, or expressions, and it is totally fine! Yet, without systemicity and constant repetition, you might get lost very quickly.

In this chapter, we are going to explain some rules of Polish grammar. Don't get discouraged—the whole process will be fun and interesting. If you want to proceed with learning Polish, you need to know why the words are ordered in a certain way in a sentence, and why some words have some strange endings.

Polish Verbs

If you want to learn Polish verbs successfully, you need to ditch English concepts that you already have in your mind. The first thing you need to know is that there are eleven different patterns of verb conjugation in Polish. Yes, eleven! And we are only talking about the present forms. If you want to learn them all by heart, don't do it—since it won't give you any good results. If you want to learn it, you need a strategy, so let's provide you with the best one!

In order not to get lost in the infinite amounts of conjugations and endings, we need to search for similarities and patterns. Essentially, nearly all Polish verbs in an infinitive form (the form without a person like *to be* in English) end with the letter [-ć]. What is more, each person has its own special ending added to the main part of the verb. Let's look at the verbs *robić* [to do], *czytać* [to read], and *śpiewać* [to sing]:

To do - robić

I do – ja robię

You do – ty robisz

He does – on robi

She does – ona robi

It does – ono robi

We do – my robimy

You do – wy robicie

They do – oni/one robią

To read – czytać

I read – ja czyta**m**

You read – ty czyta**sz**

He reads – on czyta

She reads – ona czyta

It reads – ono czyta

We read – my czyta**my**

You read – wy czyta**cie**

They read – oni/one czyta**ją**

To sing – śpiewać

I sing – ja śpiewa**m**

You sing – ty śpiewa**sz**

He sings – on śpiewa

She sings – ona śpiewa

It sings – ono śpiewa

We sing – my śpiewa**my**

You sing – wy śpiewa**cie**

They sing – oni/one śpiewa**ją**

Can you already see the pattern? Let's summarize. Despite some minor changes, the pattern remains the same:

- in the first person ja, there is always the ending [-m] or [-ę].

- in the second person ty, there is always the ending [-sz].

- in the third person on/ona/ono, there is nearly always no ending; you just delete [-ć] from the original infinitive form.

- In the first person plural, there is almost always the ending [-my].

- In the second person plural, there is almost always the ending [-cie].

- In the third person plural, there is always the ending [-ą].

The above pattern applies to *nearly* all verbs—since there are some exceptions. Yet you need to remember that some verbs undergo some minor changes like letter substitution or addition of a letter. These changes result from the fact that Polish people try to make the pronunciation a bit easier. For now, let's skip all the exceptions because the purpose of this chapter is to show you some patterns and teach you some necessary stuff. If you learn the pattern, you will be understood anyway, even though you might skip or wrongly substitute a letter. Now, let's try to remember the pattern by doing some exercises.

Exercise: Try to conjugate *grać* [to play]. Take your time and apply the endings analogically based on the examples shown.

TIP: The verb *grać* is similar to *czytać*.

To play – grać

I play –

You play –

He plays –

She plays –

It plays –

We play –

You play –

They play –

Here are the answers:

I play – ja gram

You play – ty grasz

He plays – on gra

51

She plays – ona gra

It plays – ono gra

We play – my gramy

You play – wy gracie

They play – oni/one grają

Exercise: Try to conjugate *dzwonić* [to call]. Take your time and apply the endings analogically based on the examples shown.

TIP: The verb *dzwonić* is similar to *robić*.

To call – dzwonić

I call –

You call –

He calls –

She calls –

It calls –

We call –

You call–

They call–

Here are the answers:

To call – dzwonić

I call – ja dzwonię

You call – ty dzwonisz

He calls – on dzwoni

She calls – ona dzwoni

It calls – ono dzwoni

We call – my dzwonimy

You call – wy dzwonicie

They call – oni/one dzwonią

Remember: the more you know about the language, the better. Before we move on to another step, congratulations You are making huge progress and gaining more and more confidence. It is vital to know the pattern since you are unable to learn all the different declensions by heart. Even if you somehow managed to learn them, you would hate learning Polish after a short period.

Reflexive Verbs

To learn Polish verbs successfully and use them with confidence daily, there is one more important thing you need to know—reflexive verbs. These verbs can be easily found in English—this is a group that requires using a special pronoun like *yourself/myself/themselves.* For example, *she washes herself, they watch themselves,* etc.

The good news is that the Polish group of these special reflexives is really easy to learn! Firstly, Polish reflexive verbs follow the same pattern and have more or less the same endings. One—and the only— thing you need to add to make a verb reflexive is the word *się. Się* acts like *myself/yourself/yourself/yourself/himself/themselves* in English and remains the same in each person. Let's look at some examples:

To wash oneself - myć się

I wash myself - ja myję się

You wash yourself - ty myjesz się

He washes himself - on myje się

She washes herself - ona myje się

It washes itself - ono myje się

We wash ourselves - my myjemy się

You wash yourselves - wy myjecie się

They wash themselves - oni/one myją się

To help oneself - częstować się

I help myself - ja częstuję się

You help yourself - ty częstujesz się

He helps himself - on częstuje się

She helps herself - ona częstuje się

It helps itself - ono częstuje się

We help ourselves - my częstujemy się

You help yourselves - wy częstujecie się

They help themselves - oni/one częstują się

See how easy it is? All you need to do is add *się* to the verb, and that is basically it! Now it is time to do some exercises.

TIP: You don't have to 'write a person' in Polish, as you probably remember from the first chapter. We suggest skipping pronouns—you should know them well anyway.

Exercise: Try to conjugate *kąpać się* (meaning similar to *myć się* [to wash oneself]). Don't get discouraged, even if you see some minor changes in spelling—the main idea of this exercise is to teach you some rules and patterns. As mentioned, it is impossible to memorize all the spelling patterns in different declensions by heart.

To wash oneself - kąpać się

I wash myself -

You wash yourself -

He washes himself -

She washes herself -

It washes itself -

We wash ourselves -

You wash yourselves -

They wash themselves -

Now, it's time to check the answers:

To wash oneself – kąpać się

I wash myself – kąpię się

You wash yourself – kąpiesz się

He washes himself – kąpie się

She washes herself – kąpie się

It washes itself – kąpie się

We wash ourselves – kąpiemy się

You wash yourselves – kąpiecie się

They wash themselves – kąpią się

Now you know why the word *się* is so popular in Polish and what it means. Before we move on to the next level, let's summarize all you need to know about verbs in Polish:

- Polish verbs have eleven different declensions that are closely related to the patterns of pronunciation.

- The essential part of each Polish verb is the ending—it carries information about the subject (gender/number/case).

- Each person has a different ending that remains the same in each declension. It's the most important pattern you need to learn.

- Polish reflexive verbs do not require different pronouns. All you need to do is add the word *się*. In fact, adding a pronoun is unnecessary since the ending in the verb carries all the necessary information.

Essential Polish Verbs That You Need To Know

It is time to leave grammar for a moment. Below is a list of the most important Polish verbs that might be useful. Unfortunately, there are no shortcuts—you need to learn them by heart. So stay in this chapter for a while and go through the list multiple times. The good news is that each verb contains a context—a sentence in which it might be used. You don't have to learn the sentences; focus on the verbs, and try to remember as many as possible. After you feel confident with the list, you can go straight to the quiz.

Być - to be (Jestem Paula - I am Paula)

Mieć - to have (Mam kota - I have a cat)

Iść - to go (Idę do sklepu - I'm going to the store)

Robić - to do/to make (Robię zakupy - I'm doing shopping)

Próbować - to try (Próbowałem wiele razy - I've tried many times)

Pomagać - to help (Pomagam tacie - I'm helping my dad)

Grać/bawić się - to play (Lubię bawić się na dworze - I like playing outside)

Spacerować - to walk (Lubisz spacerować? - Do you like walking?)

Uczyć się - to learn (W szkole muszę się uczyć - I have to learn at school)

Mieszkać - to live (Mieszkam w mieście - I live in a city.)

Pracować - to work (Pracuję w dużej firmie - I work in a big company)

Jeść - to eat (Chodźmy coś zjeść! - Let's go eat something!)

Pić - to drink (Ona wypiła już kawę - She has already drunk her coffee)

Pisać - to write (Piszę e-mail - I'm writing an e-mail)

Czytać - to read (On czyta książkę - He's reading a book)

Liczyć - to count (Mogę na ciebie liczyć? - Can I count on you?)

Rysować - to draw (Uczę się rysować - I'm learning how to draw)

Malować - to paint (Oni malują - They're painting)

Widzieć - to see (Nie widzę go - I can't see him)

Wyglądać/spoglądać - to look (Dobrze wyglądasz! - You look good!)

Oglądać - to watch (Oglądam telewizję - I'm watching TV)

Słyszeć - to hear (Usłyszałem dziwny głos - I've just heard a strange voice)

Słuchać - to listen (Słuchamy muzyki - We're listening to music)

Spać - to sleep (Idę spać - I'm going to sleep)

Gotować - to cook (Umiesz gotować? - Can you cook?)

Sprzątać - to clean (Muszę dzisiaj sprzątać mieszkanie - I have to clean the flat today)

Podróżować - to travel (Podrózuję do Chin - I'm traveling to China)

Jechać - to drive (Jadę do domu - I'm driving home)

Latać - to fly (Chciałbyś polecieć do Londynu? - Would you like to fly to London?)

Pływać - to swim (Nie umiem pływać - I can't swim)

Biegać - to run (Ona teraz biega - She's running now)

Siedzieć - to sit (Usiądźcie - Sit down)

Rozpoczynać - to begin (Przedstawienie zaczyna się o 8:00 - The show begins at 8 am)

Stać - to stand (Stań tutaj - Stand here)

Kłaść - to put (Gdzie mogę położyć tę paczkę? - Where can I put this parcel?)

Wychodzić - to leave (Właśnie wychodziliśmy - We were just leaving)

Przychodzić - to come (Przyjdź do mojego biura o 9:00 - Come to my office at 9 am)

Śpiewać - to sing (Nie umiem śpiewać - I can't sing)

Tańczyć - to dance (Zatańczymy? - Shall we dance?)

Pamiętać – to remember (Pamiętaj o mnie – Remember about me)

Zapominać – to forget (Zapomniałem o spotkaniu! – I've just forgotten about the meeting!)

Wybierać – to choose (Wybierz jedną opcję – Choose one option)

Zamykać – to close (Zamknij drzwi, proszę – Close the door, please)

Otwierać – to open (Czy mógłbyś otworzyć okno? – Could you open the window?)

Tworzyć – to create (Stwórzmy własny projekt! – Let's create our own project!)

Budować – to build (On buduje dom – He's building a house)

Pokazywać/przedstawiać – to show (Pokażesz mi? – Can you show me?)

Czuć – to feel (Czuję się dobrze – I feel good)

Czuć/wąchać – to smell (Czuję coś dziwnego – I'm smelling something strange)

Smakować/próbować – to taste (Spróbuj tej zupy – Taste this soup)

Myśleć – to think (Myślę, że... – I think that...)

Rosnąć – to grow (Dzieci rosną bardzo szybko – Children grow very fast)

Myć – to wash (Muszę umyć samochód – I need to wash my car)

Wierzyć – to believe (Wierzę, że... – I believe that...)

Mówić – to speak (Mów głośniej! – Speak up!)

Powiedzieć – to say (Powiedz coś! – Say something!)

Rozmawiać – to talk (Możemy teraz porozmawiać? – Can we talk now?)

Dawać - to give (Czy mógłbyś mi to dać? - Could you give me this?)

Brać - to take (Muszę wziąć dzień wolnego - I have to take a day off)

Pożyczać - to borrow (Pożyczysz mi swój samochód? - Could you borrow me your car?)

Pożyczać - to lend (Pożyczę ci mój samochód - I will lend you my car)

Skakać - to jump (On skacze bardzo wysoko - He's jumping very high)

Odejść - to quit (Odchodzę! - I quit!)

Uderzyć - to hit (Mocno mnie uderzyła! - She hit me hard!)

Strzelać - to shoot (Strzelaj! - Shoot!)

Kupować - to buy (Chcę kupić nowy samochód - I want to buy a new car)

Sprzedawać - to sell (Muszę sprzedać dom - I have to sell my house)

Wymieniać - to exchange (Czy mogę wymienić pieniądze? - Can I exchange my money?)

Wygrywać - to win (Moja drużyna wygrała zawody! - My team won the competition!)

Przegrywać - to lose (Moja drużyna przegrała zawody - My team lost the competition)

Rozumieć - to understand (Rozumiesz? - Do you understand?)

Uczyć - to teach (Uczę w szkole podstawowej - I teach at primary school)

Łapać - to catch (Łap piłkę! - Catch the ball!)

You have now learned most of (or even all) the verbs from the list. What is more, you can apply all the rules and patterns from the beginning of this chapter and make your verbs more meaningful. However, now it is time to have a short quiz and check how many verbs you know by heart.

Exercise: Write a Polish verb based on the English equivalents.

To read –

To do –

To buy –

To sell –

To learn –

To borrow –

To win –

To talk –

To watch –

To choose –

To open –

To build –

To swim –

To write –

To exchange –

To show –

To smell –

To run –

To give –

To take –

To jump –

To dance –

To leave –

To put –

To understand –

To hit –

To shoot –

To sit –

To begin –

To create –

Good job! You are confident enough to express your actions in Polish. These verbs will be really useful. In fact, sometimes it is better to say only a verb than to say nothing. A Polish person might eventually understand your intentions just by hearing one essential word. After all, communicative effectiveness is the key. Let's go to the next level.

Nouns – How Do They Work?

So you have just learned over 100 essential Polish verbs and the rules that apply to them as well. It is high time you were shown another essential ingredient of a sentence—the noun. We won't be teaching you any nouns in this chapter; instead, you will learn the rules based on which nouns are governed.

Cases:

As mentioned at the beginning of this book, seven different cases apply not only to nouns but also to adjectives. Before being too hard on yourself, please note that using a wrong case does not significantly affect communication. Although mastering the rules can be worthwhile, aiming at perfection can be daunting, especially at the beginning of your journey. Remember that if you apply a wrong suffix, your message will be ninety-nine percent understandable. Let's take a closer look at the words *książka* [book] and *komputer* [computer], to get familiar with the concept of Polish cases:

Nominative – ksią**żka**

Genitive – ksią**żki**

Dative – ksią**żce**

Accusative – ksią**żkę**

Ablative – (z) ksią**żką**

Locative – (o) ksią**żce**

Vocative – ksią**żko!**

Nominative – komput**er**

Genitive – komput**era**

Dative – komput**erowi**

Accusative – komput**er**

Ablative – komput**erem**

Locative – komput**erze**

Vocative – komput**erze**

As you can see, some of the endings look similar, yet no clear rules can be applied, as far as the suffixes are concerned. It is advisable to learn the cases gradually, in context, and by using associations. If you try to learn all variations of the same word by heart, you will find yourself overwhelmed sooner or later. So, don't worry.

Even some proper names need to be declined by case. Look at the examples below:

Francja [France] – feminine noun

Nominative – Francja

Genitive – Francji

Dative – Francji

Accusative – Francję

Ablative – (z) Francją

Locative – (o) Francji

Vocative - Francjo!

Włochy [Italy] - plural noun

Nominative - Włochy

Genitive - Włoch

Dative - Włochom

Accusative - Włochy

Ablative - (z) Włochami

Locative - (o) Włoszech

Vocative - Włochy!

Number:

As far as the grammatical number is concerned, Polish singular or plural are usually formed with different endings that correspond with gender. What is interesting in the Polish plural form is that there are only two genders—masculine and non-masculine. The usage of these endings is also not determined by any rules.

For example, the word *dom* [house] is masculine, yet it is an object. Then, its plural form, *domy* [houses], involves the ending -y. The word *mężczyzna* [man] is masculine and refers to a person. Its plural form *mężczyźni* [men] ends with -i.

Gender:

It was also mentioned at the beginning of the book that Polish masculine, feminine, or neuter do not correspond with the actual sex. The Polish language has grammatical gender, whereas English has biological gender. What is even more interesting is that Polish speakers use masculine or feminine often when talking about inanimate objects, such as pieces of furniture or fruits. For example, the Polish word *banan* [banana] is masculine, the word *truskawka* [strawberry] is feminine, and the word *mango* [mango] is neutral.

To sum up, the only way to learn different genders, numbers, and cases is by repetition and memorization. We don't want you to do some intimidating exercises involving gender, case, and number; we have just included some explanations to make you more aware of some essential differences between Polish and English. Now, equipped with the knowledge about the language, you can move on to some learning and practice in context!

Before we proceed to the next chapter, though, let's summarize what you have learned in this one:

- Polish verbs have eleven different declensions that are closely related to the patterns of pronunciation.

- The essential part of each Polish verb is the ending—it carries information about the subject (gender/number/case).

- Each person has a different ending that remains the same in each declension. It's the most important pattern you need to learn.

- Polish reflexive verbs do not require different pronouns. All you need to do is to add the word *się*. In fact, adding a pronoun is unnecessary since the ending in the verb carries all the necessary information

- Each Polish noun is declined by case, gender, and number. All the information about these three grammatical characteristics can be found in the ending of a particular noun.

- There are seven cases in Polish—nominative, genitive, dative, accusative, ablative, locative, and vocative.

- The Polish language has grammatical gender. It means that gender does not correspond with the actual sex. In fact, even an object can have a feminine or masculine gender.

- Polish plural has only two genders—masculine and non-masculine.

Chapter 4 – Greetings

In this chapter, you will learn some of the most important Polish greetings, including how to greet your friends, your boss, and even strangers on the street. Let's start with the basic daily greetings.

Polish everyday expressions are similar to the English ones with only one exception—Polish people do not use an equivalent of the English *good afternoon.* There is one expression in Polish that can be used in the morning and afternoon:

Dzień dobry! – Good morning/Good afternoon!

Let's repeat:

Dzień dobry! – Good morning/Good afternoon!

In the evening you need to say:

Dobry wieczór! – Good evening!

Let's repeat it twice:

Dobry wieczór! – Good evening!

Dobry wieczór! – Good evening!

If you want your expression to be really formal, you can add *Panie/Pani* + a name. This is how it works:

Dzień dobry Pani ... – Good morning Mrs./Ms. ...

Dzień dobry Panie ... – Good morning Mr. ...

Let's repeat. You can come up with a name and add it to the expression.

Dzień dobry Pani ... – Good morning Mrs./Ms. ...

Dzień dobry Panie ... – Good morning Mr. ...

The same rule applies to *good evening*. Let's see how it works:

Dobry wieczór Pani ... – Good evening Mrs./Ms. ...

Dobry wieczór Panie ... – Good evening Mr. ...

Let's repeat:

Dobry wieczór Pani ... – Good evening Mrs./Ms. ...

Dobry wieczór Panie ... – Good evening Mr. ...

If you want to greet your friend or a person that you have known for a while, you can use:

Cześć! – Hello/Hi!

It is important to know that the Polish *cześć!* is slightly different from the English *hello!/hi!* When you don't know someone, or you address a much older person, always use *dzień dobry* instead of *cześć*. When you are at work, it is advisable to say *dzień dobry/do widzenia (Pani/Panie)* instead of *cześć* (*cześć* is rather an informal form of address), unless you get to know your colleagues better. Also, students at school/university never say *cześć* to their teachers, and teachers do not use *cześć* when addressing to their students. If you want to address a teacher, always use *dzień dobry* and be polite, no matter how long you have known the teacher.

Now, let's repeat *cześć* at least three times since its pronunciation is quite hard:

Cześć! – Hello/Hi!

Cześć! – Hello/Hi!

Cześć! – Hello/Hi!

You can use *cześć* to say goodbye as well. It is quite a universal and multi-purpose word:

Cześć! – Bye!

Remember: *cześć* is an informal way of saying goodbye. If you want to say something formal, use:

Do widzenia! – Goodbye!

Let's repeat it twice:

Do widzenia! – Goodbye!

Do widzenia! – Goodbye!

If you want to make your goodbye even more formal, try the pattern with *Pan/Pani* + a name. Here is how it works:

Do widzenia Pani ... – Goodbye Mrs./Ms. ...

Do widzenia Panie ... – Goodbye Mr. ...

Let's repeat:

Do widzenia Pani ... – Goodbye Mrs./Ms. ...

Do widzenia Panie ... – Goodbye

After you greet someone, it is time to say *how do you do?/how are you?* etc. There are a couple of Polish phrases that you can use:

Co tam?/Co u ciebie? – How are you?/How do you do?

Let's repeat them twice:

Co tam?/Co u ciebie? – How are you?/How do you do?

Co tam?/Co u ciebie? – How are you?/How do you do?

It is important to note that expressions such as *how are you/how do you do* are perceived differently in Poland. If you ask a Polish person *how do you do?*, don't expect something like *I'm fine/I'm okay/I'm doing great*. Instead, a Polish person will tell you a couple of things about their job/school/family life, etc. So, the Polish *co tam/co u ciebie?* is slightly different from the English *how are you?*

It is time to practice a bit!

Exercise: How do you...

... greet your friend?

... say goodbye to your boss?

... say goodbye to your friend's parents?

... greet your Polish teacher in the morning?

... greet a stranger on the street in the evening?

... say goodbye to a shop assistant?

... greet your teacher in the afternoon?

... greet your new business partner in the evening?

... ask your Polish friend how does he or she do?

There are also some colloquial expressions that are mostly used by younger generations. It is good to know a couple of informal greetings as well, so let's take a look at some of them:

Siema! – Hey!

Elo! – Yo! (a very informal form of addressing your close friends)

Jak leci? – What's up?

Trzymaj się! – Take care!

Na razie! – Bye!

Dzięki! – Thanks!

Spoko!/Ok!/Okej! – Okay!/No problem! (Polish people say *okay* very often)

Let's repeat all the colloquial expressions:

Siema! – Hey!

Elo! – Yo!

Jak leci? – What's up?

Trzymaj się! – Take care!

Na razie! - Bye!

Dzięki! - Thanks!

Spoko!/Ok!/Okej! - Okay!/No problem!

Excellent! You have basically learned all of the useful expressions that you need to know to greet someone or say goodbye. Now it is time to start a real conversation. Let's move back to the first chapter for a while.

Remember how to introduce yourself? Take your time and try to say the phrases out loud...

Remember how to ask someone to introduce himself/herself? Again, take your time and pronounce the phrases...

Remember how to ask someone to introduce himself/herself formally? Think for a moment and pronounce the phrases...

Hopefully, you remember all the useful conversational phrases from the first chapter. The following is a complex exercise, but it will make you focus and wrap things up.

Exercise: Some context is provided based on what you will need regarding the Polish expressions that you have learned so far. This time, there aren't any English equivalents—it is your job to imagine a particular situation and choose an appropriate expression.

1) You are meeting your new boss for the first time. Greet him/her and introduce yourself.

2) You are meeting your close friend from Poland. Greet him/her and ask how does he/she do.

3) You are meeting your new business partner (you've invited him/her for lunch). Greet him/her, introduce yourself, and ask him/her to introduce himself/herself.

4) You are in a supermarket. Greet the shop assistant.

5)   You are meeting your new Polish teacher (your friend has just told you that he/she wants to see you in his/her office). Greet him/her and introduce yourself.

6)   You are meeting a group of your very close friends. Greet them and ask how do they do.

7)   Your friend invited a person you don't know to his birthday party (his cousin) Greet him/her, introduce yourself and ask how does he/she do.

8)   The birthday party is over, and you decide to go home. Say goodbye to all of your friends.

9)   A lunch with your business partner is over. Say goodbye to him/her.

10) You've just met your friend's mom on the street, and it's 10 pm. Greet her.

Good job! You are making huge steps towards fluency! If you are not confident enough with the previous chapters, go back and revise all the necessary phrases and vocabulary items. You will need them in each next chapter—make sure that you understand and remember most things. Let's move on to the next chapter, which is all about expanding your conversational limits.

Chapter 5 – An initial Conversation

Before we move on, let's go over some of the Polish skills that you have already learned. You can now:

- Greet someone, say hello/goodbye
- Greet someone formally using formal forms of address
- Introduce yourself
- Ask someone to introduce himself/herself
- Count to 100
- Tell the time
- Tell someone your phone number
- Ask about someone's address or tell them your address
- Use polish currency in multiple situations (e.g., while doing shopping)

As well as all the above skills, you have also learned some essential background knowledge about Polish grammar (pronouns, nouns, verbs). With all the skills and knowledge, you can now move on to more advanced Polish phrases!

How old are you?

Greeting someone and saying your name in a foreign language is a good start, yet it might be not enough. To actually have a simple conversation, you have to learn more phrases. Let's start by telling someone how old you are—you should go back to Chapter 2 and read the extract about age.

So how do you ask someone how old he/she is? Think for a second.

Ile masz lat?

Now say how old you are. If you don't remember how to express it, go back to Chapter 2. So, how can you say how old you are?

Mam... lat.

Remember that Polish people do not use the verb *być* [to be] while telling others their age. Instead, they use *mieć* [to have]. A literal translation would be *I have... years.*

Exercise: You already know Polish numbers. Try to say in Polish how old you are using different numbers.

I am 18 years old.

I am 54 years old.

I am 33 years old.

I am 97 years old.

I am 6 years old.

I am 45 years old.

I am 23 years old.

Now say your age.

Sometimes you will have to ask about someone's age politely. Here are the formal forms of the question *ile masz lat?:*

Ile ma Pan/Pani lat?

Ile mają Panie/Panowie/Państwo lat?

Let's repeat:

Ile ma Pan/Pani lat?

Ile mają Panie/Panowie/Państwo lat?

Good! Try to exercise a bit.

Exercise: Ask about someone's age politely based on the context provided.

A woman

A man

A group of women

A group of men

A group of men and women

Language

Questions about knowledge of a particular language are an inseparable part of nearly every foreign conversation. If you don't feel confident enough to handle a dialog, you can at least say that you don't know the language. Here are some essential phrases and questions that will definitely help you on your way. If you want to ask someone if he/she speaks a particular language, you need to say:

Mówisz po angielsku? – Do you speak English?

Mówisz po polsku? – Do you speak Polish?

And now let's look at the formal ways:

Czy mówi Pan po angielsku? (one male)

Czy mówi Pani po angielsku? (one female)

Czy mówią Panie po angielsku? (two or more females)

Czy mówią Panowie po angielsku? (two or more males)

Czy mówią Państwo po angielsku? (two or more males and females)

Czy mówi Pan po polsku? (one male)

Czy mówi Pani po polsku? (one female)

Czy mówią Panie po polsku? (two or more females)

Czy mówią Panowie po polsku? (two or more males)

Czy mówią Państwo po polsku? (two or more males and females)

It is advisable to use the formal forms, even though a person seems to be as old as you are. Remember: Polish people switch to the informal style after knowing someone for a while.

So, you can ask someone if he/she knows Polish/English. Now it is time to tell someone that you speak/don't speak Polish/English.

If you want to say that you **speak** Polish/English, you need to use:

Mówię po angielsku. - I speak English.

Mowię po polsku. - I speak Polish.

Let's repeat:

Mówię po angielsku. - I speak English.

Mowię po polsku. - I speak Polish.

If you want to say that you **don't speak** Polish/English, you need to use:

Nie mówię po angielsku. - I don't speak English.

Nie mówię po polsku. - I don't speak Polish.

If you want to say that you **don't speak** Polish/English **very well**, you need to use:

Nie mówię dobrze po angielsku. - I don't speak English very well.

Nie mówię dobrze po polsku. - I don't speak Polish very well.

That's a lot for the beginning. In order not to get lost, let's try some exercises.

Exercise: Try to say the following phrases in Polish.

Do you speak English? (informal way)

Do you speak Polish? (male, formal way)

Do you speak English? (female, formal way)

Do you speak Polish? (males, formal way)

Do you speak English? (females, formal way)

Do you speak Polish? (males and females, formal way)

I speak Polish.

I speak English.

I don't speak Polish.

I don't speak English.

I don't speak Polish very well.

I don't speak English very well.

Nationality and Place of Living

Another important part of an initial conversation is represented by asking about someone's address or nationality. Here we won't focus on telling the exact address—since you have already learned this skill in Chapter 2 (numbers). Instead, you will learn how to ask some basic questions about the country/nationality/city, etc.

Let's start with a broad context. If you want to ask someone about his/her nationality, you need to say:

Skąd pochodzisz? – Where are you from?

If you want to keep the polite style, you need to say:

Skąd Pan/Pani pochodzi?

Skąd Panowie/Panie/Państwo pochodzą?

If you want to tell someone where you are from, you need to say:

Pochodzę z... – I am from...

To add even more context, let's learn some vocabulary. You are about to learn some country names in Polish. Take your time and repeat all the names multiple times. As long as you get comfortable with the new piece of vocabulary, you can go further.

Countries - kraje:

Polska - Poland

Wielka Brytania - UK/Great Britain

Stany Zjednoczone/USA - the United States/the USA

Niemcy - Germany

Francja - France

Hiszpania - Spain

Czechy - the Czech Republic

Włochy - Italy

Portugalia - Portugal

Grecja - Greece

Holandia - the Netherlands

Belgia - Belgium

Węgry - Hungary

Słowacja - Slovakia

Ukraina - Ukraine

Turcja - Turkey

Dania - Denmark

Norwegia - Norway

Szwecja - Sweden

Finlandia - Finland

Chorwacja - Croatia

Irlandia - Ireland

Islandia - Iceland

Rosja - Russia

Chiny - China

Japonia - Japan

Australia - Australia

Brazylia - Brazil

Argentyna - Argentina

Kolumbia - Colombia

Meksyk - Mexico

Kanada - Canada

Egipt - Egypt

Izrael - Israel

Continents - kontynenty:

Ziemia - the Earth

Europa - Europe

Azja - Asia

Australia - Australia

Afryka - Africa

Antarktyda - Antarctica

Ameryka Północna - North America

Ameryka Południowa - South America

Ameryka Środkowa - Central America

Before we practice, there is one thing that you need to know. The Polish verb *pochodzić z* [to come from] makes the country appear in a different case (namely, the genitive case). So, if you want to say that you come from Europe, you can't use *Pochodzę z Europa*. Instead, you have to say *Pochodzę z Europy*. Here are more examples:

Pochodzę z Polski. - I come from Poland.

Pochodzę z Wielkiej Brytanii. - I come from Great Britain.

Pochodzę z Niemiec. - I come from Germany.

Pochodzę z Chin. - I come from China.

Pochodzę z Ukrainy. – I come from Ukraine.

Of course, all these cases are difficult to grasp at the beginning, so don't get discouraged. Even though you forget about using the genitive case, you will be understood anyway. Keep in mind that communicative effectiveness, not 100 percent accurate use, is the key. We have included some grammatical explanations to make your learning less ambiguous.

Let's practice.

Exercise: Try to say in Polish the following phrases.

I come from Poland.

I come from the USA.

I come from Great Britain.

I come from Germany.

I come from China.

I come from Belgium.

I come from Turkey.

I come from Ukraine.

I come from Sweden.

I come from Japan.

I come from Australia.

Excellent! You have learned some essential vocabulary and useful phrases connected to country/nationality. Now it is time to move to the narrow context. If you want to ask someone about his/her place of living, you need to say:

Gdzie mieszkasz? – Where do you live?

If you want to keep the polite style, you need to use the following phrases:

Gdzie Pan/Pani mieszka? – Where do you live? (one male/one female)

Gdzie Panie/Panowie/państwo mieszkają? – Where do you live? (females/males/males and females)

If you want to tell someone where you live, you need to use the following phrase:

Mieszkam w/na... (city/region etc.) – I live in...

Pretty easy, isn't it? To introduce more context, we will provide some useful vocabulary. You can use the new words to practice the *where do you live* phrase:

w Londynie – in London

w Nowym Jorku – in New York

w Warszaawie – in Warsaw

w Krakowie – in Cracow

w mieście – in a city

w dużym mieście – in a big city

w małym mieście – in a small town

na wsi – in the countryside

w domu – in a house

w bloku – in a block of flats

na północy kraju – in the north of the country

na południu kraju – in the south of the country

na wschodzie kraju – in the east of the country

na zachodzie kraju – in the west of the country

w pobliżu dużego miasta – near a big city

w centrum miasta – in the city center

na przedmieściach – in the suburbs

w górach – in the mountains

Try to go through the new set of vocabulary many times and try to remember as many new items as possible. There is no time pressure—

you can always go back to the previous chapters if you want to make a short revision. If you are confident enough with the above list, you can practice a bit with the phrase.

Exercise: Try to say in Polish the following phrases.

Where do you live? (informal)

Where do you live? (formal, male)

Where do you live? (formal, female)

Where do you live? (formal, males)

Where do you live? (formal, females)

Where do you live? (formal, males and females)

I live in Warsaw.

I live in Cracow.

I live in a big city.

I live in the suburbs.

I live in the north of the country.

I live in the countryside.

I live in a house.

I live in a block of flats.

I live in the city center.

I live in the mountains.

I live near a big city.

Good job! You are making huge progress! You have learned many new vocabulary items and can incorporate these new items in a real context. Keep it up!

Useful Conversational Phrases

Sometimes a conversation doesn't go as planned. Even though you will have well-prepared scenarios in your head, most of the time, face-to-face interaction will always be surprising. You have to remember that every real dialog (not via SMS or any other instant messenger) requires improvisation. Thus, we have prepared a list of useful phrases that might be helpful during the initial foreign conversation you will take part in.

Some of the phrases that you are about to learn have already been introduced in the previous chapter, yet in a slightly different context. Go through the following list multiple times and repeat each item. As soon as you feel confident with using these expressions, you can go straight to the exercises.

Tak – Yes

Nie – No

Miło mi cię poznać. – Nice to meet you!

A ty? – And you?/How about you?

Ja też. – Me too.

Ja też nie. – Me neither.

Czy mogę ci jakoś pomóc? – How can I help you?

Nie, dziękuję. – No, thank you.

Myślę, że tak. – I think so.

Myślę, że nie. – I don't think so.

Oczywiście. – Of course/Sure.

Nie ma problemu. – No problem.

Czy mógłbyś/mogłabyś przeliterować? – Could you spell it?

Czy mógłbyś/mogłabyś powtórzyć? – Could you repeat?

Nie rozumiem. – I don't understand.

Powodzenia! – Good luck!

Dobry pomysł! – Good idea!

Myślę, że to dobry pomysł. – I think it's a good idea.

Niech pomyślę... – Let me think...

Poczekaj chwilę. – Wait a moment.

Przepraszam. – Excuse me/I'm sorry

Przepraszam. Muszę już iść. – I'm sorry. I have to go.

Przepraszam za spóźnienie. – Sorry for being late.

Przepraszam, która jest godzina? – Excuse me, what time is it?

Przepraszam, gdzie jest...? – Excuse me, where is...?

Czy mógłbyś/mogłabyś pokazać mi gdzie jest...? – Could you show me where... is?

Czy mógłbyś/mogłabyś pokazać na mapie? – Could you show me on the map?

Here are another two exercises—one easier, and one more difficult. Let's see how well you know the new set:

Exercise: Try to say in Polish the following phrases.

Nice to meet you.

How about you?

Yes.

No.

I think so.

Could you repeat?

Could you spell it?

Good luck!

Wait a moment.

I am sorry.

I don't understand.

Sorry for being late.

Sure.

Me neither.

No problem.

Excuse me.

Excuse me, where is?

How can I help you?

I don't think so.

I don't understand.

Let me think.

Good job! These phrases will definitely make your language journey way easier. Yet knowing them by heart and repeating/translating them will not give you the conversational confidence. Thus, here is a more difficult exercise.

Exercise: Try to say the appropriate Polish phrase based on the context provided. Sometimes there is more than one correct answer. Let your imagination choose what is best.

a) A friend asks you to do him/her a favor. What do you say?

b) The meeting at work has already started. What do you say as soon as you come in?

c) Your friend suggests going to the cinema tonight. What do you say?

d) You don't understand your Polish friend. What do you say?

e) You didn't hear what your friend said, and you want him/her to repeat himself/herself. What do you say?

f) You need to think for a moment. What do you say?

g) You want a stranger to show you a place on the map. What do you say to him/her?

h) You've just met your friend's sister. What do you say to her?

i) You want to apologize for something. What do you say?

j) You want to know what time it is. How do you ask your friend?

k) You want to know what your friend thinks about a certain problem. How do you ask him/her?

l) You see a child crying. What do you say to him/her?

You have just learned some very useful conversational expressions in context. Congratulations! Now it is time to face more linguistic challenges!

Likes/dislikes and Opinion

After introducing yourself and talking about some general facts like your age or place of living, it is time to make your conversation more interesting. The best way to learn something more about a person is to ask him/her some questions concerning interests/likes and dislikes. Thus, we have prepared another important ingredient of a conversation—asking about someone's opinion.

You can ask someone about his/her likes/dislikes in many ways, but let's start from the simplest version. In Polish, it looks like this:

Co lubisz? – What do you like?

Co lubisz najbardziej? – What do you like the most?

A formal version looks like this:

Co Pan/Pani lubi (najbardziej)? – What do you like (the most)?

Co Panie/Panowie/Państwo lubią (najbardziej)? – What do you like (the most)?

If you want to share your opinion, you can say:

Lubię... – I like...

Najbardziej lubię... – I like... the most.

Nie lubię... – I don't like...

Najbardziej nie lubię... – I don't like... the most

Good start! You can use the Polish *lubię/nie lubię* expression when talking not only about things but also activities. Yet you need to keep in mind that formulating these expressions is a bit different compared to English, and we are about to show you in what ways.

At first, let's try to say that you like *ciasto* [a cake].

Lubię ciasto.

Now, try to say that you don't like cake.

Nie lubię ciasta.

What has changed? You have probably noticed that it is no longer *ciasto*, but *ciasta*. The ending has changed since the *nie lubię* phrase requires applying a different case (namely, the genitive). Unfortunately, Polish cases are so advanced that they would all require writing another book. For now, let's just keep in mind that they exist. Even though you say *nie lubię ciasto* (which is incorrect), your message will be understood anyway—your Polish will just be sounding foreign, that's all.

Now, let's try to say that you like playing football.

Lubię grać w piłkę nożną.

Now you don't like playing football:

Nie lubię grać w piłkę nożną.

Have you noticed the pattern? When talking about activities, the Polish *lubię/nie lubię* phrase always requires an infinitive form of a particular verb. So the literal translation into English would look like this: *I like to play football/I don't like to play football.*

Of course, many other useful words can describe your likes/dislikes, not only *lubię/nie lubię*. Using them will make your Polish usage more advanced and interesting. The rule of using these word is the same as in *lubię/nie lubię*.

Uwielbiam/kocham – I love

Nienawidzę – I hate

Nie cierpię – I can't stand

Wolę/preferuję – I prefer

These are the most popular expressions that will give you a real boost. Try to go through them twice or more in order to remember them.

Uwielbiam/kocham – I love

Nienawidzę – I hate

Nie cierpię – I can't stand

Wolę/preferuję – I prefer

Good job! Now it is time to learn some useful words describing activities. You can apply them to the *like/love/hate* expressions and share your opinion. It is pretty easy! Take your time and learn these expressions carefully. The exercises will be demanding since you are not just a beginner. We have made a list of activities in the infinitive form—since you need to remember that Polish *like/love/hate* phrases require using an infinitive form:

Jeździć na rowerze – to ride a bike

Jeździć konno – to ride a horse

Oglądać telewizję – to watch TV

Chodzić do szkoły – to go to school

Uczyć się – to study

Grać w gry komputerowe – to play computer games

Rysować – to draw

Śpiewać – to sing

Grać na gitarze – to play the guitar

Grać na pianinie – to play the piano

Wychodzić na miasto – to go out

Spędzać czas z przyjaciółmi – to hang out with friends

Chodzić do pracy – to go to work

Jeździć samochodem – to drive a car

Chodzić na siłownię – to go to the gym

Pływać – to swim

Robić grilla – to have a barbeque

Jeść owoce – to eat fruit

Imprezować – to party

Podróżować – to travel

Biegać – to run

Chodzić na spacery – to go for a walk/to walk

Pisać – to write

Czytać książki – to read books

Robić zakupy – to do the shopping

Chodzić do galerii – to go to the shopping center

Excellent! Knowing these activities will make your Polish more advanced! Let's try something more difficult.

Exercise: Try to say in Polish the following expressions.

I like riding a bike.

I hate doing shopping.

I love spending time with my friends.

I don't like running.

I hate reading books.

I love walking.

I like playing the guitar.

I hate singing.

I love riding the horse.

I love going out.

I hate going to school.

I like driving a car.

I love hanging out with my friends.

I love traveling.

I don't like drawing.

I hate studying.

Excellent! Before we move on, let's explore one more thing that might be useful—questions about some specific opinion. In other words, you are about to learn how to ask someone if he/she likes a particular thing. It goes like this:

Lubisz...? – Do you like...?

The rule stays the same. When you ask about activities, they stay in the infinitive form. For example:

Lubisz pływać? – Do you like swimming?

Lubisz jeździć na rowerze? – Do you like riding a bike?

Let's try a short exercise.

Exercise: Try to ask the following questions in Polish.

Do you like singing?

Do you like walking?

Do you like partying?

Do you like drawing?

Do you like going shopping?

Do you like driving a car?

Do you like riding a horse?

Do you like reading books?

Do you like watching TV?

Do you like running?

Do you like playing computer games?

Do you like studying?

Excellent! You are getting more and more confident with your Polish! Now it is time to expand on the likes/dislikes topic and teach you how to express an opinion about things, not activities. Of course, before the exercises, you need to know some basic words that you can use when sharing your opinion. Try to remember as many words as possible.

Below is a list of common food and drink. When it comes to sharing an opinion about things, you need to remember that different cases should be applied. Thus, we have written the forms that need to be used with like/love/hate phrases. Cases are tough but don't get discouraged. Even Polish people struggle with them. Let's begin:

Ziemniaki (ziemniaków) - potatoes

Pomidory (pomidorów) - tomatoes

Ogórki (ogórków)- cucumbers

Papryka czerwona (paprykę czerwoną/papryki czerwonej) - red pepper

Cebula (cebulę/cebuli) - onion

Banan (banana) - banana

Jabłka (jabłek) - apples

Pomarańcza (pomarańczę/pomarańczy) - orange

Grejfrut (grejpfruta) - grapefruit

Cytryna (cytrynę/cytryny) - lemon

Gruszka (gruszkę/gruszki) - pear

Brzoskwinia (brzoskwinię/brzoskwini) - peach

Kiełbasa (kiełbasę/kiełbasy) - sausage

Boczek (boczku) - bacon

Kurczak (kurczaka) - chicken

Czekolada (czekoladę/czekolady) - chocolate

Ciastka (ciastek) - cookies/biscuits

Woda mineralna (wodę mineralną/wody mineralnej) - mineral water

Woda gazowana (wodę gazowaną/wody gazowanej) - sparkling water

Cola (colę/coli) - cola

Czerwone wino (czerwonego wina) - red wine

Białe wino (białego wina) - white wine

Whisky - whiskey

Good job! You don't have to learn by heart different case forms of a particular thing. We will be repeating throughout the whole book that communicative effectiveness is the key. If you want to be 100 percent accurate, your learning process will be much slower. It is good to make mistakes and learn from them.

Now let's try to exercise.

Exercise: Try to say in Polish the following expressions.

I like whiskey.

Do you like chocolate?

Do you like sparkling water?

I don't like bananas.

I don't like mineral water.

I love cola.

I hate white wine.

Do you like red wine?

I love bacon.

I hate sausages.

Do you like apples?

Do you like chicken?

I love cookies.

Do you like orange?

I hate red pepper.

I love cucumbers.

I love grapefruit.

Do you like pear?

Feelings and Emotions

In this section, you will learn how to ask someone about his/her mood and how to express your feelings through the Polish language.

To ask someone about his/her mood or feelings, you need to use the following expression:

Jak się czujesz? – How do you feel?

The polite version looks like this:

Jak się Pan/Pani czuje? – How do you feel? (male/female)

Jak się Panowie/Panie/Państwo czują? – How do you feel? (males/females/males and females)

If you want to tell someone about your mood//feelings, you can use the following expressions:

Jestem ... – I am ...

Czuję się ... – I feel ...

Pretty easy, isn't it? Unfortunately, it is not the whole story though. While the expression itself is quite simple, the word that expresses your feelings introduces some complications. You need to apply a different ending to the adjective, depending on your sex. Males usually apply the ending -*y*, whereas females apply -*a*. Without further theoretical explanations, let's go straight into examples since you will grasp the idea based on a real context. Below is a list of basic adjectives describing feelings. On the "Polish side" there are two versions—the first is for males and the second is for females. Try to remember as many words as possible. You will need them for further practice!

Szczęśliwy/Szczęśliwa – happy

Smutny/smutna – sad

Zmęczony/zmęczona – tired

Pewny/pewna siebie – confident

Poekscytowany/podekscytowana – excited

Zainteresowany/zainteresowana – interested

Zaskoczony/zaskoczona – surprised

Znudzony/znudzona – bored

Zdenerwowany/zdenerwowana – nervous

Głodny/głodna – hungry

Spragniony/spragniona – thirsty

Śpiący/śpiąca – sleepy

Chory/chora – sick

Obolały/obolała – sore

Oszołomiony/oszołomiona – dizzy

Wkurzony/wkurzona – angry

Usatysfakcjonowany/usatysfakcjonowana – satisfied

Dumny/dumna – proud

Sfrustrowany/sfustrowana – frustrated

Przestraszony/przestraszona – scared

Rozczarowany/rozczarowana – disappointed

Good job! It is time to practice these words in a real context. Remember about choosing a form that corresponds with your sex.

Exercise: Try to say the following phrases in Polish.

I feel tired.

I am hungry.

How do you feel?

I feel angry!

How do you feel? (formal, male)

I feel dizzy.

I am surprised.

How do you feel? (formal, female)

I feel sick.

I am excited.

How do you feel? (formal, males)

I feel thirsty.

I am proud.

How do you feel? (formal, females)

I feel sore.

I am confident.

How do you feel? (formal, males and females)

I feel bored.

I am disappointed.

I feel sleepy.

I am nervous.

I am sad.

I feel happy.

I am scared.

Very good! If you have problems with a particular structure, don't hesitate to go back to the previous chapters. Learning a foreign language is a demanding process and takes time.

Before we go on to the next chapter, here are some exercises as a revision of the knowledge you have already acquired. Prepare yourself for multiskill practice! If you feel confident enough and don't need more time, try these exercises now.

Revision

This section is designed to test your knowledge and everything you have already learned about the Polish language. The exercises contain items and expressions picked randomly from different sections.

Exercise 1 – Try to say the following expressions in Polish:

I love walking.

I like playing the guitar.

I hate singing.

I love riding the horse.

I love going out.

I hate going to school.

I like driving a car.

I feel sore.

I am confident.

How do you feel? (formal, males and females)

I feel bored.

I am disappointed.

I feel sleepy.

I am nervous.

I am sad.

Do you like singing?

Do you like walking?

Do you like partying?

Do you like drawing?

Wait a moment.

I am sorry.

I don't understand.

Sorry for being late.

Sure.

Me neither.

No problem.

Excuse me.

I am 97 years old.

I am 6 years old.

I am 45 years old.

I am 23 years old.

I live in a house.

I live in a block of flats.

I live in the city center.

I live in the mountains.

I live near a big city.

Exercise 2 – There will be a couple of guided dialogs with English expressions to translate. Try to say everything in Polish.

Dialog 1:

- Hello. I am Sarah.

- Hello. I am Ania. How old are you?

- I am 16. And you?

- I am 23. Where are you from?

- I am from the USA, and you?

- I am from Poland.

- Nice to meet you.

Dialog 2:

- What do you like the most?

- I like riding a bike and play computer games. And you?

- I like riding a bike and singing. I don't like playing computer games.

- Okay. I don't like doing shopping.

Dialog 3:

- Where are you from?

- I am from Poland, and you?

- I am from England. Where do you live?

- I live in Warsaw. And you?

- I live in London.

Dialog 4:

- How do you feel?

- I feel tired. And you?

- I am hungry. What do you like?

- I like ice cream and bananas, and you?

- I like chicken and cola.

Exercise 3 – There will be a couple of situations that will require different expressions, but you won't be provided with the English versions. The only thing you will know is the context. Try to come up with Polish expressions based on the context provided:

- You want to apologize for something. What do you say?

- You want to know what time it is. How do you ask your friend?

- You want to know what your friend thinks about a certain problem. How do you ask him/her?

- You see a child crying. What do you say to him/her?

- You've just met your friend's brother. Introduce yourself, say a couple of phrases about yourself (your place of living/your age) and ask him how old he is.

- You are talking about favorite foods with your friend. Tell him/her what you like the most and ask him/her what he/she likes the most.

- You are talking about favorite ways of spending free time with your friend. Tell him/her what you like the most and ask what he/she likes the most.

- You've just met your new boss. Introduce yourself, tell him/her about your place of living/your age, and ask him/her how he/she feels.

- Your friend wants to know how you feel today. Tell him/her and ask how he/she feels today.

- Your teacher is asking you how you feel. Tell him/her and ask how he/she feels today.

- You've just met your new teacher. Introduce yourself, tell a couple of things about your age/place of living, etc.

- Ask your friend's parents about their favorite ways of spending free time.

- Ask your coworker about his/her favorite food.

- You got lost in the city center. Introduce yourself to a stranger and tell him/her where you are from. Then, ask him/her to show you the way on the map.

Good job! You are confident enough to have a basic conversation in Polish. With such knowledge, you will be able to use Polish in different situations, formal and informal. This chapter has equipped you with the basic skills that will be helpful no matter what situation you will be faced with.

Chapter 6 – At Work

If you have got this far, you've probably learned the basics of the Polish language. In this chapter, you are going to learn vocabulary connected to jobs and the working environment as well as some useful phrases.

Profession

No matter where you live, questions concerning your way of living appear very often. It is good to know how they sound in Polish, so here they are:

Gdzie pracujesz? – Where do you work?

Kim jesteś z zawodu? – What is your profession?

Co robisz w życiu? – What do you do? (general question)

If you want to tell someone about your profession, you need to use the following phrases:

Jestem... – I am a/an...*

Pracuję jako... – I work as a...

*The phrase *jestem...* requires using a different case, whereas the phrase *pracuję jako...* does not change the case of the noun. To show

how these phrases work, let's take the word *lekarz* [doctor]. The first phrase would look like this:

Jestem lekarz**em**.

The second phrase would look like this:

Pracuję jako lekarz.

As always, using the wrong case will not entirely affect the understanding of your message. You don't have to learn all the declensions. The best way to master the inflectional system is to use the language and learn from your mistakes.

Now it is time to learn some new vocabulary. Below is a list of popular professions. Go through the list multiple times and try to remember as many words as possible. We have included the second form to allow you the opportunity to practice both ways of telling someone about your profession.

Professions:

Lekarz (lekarzem) – a doctor

Nauczyciel (nauczycielem) – a teacher

Biznesmen (biznesmenem) – a businessman

Bizneswoman (bizneswoman) – a businesswoman

Prawnik (prawnikiem)– a lawyer

Pielęgniarka (pielęgniarką) – a nurse

Sprzedawca (sprzedawcą) – a shop assistant

Księgowy/księgowa (księgowym/księgową) – an accountant

Strażak (strażakiem) – a firefighter

Żołnierz (żołnierzem) – a soldier

Policjant (policjantem) – a policeman

Policjantka (policjantką) – a policewoman

Szef kuchni (szefem kuchni) – a chef

Kucharz (kucharzem) - a cook

Kelner (kelnerem) - a waiter

Kelnerka (kelnerką) - a waitress

Pilot (pilotem) - a pilot

Naukowiec (naukowcem) - a scientist

Listonosz (listonoszem) - a postman

Tłumacz (tłumaczem) - a translator

Mechanik (mechanikiem) - a mechanic

Hydraulik (hydraulikiem) - a plumber

Malarz (malarzem) - a painter

Aktor (aktorem) - an actor

Aktorka (aktorką) - an actress

Kierowca (kierowcą) - a driver

Sprzątacz/sprzątaczka (sprzątaczem/sprzątaczką) - a cleaner

Dentysta (dentystą) - a dentist

Rolnik (rolnikiem) - a farmer

Inżynier (inżynierem) - an engineer

Kierownik/menedżer (kierownikiem/menadżerem) - a manager

Fotograf (fotografem) - a photographer

Muzyk (muzykiem) - a musician

Sekretarz/sekretarka (sekretarzem/sekretarką) - a secretary

Kierowca taksówki (kierowcą taksówki) - a taxi driver

Pisarz (pisarzem) - a writer

Opiekun/opiekunka (opiekunem/opiekunką) - a babysitter

Piekarz (piekarzem) - a baker

Fryzjer (fryzjerem) - a hairdresser

Filmowiec (filmowcem) – a filmmaker

Dziennikarz (dziennikarzem) – a journalist

Ksiądz (księdzem) – a priest

Weterynarz (weterynarzem) – a vet

Psycholog (psychologiem) – a psychologist

Badacz (badaczem) – a researcher

Exercise: Try to say the following phrases in Polish.

I am a researcher.

I work as a dentist.

I work as a firefighter.

I am an actor.

I work as a filmmaker.

I am a waiter.

I am a waitress.

I work as an accountant.

I am a businessman.

I am a businesswoman.

I work as a cleaner.

I am a cook.

I work as a hairdresser.

I work as a plumber.

I am a taxi driver.

I am a journalist.

I work as a mechanic.

I am a farmer.

Good job! You have learned how to tell someone about your profession. Now it is time to move on to some advanced vocabulary connected to the work environment and some specific phrases that will make you more confident with your Polish.

Working Environment

It is time to learn some advanced phrases! At first, we will give you some vocabulary. After learning some essential words, you will have the opportunity to learn some phrases that might be very useful, especially if you are planning to work in Poland. Let's start!

Miejsce pracy – workplace

Biuro – office

Praca – job

Fabryka – factory

Firma – company

Siedziba firmy – headquarters

Korporacja – corporation

Pracownik – employee

Pracodawca – employer

Szef/szefowa – boss

Koledzy z pracy – colleagues/coworkers

Praca zdalna – remote working

Pracownik fizyczny – blue-collar worker

Pracować – work

Wypłata – salary

Zarobki – earnings/wages

Brutto – gross

Netto – post-tax

Podatek – tax

Awans – promotion

Dostać awans – to get a promotion

Dostać pracę – to get a job

Być zwolnionym – to be dismissed

Być zwolnionym natychmiastowo – to be fired

Zredukować personel – to make people redundant

Podwyżka – pay rise

Dostać podwyżkę – to get a pay rise

Praca na cały etat – full-time job

Praca na pół etatu – part-time job

Praca dodatkowa – side job

Praca zmianowa – shift job

Nocna zmiana/nocka – night shift

Rozmowa o pracę – job interview

Umowa o pracę – job agreement

Życiorys (CV) – curriculum vitae (CV)

Podanie o pracę – job application form

Stanowisko – position

Kwalifikacje – qualifications

Wymagania – requirements

Umiejętności – skills

Wykształcenie – education

Doświadczenie zawodowe – job experience

Dział kadr – personnel department/HR

Dział obsługi klienta – customer service department

Dział wsparcia technicznego – help desk

Wyjazd służbowy – business trip

Notatka służbowa – memo

Spotkanie - meeting

Urlop - leave

Urlop macierzyński - maternity leave

Urlop zdrowotny - sick leave

Urlop bezpłatny - unpaid leave

Płatny urlop wypoczynkowy - paid vacation leave

It is time to practice and memorize the words! Let's check what you remember.

Exercise: Try to find the English equivalents for these Polish words.

Korporacja

Pracownik

Pracodawca

Szef/szefowa

Kwalifikacje

Wymagania

Umiejętności

Notatka służbowa

Spotkanie

Urlop

Pracować

Wypłata

Zarobki

Brutto

Netto

Podatek

Doświadczenie zawodowe

Dział kadr

Dział obsługi klienta

Dział wsparcia technicznego

Wyjazd służbowy

Dostać awans

Dostać pracę

Być zwolnionym

Być zwolnionym natychmiastowo

Praca na cały etat

Praca na pół etatu

Excellent! You have learned plenty of essential words that will help you survive in the Polish working environment! Now it is time to go further and learn some very useful phrases. Take your time and repeat them multiple times. Try to remember as many phrases as possible.

Proszę przesłać CV oraz podanie o pracę. – Please, send your CV and a job application form.

Pracuję na pół etatu. – I have a part-time job.

Pracuję w dużej firmie. – I work in a big company.

Jestem nauczycielem/nauczycielką. Pracuję w szkole średniej. – I am a teacher. I work at a high school.

Gdzie znajduje się firma w której pracujesz? – Where is the company you work at located?

Firma znajduje się w Warszawie. – The company headquarters is located in Warsaw.

Pracuję w systemie zmianowym. – I have a shift job.

O której godzinie kończysz pracę? – What time do you finish your work?

Dziś kończę o 17:00. – Today I'm finishing at 5:00 pm.

Dziś idę na nockę. – Today I'm working a night shift.

Jakie wykształcenie Pan/Pani posiada? – What educational background do you have?

Ukończyłem/ukończyłam uniwersytet. – I graduated/graduated university.

Jakie umiejętności Pan/Pani posiada? – What skills do you have?

Czy posiada Pan/Pani prawo jazdy? – Do you have a driving license?

Tak, posiadam prawo jazdy. – Yes, I have a driving license.

Jakie jest Pana/Pani doświadczenie zawodowe? – What is your job experience?

Pracowałem dla firmy... od 2011 roku. – I worked for the company... since 2011.

Prosimy skontaktować się z naszym działem wsparcia technicznego. – Please, contact our help desk.

Proszę przesłać podanie o pracę do działu kadr. – Please, send your application form to the personnel department.

Dostałem/dostałam awans! – I got a promotion!

Czy mogę wziąć dzień wolnego? – Can I take a day off?

Jestem chory/chora. Jutro nie mogę przyjść do pracy. – I am sick. I can't go to work tomorrow.

Good job! Now it is time to practice. However, we haven't made it easy—you need to come up with a Polish phrase on your own, not to translate directly from English!

Exercise: Try to come up with a suitable Polish phrase. There are no straight answers—everything depends on your imagination!

    a) Ask your colleague what time he/she finishes his/her job

    b) Tell your friends that you got a promotion

c) Tell your interviewer that you've graduated from university

d) Ask your boss to give you a day off

e) Tell your boss that you are sick and you can't go to work tomorrow

f) Tell your friend what time you finish work

g) Tell your interviewer that you have a driving license

h) Tell your business partner about the location of your company's headquarters

i) Tell your interviewer about your previous job experience.

Good job! You are confident enough to join the Polish working environment. There is much more to learn, yet knowing these phrases and words will give you a good start.

Chapter 7 – At School/At The University

Due to globalization and open borders, especially in the European Union, many students have the opportunity to study abroad. Many interesting exchange programs enable you to spend a year in a different country while learning the same subjects. Even some younger learners can go abroad on their own by taking part in a language camp or a school trip.

If you are considering choosing Poland as your target country, it is a good choice! Even though most of your friends will speak English, you need to familiarize yourself with some essential vocabulary and phrases that will help you survive the first days/weeks in a Polish school. Thus, we have chosen the most important Polish words or phrases that you might be faced with during your school trip/exchange year. Here we go!

School subjects

You will probably feel lost during your first days in a completely different environment, especially while looking for classrooms, classes, and teachers. It is good to know your lesson plan in advance;

thus, the following list includes a list of school subjects that you definitely need to know:

Edukacja – education

Język polski – Polish

Matematyka – mathematics/maths

Język obcy – foreign language

Język angielski – English

Język niemiecki – German

Język hiszpański – Spanish

Geografia – geography

Historia – history

Biologia – biology

Chemia – chemistry

Fizyka – physics

Religia – religion

Wychowanie fizyczne (WF) – physical education (PE)

Muzyka – music class

Plastyka – art class

Informatyka – IT class

Godzina wychowawcza – form period/homeroom period

Zajęcia dodatkowe – extracurricular activities

Kółko zainteresowań – special interest group

Zajęcia wyrównawcze – remedial class

Gimnastyka korekcyjna – remedial exercises

Zajęcia praktyczne – practical class

Zajęcia do wyboru – elective courses

Zajęcia wychowawcze – advisory class

Zajęcia wieczorowe – night class

Exercise: Try to come up with an English equivalent of the following Polish school subject.

Geografia

Historia

Biologia

Chemia

Fizyka

Religia

Język polski

Matematyka

Język obcy

Język angielski

Religia

Wychowanie fizyczne (WF)

Muzyka

Plastyka

Informatyka

Zajęcia praktyczne

Zajęcia do wyboru

Zajęcia wychowawcze

Zajęcia wieczorowe

Good job! Knowing your lesson plan will give you confidence during your first days at school. Yet to make your experience even less stressful, you need to know some basic words connected to the school environment. As always, try to remember as many words as possible and go through the list multiple times.

School Environment

Nauczyciel - teacher

Uczeń - student

Dyrektor szkoły - school head teacher/school principal

Sala lekcyjna - classroom

Lekcja - lesson

Zajęcia - class

Stołówka - cafeteria/canteen

Sklepik szkolny - tuck shop

Szatnia - changing room

Sala gimnastyczna - school gym

Boisko szkolne - school playground

Sekretariat szkolny - school's secretary office

Biblioteka szkolna - school library

Czytelnia - a reading room

Sala komputerowa - IT suite

Gabinet dyrektora - head teacher's office

Woźny - caretaker

Dzwonek szkolny - school bell

Przerwa - break

Przerwa śniadaniowa - lunch break

Świetlica szkolna - afterschool club

Autobus szkolny - school bus

Wycieczka szkolna - school trip

Sprawdzian/test - test

Ocena - grade (oceny - grades)

Kartkówka - short quiz

Egzamin państwowy - state exam

Uczyć się - to learn/to study

Uczyć się na pamięć - to learn by heart

Wkuwać - swot/cram

Zaliczyć/zdać test - to pass a test

Oblać test/nie zaliczyć testu - to fail a test

Pisać egzamin - to take a test

Poprawiać test - to retake a test

Egzamin poprawkowy/poprawka - retake

Dziennik lekcyjny - register

Prezentacja - presentation

Egzamin ustny - oral exam

Egzamin pisemny - written exam

Zadanie domowe - homework

Projekt - project

Praca w grupach - group work

Praca w parach - pair work

Rozmowa - conversation

Dyskusja - discussion

There have been many new words to memorize; thus, it is time to practice and ensure that you have made the most of your learning.

Exercise: Try to come up with a Polish equivalent of the following English words.

IT suite

head teacher's office

caretaker

school bell

break

to fail a test

to take a test

to retake a test

retake

register

changing room

school gym

school playground

school's secretary office

school library

oral exam

written exam

homework

project

group work

teacher

student

school head teacher/school principal

classroom

Excellent! You have made huge progress and communication in Polish. To give you a boost, below are some essential phrases that might be very useful during your Polish schooldays. Take your time and repeat each phrase a few times:

Dzień dobry, uczniowie! – Good morning, students!

Dzień dobry, Panie/Pani... – Good morning, Mr./Mrs./Ms.

Siadajcie, proszę. – Sit down, please.

Otwórzcie podręczniki na stronie 46. - Please, open your books on page 46.

W pyszłym tygodniu odbędzie się kartkówka ze słówek. - Next week there will be a short vocabulary quiz.

Przepraszam, czy mogę wyjść do toalety? - Excuse me, can I go to the toilet?

Zadania 3, 4, 5 to zadanie domowe na przyszły tydzień. - Exercises 3, 4, 5 are homework for the next week.

Robert, czy mógłbyś wytrzeć tablicę? - Robert, could you clean the blackboard, please?

Dziś będziemy mówić o dzikich zwierzętach. - Today we will be talking about wild animals.

Czy mógłbyś to przeliterować? - Could you spell it out?

Przepraszam, gdzie jest stołówka? - Excuse me, where is the school canteen?

Przepraszam, jak dojdę do sali gimnastycznej? - Excuse me, how can I get to the gym?

O której kończy się lekcja? - What time does the lesson end?

Lekcja kończy się o godzinie 9:45. - The lesson ends at 9:45 am.

Jakie przedmioty mamy dzisiaj? - Which classes do we have today?

Dzisiaj mamy matematykę, fizykę, informatykę, WF i geografię. - Today we have maths, physics, IT, PE, and geography.

O której godzinie odjeżdża autobus szkolny? - What time does the school bus leave?

Autobus szkolny odjeżdża o 15:00, zaraz po ostatniej lekcji. - The school bus leaves at 3:00 pm, right after the last lesson.

Dzisiejsze zajęcia są odwołane. - Today's classes have been canceled.

Now it is time to practice a bit. We won't ask you for a translation; you will need to come up with a suitable phrase on your own.

Exercise: Try to come up with a suitable Polish phrase. There are no straight answers—everything depends on your imagination!

a) You don't know what time the school bus leaves. Ask your friend.

b) You don't know what time the lesson ends. Ask your friend.

c) You don't know what classes you have today. Ask your friend.

d) You had a problem with understanding a word. Ask your friend to spell it out.

e) You don't know where the school canteen is. Ask your friend.

f) Your PE lesson is starting in five minutes, but you don't know where the gym is. Ask your friend to give you directions.

g) Your friend wants to know what time the school bus leaves. Tell him/her.

h) Your teacher wants to know your name. Introduce yourself.

i) Your friend wants to know what classes your class has today. Tell him/her.

j) Your friend wants to know what time the lesson ends. Tell him/her.

At the University/College

Whether you have decided to study in Poland or take part in a student exchange program, it doesn't matter. Poland is a beautiful country, and you will enjoy your stay. In order not to get lost, it is advisable to know at least some basic words and phrases connected to the academic environment:

Uniwersytet - University/college

Stopień naukowy - degree

Student - student

Wykładowca - lecturer

Wykład - lecture

Sala wykładowa - lecture room

Aula - lecture hall

Licencjat - bachelor's degree

Magister - master's degree

Dyplom/świadectwo - diploma

Zajęcia praktyczne - practicals

Praktykant - trainee

Notatki - notes

Robić notatki - to take notes

Wygłaszać mowę - to give a speech

Przygotowywać prezentację - to prepare a presentation

Badanie - research/study

Przeprowadzać badanie - to conduct research

Wyniki badania - results of the study

Rektor uniwersytetu - college president/university president

Egzamin - exam

Sesja egzaminacyjna - exam session

Zaliczenie warunkowe - conditional promotion

Rok studiów - college level

Praca dyplomowa - thesis

Praca licencjacka - bachelor's thesis/BA thesis

Praca magisterska - master's thesis/MA thesis

Studia zaoczne - part-time studies

Studia dzienne - full-time studies

Kampus uniwersytecki - the university campus

Dziekanat - deanery/dean's office

Doktorat - doctorate

Praca doktorancka - Ph.D. thesis

Absolwent - graduate

Absolutorium - graduation ceremony

Wydział - institute

Władze szkoły - school authorities

Rekrutacja - recruitment

Egzaminy wstępne - entrance exams

Wymiana studencka - student exchange program

Indeks - student book

Legtymacja studencka - student ID card

Kredyt studencki - student loan

Akademik - residence hall/dormitory

Europejski System Transferu Punktów (ECTS) - European Credit Transfer System (ECTS)

Good! However, if you don't feel confident enough, go back over these and try to repeat them out loud as many times as possible. Eventually, all these new words won't be new at all.

Time to practice!

Exercise: Try to find the English equivalents of the following Polish words.

Praca licencjacka

Praca magisterska

Studia zaoczne

Studia dzienne

Wymiana studencka

Indeks

Legitymacja studencka

Kredyt studencki

Akademik

Rektor uniwersytetu

Egzamin

Sesja egzaminacyjna

Student

Wykładowca

Wykład

Sala wykładowa

Aula

Praktykant

Notatki

Robić notatki

Excellent! You have learned many new words connected with the academic environment. To feel even more confident with your Polish, you need to learn some phrases. Below are some expressions that might help you during your college days/exchange. There are many of them, but don't get discouraged. Try to remember as many as possible and repeat them out loud:

Przepraszam, gdzie znajduje się dziekanat? – Excuse me, where is the dean's office?

Dziekanat znajduje się na trzecim piętrze. – The dean's office is on the third floor.

Przepraszam, gdzie znajduje się aula C1? - Excuse me, where is the lecture hall C1?

Aula C1 jest na czwartym piętrze. - C1 is on the fourth floor.

Dzisiejsze wykłady są odwołane. - All of today's lectures have been canceled.

Wyniki egzaminów zimowych są dostępne na stronie internetowej wydziału. - Winter exams results are available on the website of our institute.

Ten wykład jest nieobowiązkowy. - This lecture is non-mandatory.

Przepraszam, o której rozpoczyna się ostatni wykład? - Excuse me, what time does the last lecture start?

Ostati wykład zaczyna się o 17:00. - The last lecture starts at 5:00 pm.

Dzień dobry, chciałbym/chciałabym wypożyczyć książkę. - Hello, I would like to borrow a book.

Jaka książka Pana/Panią interesuje? - What book are you looking for?

Szukam... - I am looking for...

Proszę chwilkę poczekać. - Wait a moment, please.

Czy to jest książka, której Pan/Pani szuka? - Is that the book you are looking for?

Tak, to dokładnie ta. - Yes, exactly.

Czy mogę zobaczyć Pana/Pani legitymację studencką? - May I see your student ID card?

Oczywiście, proszę. - Of course, here you are.

Dzień dobry, chciałbym/chciałabym wziąć udział w wymianie studenckiej. - Hello, I would like to take part in a student exchange program.

Jaki kraj chciałby Pan/chciałaby Pan odwiedzić? - What country would you like to visit?

Jestem zainteresowany/zainteresowana studiowaniem w Polsce. - I am interested in studying in Poland.

Świetny wybór! Może Pan/Pani skorzystać z naszego nowego programu trwającego pół roku. - Great choice! You can take part in our new program that is a half year long.

Jakie uczelnie w Polsce mogę wybrać? - Which Polish universities can I choose?

Czy w Polsce będę musiał/musiała zdawać egzaminy? - Do I have to take all the exams in Poland?

Tak, wszystkie egzaminy będzie musiał Pan/musiała Pani napisać w Polsce. - Yes, you will have to take all the exams in Poland.

Czy mogą wziąć udział w programie na ostatnim roku studiów? - Can I take part in the exchange program in the last year of my studies?

Niestety, nie może Pan/Pani wziąć udziału w wymianie na ostatnim roku. - I'm sorry, you can't take part in the exchange in the last year.

Dlaczego? - Why?

Ponieważ musi Pan/Pani przeprowadzić badanie i napisać pracę tutaj. - Because you have to conduct the study and write your thesis here.

Exercise: Try to come up with a suitable Polish phrase. There are no straight answers—everything depends on your imagination!

  a) You are looking for the lecture room D2. Ask your friend where it is.

  b) Tell the librarian that you want to borrow a book.

  c) Tell the college employee that you want to take part in a student exchange program.

d) You want to know if you have to take all the exams. Ask your lecturer.

e) You don't know what time the lecture starts. Ask your friend.

f) Your friend wants to know if the next lecture is mandatory. Tell him/her that it isn't.

g) Your friend wants to know what time the last lecture starts. Tell him/her.

h) Tell your friends that all lectures have been canceled today.

i) You are looking for the dean's office. Ask your friend to show you where it is.

j) Tell the college employee that you want to study in Poland.

Excellent! The above words and phrases will help you survive in the Polish academic environment, at least during the first weeks. If you don't feel confident enough, go through the exercises and lists again and again.

Chapter 8 – Food and Drink

Food and drink are one of the most important things on your trip to a foreign country. Whether you are going to eat out or cook at a hostel/apartment, you will have to know some basic vocabulary. Here are the most essential words:

Dairy Products – produkty mleczne:

Mleko – milk

Śmietana – cream

Ser żółty – cheese

Twarożek – cottage cheese

Jogurt – yogurt

Masło – butter

Margaryna – margarine

Maślanka – buttermilk

Bakery – pieczywo:

Chleb – bread

Chleb pszenny – wheat bread

Świeży chleb – fresh bread

Chleb żytni – rye bread

Chleb tostowy – toast bread

Bułka – bread roll

Bagietka – baguette

Pączki – donuts

Ciastka – biscuits/cookies

Vegetables – warzywa:

Ziemniak – potato

Pomidor – tomato

Ogórek – cucumber

Papryka czerwona – red pepper

Cebula – onion

Kapusta – cabbage

Sałata – lettuce

Marchewka – carrot

Brokuł – broccoli

Kalafior – cauliflower

Fasola – beans

Czosnek – garlic

Dynia – pumpkin

Szpinak – spinach

Pietruszka – parsley

Soja – soy

Seler – celery

Jarmuż – kale

Burak – beet/beetroot

Batat – sweet potato

Fruits - owoce:

Banan - banana

Jabłko - apple

Pomarańcza - orange

Grejfrut - grapefruit

Cytryna - lemon

Gruszka - pear

Brzoskwinia - peach

Kokos - coconut

Ananas - pineapple

Śliwka - plum

Arbuz - watermelon

Truskawka - strawberry

Malina - raspberry

Jagoda - blueberry

Wiśnia - cherry

Awokado - avocado

Orzech włoski - a walnut

Meat - mięso:

Kiełbasa - sausage

Bekon - bacon

Kurczak - chicken

Drób - poultry

Wołowina - beef

Wieprzowina - pork

Baranina - lamb

Szynka - ham

Mięso mielone - minced meat

Kabanos - a kabanos sausage (a snack stick sausage)

Salami - salami

Sweets/Candy - słodycze:

Czekolada - chocolate

Ciastka - cookies/biscuits

Cukierki czekoladowe - bonbons

Delicje - jaffa cakes

Batonik - chocolate bar

Żelki - jelly beans/gummy bears

Deser - dessert

Galaretka - jelly

Wafelek - wafer

Lody - ice cream

Lizak - lollipop

Krówka - fudge

Landrynki - hard candy

Beverages - napoje:

Woda w butelce - bottled water

Woda mineralna - mineral water

Woda gazowana - sparkling water

Cola - cola

Napoje gazowane - fizzy drinks

Sok pomarańczowy - orange juice

Sok jabłkowy - apple juice

Koktajl owocowy - fruit cocktail/smoothie

Kawa - coffee

Kawa rozpuszczalna – instant coffe

Kawa czarna – black coffee

Kawa z mlekiem – white coffee

Herbata – tea

Gorąca czekolada – hot chocolate

Piwo – beer

Wódka – vodka

Czerwone wino – red wine

Białe wino – white wine

Whisky – whiskey

Other Groceries:

Jajka – eggs

Mąka – flour

Sól – salt

Pieprz – pepper

Cukier – sugar

Cukier brązowy – cane sugar

Ryż – rice

Olej – oil

Oliwa z oliwek – olive oil

Przyprawy – spices

Miód – honey

Płatki kukurydziane – corn flakes

Płatki śniadaniowe – cereal

Go through the list many times and repeat each word out loud. It is good to know at least some basic names since many grocery shops in Poland are not like supermarkets. When you want to buy something in a small shop, you need to go straight to the shop assistant and tell him or her what you want. Otherwise, you won't be able to buy anything.

When it comes to Polish supermarkets, they are quite common too; you can find at least one, even in a small town. When it comes to the bigger cities, there are many supermarkets everywhere; however, they are not as big as the American ones. One of the most popular Polish supermarkets is Biedronka [the Ladybird]. You will also find some foreign supermarkets, such as Tesco, Lidl, Kaufland, Intermarche, and Carrefour, and some smaller franchises, such as Żabka [the Frog], Stokrotka [the Daisy], Małpka [the Monkey], and Polo Market.

For now, let's pretend that you are not in a supermarket but a small grocery shop. You want to cook something in the shared kitchen in your hostel and are looking for the ingredients. Your task is simple—you need to tell the shop assistant what you want.

If you want to buy something, you need to say:

Poproszę... - please...

Exercise: Try to buy products from your shopping list. The shop assistant doesn't know a word of English!

    a) Eggs, flour, sugar, mineral water, honey, and cereal

    b) Tea, chocolate, beer, bread, and yogurt

    c) Parsley, apple, sausage, ham, and milk

    d) Rice, salt, pepper, tomatoes, and potatoes

    e) Ice cream, avocado, fresh bread, and butter

Good job! It is important to know that you need to use polite language while speaking with a shop assistant. So don't say *cześć!*—use *dzień dobry!/do widzenia* instead.

Here are more phrases that might be useful while doing shopping:

Przepraszam, ile to kosztuje? - Excuse me, how much does it cost?

Czy mogę zapłacić gotówką? - Can I pay with cash?

Czy chciałby Pan/chciałaby Pani zapłacić kartą czy gotówką? - Would you like to pay with cash or with a credit card?

Czy mogę prosić o paragon? - Can I have a receipt, please?

Proszę wprowadzić PIN. - Enter your PIN code, please.

Dziś polecamy... - I recommend buying... today.

Ok, wezmę to. - Okay, I'll take it.

Nie, dziękuję. - No, thanks.

Czy mogę zwrócić ten produkt? - Can I return this product?

Przepraszam, gdzie znajdę owoce? - Excuse me, where can I find fruit?

Tak, w sekcji artykułów spożywczych - Yes, they are in the produce section.

Czy chciałby Pan/chciałaby Pani torbę? - Would you like a plastic bag?

Ten produkt jest obecnie wyprzedany. - This item is currently out of stock.

Czy ten produkt jest w promocji? - Is this product on sale?

Chciałbym/Chciałabym zapłacić gotówką. - I would like to pay with cash.

Chciałbym/Chciałabym zapłacić kartą. - I would like to pay with a credit card.

Proszę, oto reszta. - Here's your change.

Czy jest Pan/Pani członkiem naszego klubu? - Are you a member of our loyalty program?

Czy ma Pan/Pani jakieś drobne? - Have you got any change?*

*Keep in mind: It's quite common that cashiers in Poland ask about the change. If you buy only one thing and give them a bank note, you might be asked to provide some change.

It is time to practice! All you need to do is to react in Polish:

a) Tell the shop assistant that you want your receipt.

b) You want to know if a particular product is on sale. Ask the shop assistant.

c) You're looking for fresh bread. Ask the shop assistant to tell you where it is.

d) Tell the shop assistant that you want to pay with cash.

e) Tell the shop assistant that you want to pay with a credit card.

f) Ask the shop assistant whether you can return a product.

g) Buy eggs (by telling the shop assistant that you want to)

h) Buy fresh bread (by telling the shop assistant that you want to)

i) Buy coffee (by telling the shop assistant that you want to)

j) Buy mineral water (by telling the shop assistant that you want to)

Good job! You are no longer afraid of doing shopping, even in small grocery shops. If you want to use your Polish and practice, we recommend only choosing small shops.

At the Restaurant

When you visit a different country, you probably want to try its cuisine. The best way to do this is to visit restaurants and cafés. Even though most of the staff will probably speak fluent English, it is nice to, at least, say "Thank you!" in the foreign language when visiting a restaurant. And if you go to less known places, don't be surprised when your waiter won't understand English! After all, knowing some basic vocabulary used at a restaurant will make you more confident during your trip to Poland. The following words and phrases will make your trip to a Polish restaurant way easier:

Menu - menu

Śniadanie - breakfast

Lunch - lunch

Obiad - dinner

Kolacja - supper

Przystawki - starters/appetizers

Danie główne - main course/main dish

Zimne napoje - cold drinks

Gorące napoje - hot drinks

Kelner - waiter

Kelnerka - waitress

Szef kuchni - chef

Rachunek - bill

Rezerwacja - reservation

Danie dnia - today's special/dish of the day

Zarezerwować stolik - to book a table

Zapłacić gotówką - to pay with cash

Zapłacić kartą - to pay with a credit card

Złożyć zamówienie - to place the order

Napiwek - a tip (leaving huge tips or leaving tips at all is not a very common thing in Poland. If you don't leave a tip, it is absolutely fine).

Exercise: Say in Polish the following words.

lunch

dinner

supper

starters/appetizers

main course/main dish

cold drinks

hot drinks

waiter

waitress

chef

bill

reservation

today's special/dish of the day

Good! Now it is time to learn some phrases that will enable you to order a meal and communicate with the waiter/waitress in Polish:

Dzień dobry, chciałbym/chciałabym zarezerwować stolik dla ... osób. - Good morning, I would like to book a table for... people.

Dobry wieczór, mam rezerwację dla dwóch osób. - Good evening, I have a reservation for two people.

Dzień dobry, czy mogę przyjąć zamówienie? - Good morning, can I take your order?

Chciałbym/Chaciałabym... - I would like...

Czy mógłby/mogłaby mi Pan/Pani polecić coś do jedzenia? - Could you recommend something to eat?

Czy mógłby/mogłaby mi Pan/Pani polecić coś do jedzenia? - Could you recommend something to drink?

Czy chciałby/ chciałaby Pan/Pani coś do picia? - Would you like something to drink?

Przepraszam, czy mogę dostać menu? - Excuse me, can I have a menu, please?

Jakie jest dzisiejsze danie dnia? - What dish is today's special?

Chciałbym/chciałabym zapłacić kartą. – I would like to pay with a credit card.

Chciałbym/chciałabym zapłacić gotówką. – I would like to pay with cash.

Chciałbym/Chciałabym zapłacić. – I would like to pay. *

*The service in Polish restaurants looks slightly different; don't expect your waiter to come to you every five minutes and check if everything is okay with the meal. If you want to pay, you just need to call the waiter and say that you want your bill.

Now it is time to practice. As always, try to choose the best Polish phrase:

     a) Tell your waiter/waitress that you want a menu.

     b) You want to know what is today's special. Ask your waiter.

     c) Tell your waiter/waitress that you want to pay.

     d) Tell your waiter/waitress that you want to pay with cash.

     e) Tell your waiter/waitress that you want to pay with a credit card.

     f) Book a table for five people.

     g) Ask your waiter to recommend something to eat.

     h) Ask your waiter to recommend something to drink.

Excellent! If you want to order a particular meal, you just say *poproszę* + the name of the meal (just as in the shopping section). For example:

Poproszę kawę. – One coffee, please.

Remember that *poproszę* changes the case of the noun (here: the name of a meal/product). Yet if you forget about applying the case (accusative), you will be understood anyway. Just don't feel ashamed of the way your Polish sounds. If your waiter/waitress understands you very well, you are successful.

Now it is time for something extra. Let's just chill out and stop memorizing phrases and vocabulary for a moment. Below is a list of traditional Polish meals that are definitely worth trying:

Kotlet schabowy - a breaded **pork** cutlet; made of **pork tenderloin** (with the bone or without), or a **pork chop**.

Pierogi - Polish dumplings; they come with different fillings (e.g., cheese, jam, fruits, meat, cabbage, mushrooms).

Bigos - very spicy stew based on **sauerkraut** and meat.

Gołąbki - cabbage leaves filled with spiced minced meat and rice.

Kiełbasa - a Polish sausage; yet it differs significantly from the English equivalent. It comes in different versions (e.g., fresh, smoked) and is made of different types of meat (pork, lamb, veal, game, beef, etc.).

Kapusta kiszona - sauerkraut.

Ogórek konserwowy - a pickled cucumber; rather sweet and vinegary in taste. Sałatka warzywna **(sałatka jarzynowa)** - vegetable salad; a traditional Polish side dish based on cooked vegetables (potato, carrot, parsley root, celery root) with eggs, pickled cucumbers, and mayonnaise.

Żurek - very traditional Polish sour rye soup; it contains eggs, Polish sausage, diced potatoes, diced carrots, meat, and mushrooms.

Pyry z gzikiem (Upper Poland) - potatoes (pyry) served with gzik (**quark** with **sour cream**, onion, and chives).

Bryndza **(Lesser Poland)** - sheep milk cheese.

Oscypek **(Tatra Mountains)** - hard, salty cheese from non-pasteurized **sheep's milk;** smoked over a fire and often served with some cranberry jam.

Cepeliny **(Podlasie)** - large and long potato dumplings filled with meat.

Kluski śląskie **(Silesia)** - round dumplings made of potatoes that are served with gravy.

These are the traditional dishes, yet there are many new Polish dishes worth trying. For example, if you are into street food, try *zapiekanka*–a short baguette topped with ham, mushrooms, tomato sauce, different vegetables, and mayonnaise. *Zapiekanka* comes in different varieties and sizes.

Apart from traditional cuisine, many restaurants offer food from all around the world (Italian, Chinese, Indian, etc.), so don't expect only restaurants that serve *pierogi* and *żurek*. Moreover, if you are on a plant-based diet, you will be surprised how many vegan restaurants can be found in Poland. In fact, Warsaw is in the top ten of European cities with the biggest amount of vegan and vegetarian restaurants.

Chapter 9 – Entertainment

A good trip consists of sightseeing and some entertainment. If you go on a trip on your own, it is up to you how you spend your time. Thus, keep in mind that Polish cities offer plenty of opportunities to enjoy in your free time. Moreover, the nightlife is amazing.

Cinema/Movies

Cinemas are quite popular in Poland. Cities such as Warsaw, Cracow or Poznan contain at least ten different cinemas, and some smaller cities offer at least one. The tickets usually are more expensive on weekends, so if you want to choose the cheapest way, go to the cinema on Wednesday or Thursday. Sometimes, tickets on weekends can cost twice as much! Below are some vocabulary and phrases that might be useful during your trip to the cinema:

Kino - cinema

Film - film/movie

Film akcji - action film

Thriller - thriller

Gatunek filmowy - a movie genre

Komedia romantyczna - romantic comedy

Komedia - comedy

Horror – horror film

Film historyczny – historical film

Film przygodowy – adventure film

Film science fiction – science-fiction film

Musical/film muzyczny – musical

Sala kinowa – screening room

Miejsce – seat

Rząd – row

Ekran – screen

Bar przekąskowy – snack bar

Popcorn – popcorn

Zimne napoje – cold beverages

Bilet do kina – cinema ticket

Now let's try a short exercise that will help you remember the words you have just learned.

Exercise: Say in Polish the following words.

seat

row

screen

snack bar

popcorn

cold beverages

cinema ticket

historical film

adventure film

science-fiction film

musical

cinema

film/movie

action film

thriller

a movie genre

romantic comedy

Before you go to the cinema, you have to, of course, choose your movie. We have prepared a short exercise that will allow you to discuss your favorite films with your friend. Remember the chapter in which we practiced likes/dislikes and like/love/hate phrases? It is time to use them again.

Exercise: There are a few situations. Using your previous knowledge and vocabulary from this chapter, try to discuss your favorite kind of film with your friend.

a) Tell your friend that you don't like romantic comedies.

b) Ask your friend what movie genre he/she likes the most.

c) Tell your friend that you love thrillers.

d) Tell your friend that you hate horror films.

Very good! You have chosen the film, so it is time to go to the cinema. Here are the most useful phrases:

Dzień dobry, poproszę dwa blilety. - Hello, two movie tickets, please.

Jaki film chciałby Pan/chciałaby Pani obejrzeć? - Which film would you like to see?

Chciałbym/chciałabym obejrzeć ten film. - I would like to see this film.

Proszę wybrać swoje miejsce. - Please, choose your seat.

Czy te dwa miejsca są wolne? - Are these two seats free?

Przykro mi, te miejsca nie są już wolne. - I'm sorry, these two are not available.

Czy mogę zabrać jedzenie i napoje na salę? - Can I take food and drink to the screening room?

Może Pan/Pani zabrać tylko jedzenie i picie zakupione w naszym barze. - You can take the food and beverages from our snack bar.

Przepraszam, gdzie jest bar z przekąskami? - Excuse me, where is the snack bar?

Dzień dobry, chciałbym/chciałabym kupić dwa duże popcorny. - Hello, I would like to buy two large popcorns.

Dobrze, czy coś do picia? - Okay, would you like something to drink?

Poproszę dwie duże cole. - Two large cokes, please.

Przepraszam, gdzie jest sala numer 8? - Excuse me, where is room number 8?

Prosimy o wyłączenie telefonów. - Please, switch off your phones.

Nagrywanie filmów jest zabronione. - Recording is not allowed.

Let's go through a short exercise.

Exercise: Try to choose the best Polish phrase.

  a) Buy two tickets.

  b) Ask the employee if these two seats are available.

  c) Order two large cokes.

  d) Ask the employee where room 8 is.

  e) Ask the employee where the snack bar is.

  f) Ask your friend which film he/she would like to see.

Excellent! You can go to the Polish cinema and order tickets in Polish.

At the Theater/Opera

Although theaters are not that popular when compared to previous decades, you can still enjoy some places that are worth visiting. Theaters in Poland can be found in cities such as Warsaw, Krakow, etc. Here is a list of the most important words connected to art:

Teatr – theater

Teatr muzyczny – musical theatre

Sztuka – play

Spektakl/przedstawienie – performance

Występować – perform

Aktor/aktorka – actor

Główna rola – lead/major role

Balet – ballet

Balet klasyczny – classical ballet

Kurtyna – curtain

Rekwizyt – prop/stage prop

Scena – stage

Opera – opera

Opera – opera house

Operetka – operetta

Musical – musical

Chór – choir

tancerz/tancerka – dancer

śpiewak operowy – opera singer (masculine)

śpiewaczka operowa – opera singer (feminine)

It is time to memorize the vocabulary through practice.

Exercise: Say the Polish equivalents of the English words below.

stage

opera

opera house

operetta

musical

choir

play

performance

perform

actor

ballet

classical ballet

curtain

prop/stage prop

Good! You are about to be ready to go to the Polish theater. Now imagine that you are sitting with your friend at a café and talking about art.

Exercise: Try to say it in Polish.

        a) Tell your friend that you love ballet.

        b) Tell your friend that you would like to see a play.

        c) Tell your friend that you don't like the major role in the play.

        d) Ask your friend if he/she likes ballet.

        e) Ask your friend if he/she likes opera.

        f) Tell your friend that you love musicals and ask if he/she does too.

Music and Nightlife

If you are in a different country, you definitely need to try the nightlife and get familiar with the music. There are plenty of nightclubs, pubs and good parties in each city in Poland. Moreover, parties do not finish at 2:00 am or 3:00 am, and Polish nightclubs are usually open till the early morning, so 6:00 am or even 7:00 am—yes, in Poland, you can party all night long! Apart from parties, many pubs offer live concerts, performances, and karaoke contests.

Let's learn some vocabulary connected to music:

Muzyka - music

Gatunek muzyczny - a music genre

Rock - rock music

Pop - pop music

Hip-hop - hip-hop

Muzyka taneczna - dance music

Koncert - a concert

Występ - a performance

Karaoke - karaoke

Płyta - an album

Utwór - a track

Piosenka - a song

Piosenkarz (male)/piosenkarka (fem.) - a singer

It is time to practice.

Exercise: Try to say these English sentences in Polish.

a) Tell your friend that you like rock music.

b) Ask your friend what music genre he/she likes the most.

c) Tell your friend that you don't like pop music.

d) Tell your friend that you love dance music.

Good! You can now discuss your favorite music.

Now, it is time to party:

Nocne życie - nightlife

Klub nocny/klub - nightclub

Klub muzyczny - music club

Bar/pub - bar/pub

Dyskoteka - disco

Barman - barman/bartender

Barmanka - barmaid/bartender

Parkiet - dance floor

Tańczyć - dance

Muzyka - music

Karaoke - karaoke

Śpiewać - sing

Imprezować - party

Spędzać czas z przyjaciółmi - spend time with friends

Zespół muzyczny - music group

DJ/didżej - DJ/club DJ

Drink/koktajl - cocktail

Loża VIP - VIP lounge

Ochroniarze - security guards

The words above are worth knowing if you want to party in Poland. Go through the list once again if you have forgotten most of the new words. If you haven't, let's practice.

Exercise: Say the Polish equivalents of the English words below.

music group

DJ/club DJ

cocktail

VIP lounge

security guards

music

karaoke

sing

party

nightlife

nightclub

music club

bar/pub

disco

barman/bartender

Excellent! You have learned a few words that might help you order your favorite drink or go to your favorite club. It is time to put these words in a real context by learning some useful phrases:

Cześć, chciałbym/chciałabym zamówić dwa koktajle. - Hi, I would like to buy two cocktails.

Oczywiście, jakie drinki? - Of course, which drinks?

Poproszę dwa z owocami. - I would like two drinks with some fruit.

Oczywiście. Czy mam dorzucić kostki lodu? - Of course. Would you like some ice cubes?

Tak, poproszę. - Yes, please.

Cześć, czy mogę prosić o kartę napojów? - Hi, can I have a cocktail menu?

Cześć, oto karta napojów. - Hi, here is the cocktail menu.

Przepraszam, o której startuje impreza? – Excuse me, what time does the party start?

Dobry wieczór, chciałbym/chciałabym zamówić lożę VIP dla 9 osób. – Hello, I would like to book a VIP lounge this night for nine people.

Oczywiście, to będzie 200 zł. – Of course, that will be 200 zł.

Exercise: Try to say the following in Polish.

a) Order four cocktails and one beer.

b) You don't know what time the party starts. Ask your friend.

c) Book the VIP lounge.

d) Ask the bartender to show you the cocktail menu.

Good job! Partying in Poland is no longer be a problem for you.

Short Revision

Let's sum up the whole entertainment chapter and get straight into practice.

Exercise: Try to say the following in Polish.

a) You are talking with your friend about movies. Tell him/her that you like romantic comedies, but you hate action films. Then, ask him/her what type of film he/she likes the most.

b) You are in a nightclub. Go to the bartender and order three drinks. Then go to the manager and book a VIP lounge for your friends.

c) You are in the cinema with your friend. Buy two tickets for the movie. Then go to the snack bar and buy two large popcorns and two large cokes.

d) You are talking with your friend about music. Tell him/her that you love pop music and rock music and that you hate dance music. Then ask him/her about his/her favorite music genre.

e) You are in the cinema. As your friend which film he/she would like to see.

f) Ask your friend if he/she likes ballet.

g) Ask your friend if he/she likes opera.

h) Tell your friend that you love ballet.

i) Tell your friend that you would like to see a play.

j) You don't know what time the party starts. Ask your friend.

Afterword

You have now faced an intensive language course and demanding exercises, but your language journey isn't over yet; this is just the beginning. This book should have been informative, educational, and provided a solid foundation of the Polish language. Now, being equipped with the basic knowledge, you are able and willing to continue your journey.

Remember that this book is not a one-time read. Every time you forget a word or a phrase, go back to whichever chapter you need. After all, systematic and consistent learning is all that counts. If you have the opportunity to go to Poland, don't hesitate—pack your things! Plus, a real, face-to-face conversation will teach you more than a hundred books ever could.

Let's summarize what you learned in this book:

    a) The basics of Polish—pronouns, verbs, nouns

    b) Grammatical background information

    c) The difference between formal and informal style

    d) Introducing yourself

    e) Counting to 100

    f) Discussing your likes/dislikes

g) Telling others about your mood and feelings

h) Telling others your telephone number, address, age, place of living, etc.

i) Doing shopping

j) Ordering a meal in a restaurant

k) Going to a nightclub/cinema/theater

l) Using Polish in an academic/school environment

m) Using Polish in a working environment

n) ...and many more!

Getting to an advanced level requires self-discipline and dedication. Mastering a language is a tough and very long process, yet the result will always be rewarding. Good luck on your onward journey into the Polish language!

Finally, if you found this book useful in any way, a review on Amazon is always appreciated.

Part 2: Polish Short Stories

11 Simple Stories for Beginners Who Want to Learn

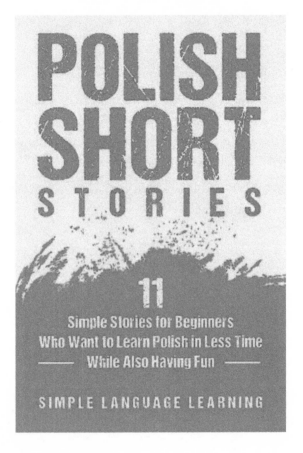

Introduction

Traveling has become so popular that most people cannot imagine a summer without a short trip to another country. They want to meet new people, learn about different traditions and customs, and celebrate the opportunities they now have. The urge to learn at least one foreign language is now of great importance.

How can I learn a foreign language? This question repeatedly appears in each learner's mind. If you want to master a new language, you need to operate within its key components—reading, listening, vocabulary, grammar, writing, and speaking.

If you have purchased this book, then you are probably not interested in participating in boring language classes or memorizing endless vocabulary columns and grammar rules. So, your question might really look like: **How can I learn a foreign language quickly and efficiently?** The good news is that the solution is right here!

What this book is NOT

This book is NOT a textbook! It will teach you the basics of the Polish language without making you memorize grammar rules and dialogs. While reading, you won't feel like studying or learning—this book will make you relax and have fun.

At this point, you might probably ask yourself, **"So, what is this book really about?"** Well, you are about to read eleven short and catchy Polish stories that will move you closer to your aim—acquiring the Polish language.

Each story consists of the original Polish text and the English translation so that you can follow the plot. After reading each story, you will be provided with a summary in the original language, as well as in English. What is more, the original text of the story will contain some words in bold (in fact, the most difficult ones) that will be translated for you. At the end of each chapter, you will find a set of questions to the text in Polish and English. Pay attention to the details. Of course, you can go back to the original story whenever you want. After all, this book is NOT a test—it has been written to make your language journey fun and easy.

Why reading?

Reading in a foreign language will give you the foundations. No one starts using a foreign language without a certain amount of exposure. Unlike regular textbooks, this book will allow you to practice your language based on real context—the key element to foreign language exposure. Would you like to practice speaking in a foreign language with a real Polish person or with a dialog played from a CD? The odds are that you are looking for a real thing. Therefore, you will enjoy reading the short stories since they portray the real language—not some artificial, out-of-context stuff. Moreover, reading in a foreign language has been proven to have real advantages:

1. **Your vocabulary expands exponentially** – reading in a foreign language is the best way to broaden your vocabulary range. Each new word is placed in a real context so that you can easily remember when and how to use it.

2. **Reading teaches you how to write** – what's the best way to learn how to write in a foreign language? Of course, it's reading! You need to remember that writing in a foreign language can't be based on the style of your native language— each language is unique! Through reading, you familiarize yourself with some features of the written form of your target foreign language.

3. **Reading is fun** - everyone enjoys reading! And you have the opportunity to read some interesting short stories wherever you want—at home, on the beach or in a café.

4. **Reading will make you learn the language way faster** - you will be surprised how much you will learn just by reading some stories and doing simple exercises.

Tips for faster and better reading in a foreign language

Reading is a skill that requires practice. The more effort, the better the results. If you read one book a year (probably on vacation), do not expect outstanding outcomes. To read quickly and efficiently, you need to do it regularly, no matter what language you are faced with. Before you see the tips, remember: systematicity is the key.

1. **Start with simple texts** - if you're a beginner, try to start with some "guided readings" (like this book, for example). You will be provided with translations, explanations, and exercises that will prevent you from getting lost.

2. **You don't have to understand 100 percent of the text** - especially if you're a beginner. If you grasp the general idea of the story, you're already successful.

3. **Try to focus on new words** - there will be some words that you haven't seen before. Try to discover the situation in which they are used and try to guess the meaning. These simple exercises will make you memorize new words way faster.

4. **Adjust the reading to your own needs** - sometimes, you will see many unknown words just within one paragraph or even one sentence. But don't get discouraged. Try to analyze the pieces slowly and translate the words.

5. **Take your time and just relax** - reading in a foreign language may be a bit overwhelming, especially at the beginning. Just take your time and celebrate small wins.

6. **Have fun!** - This book is neither a textbook nor a test! You can check translations in a dictionary, or even translate

entire sentences that are really problematic. As long as you work with the target language, you win.

A few notes about the Polish language

Your decision to learn a foreign language is probably a bit more specific—you decided to learn Polish. Whatever your motivation is, though, you won't be disappointed. Before you immerse yourself in learning, the following is some basic information about both the country of Poland and the Polish language.

The country of Poland was founded in 966 AD—the year of declaring Christianity as a national religion by the first Polish king. Poland is located in Central Europe and shares its borders with Germany in the west, The Czech Republic and Slovakia in the south, and Ukraine, Belarus, Lithuania, and a tiny bit of Russia in the north. In the north, it also has access to the Baltic Sea (around 400 km of the coastline).

Polish is certainly not one of the most spoken languages in the world since it is the official language of Poland exclusively. It has around 38 million speakers in Poland, but many immigrants in countries such as the USA, UK, Germany, Norway or Ireland are Polish. The Polish Community Abroad includes, for example, more than one million Poles in the UK and nearly one million in the States. What is interesting is that many Americans are of Polish origin due to the mass emigration caused by the difficult political situation in Poland in the eighteenth and nineteenth centuries.

Many native speakers of English consider Polish (along with Chinese, Arabic, and Japanese) as one of the hardest languages to learn due to its heavy inflectional system and, probably, pronunciation. It may be partially true; however, the beginning is always the toughest part of any language journey, yet speaking one of the hardest languages in the world is quite an achievement.

Polish is a Slavic language, yet its written form is not based on the Cyrillic alphabet but the Latin script. Therefore, Polish sounds can be tough to learn, especially some unusual consonant clusters like *szcz* or *dż dż*. However, the more you practice the pronunciation, the more automatic it becomes. The beginning is always the hardest part of any language journey since your first language data interfere with the new data that come into your mind. This book will teach you the vocabulary and grammar basics, along with some cultural background. With just fifteen to twenty minutes of practice a day, you can have a decent conversation in the target language, and your use of Polish will improve. Now look at some features of Polish that English speakers might find unusual and are not familiar with:

• The Polish language contains seven cases (nominative, genitive, dative, accusative, ablative, locative, and vocative). The cases might make the process of learning a bit overwhelming at the beginning, but there's nothing to be afraid of.

• The Polish gender system is very different from the English one—since gender in Polish is grammatical, whereas it is biological in English. For instance, the Polish word *stół* [table] is masculine, *książka* [book] is feminine, and *jajko* [egg] is neutral.

• Polish is a highly inflectional language—it means that nouns, verbs, and other parts of speech can have different endings or prefixes, depending on the case, gender, number, tense, and other features.

• Due to the abundance of inflections, Polish sentences can be created in multiple ways. Unlike English, Polish does not require a fixed order (such as subject + verb + object). Although there are more popular patterns, you can place each word in a sentence randomly and it will be grammatically correct (of course, there are some minor exceptions).

• All Polish women's first names end with the vowel "a", except for the ones with foreign origin.

• Polish shares many grammatical and lexical features with the other Slavic languages, such as Czech or Slovak.

- Because of the influence of the inflectional system, Polish people add inflections to foreign names. For instance, you can notice different suffixes added to Harry Potter or Spiderman in different cases (like Harrego Pottera, Spidermana, Harremu Potterowi, Spidermanowi, etc.).

- There are only three grammatical tenses in Polish: past, future, and present. The rules of forming tenses are quite different, too, since tenses are created by adding a suffix or prefix in most cases.

- Polish people put a lot of stress on formal forms of address. It is highly advisable to address a person you don't know or your boss/teacher with a word, *Pan/Pani,* instead of just *you.* Addressing someone by using the *you* form in situations like a job interview or a formal meeting is considered rude.

Equipped with some knowledge about the Polish language and the process of fast and efficient reading, you are ready to start your language learning journey!

Chapter 1 – Rozmowa o pracę [A job interview]

Był **mglisty**, zimny poranek. Patrząc na ulicę pełną ludzi spieszących się do pracy, Tomek wyobraził sobie swoją wymarzoną posadę. Siedział przy biurku na najwyższym piętrze wieżowca i popijał świeżą kawę...

It was a cold, foggy day. Looking at the street full of people rushing to their work, Tomek imagined his dream job. He was sitting at his desk and drinking freshly ground coffee...

Wtem, **światło na ulicy** zmieniło się na zielone. Tomek był już o krok od miejsca, w którym wyobrażał sobie swoją przyszłą pracę. Najpierw jednak, musiał przejść **rozmowę kwalifikacyjną**, która miała odbyć się równo za godzinę.

Suddenly, the traffic lights turned green. Tomek was really close to the place which he had imagined working in. Before all that, however, he had to pass the job interview, which was to begin in an hour.

Tomek był bardzo **zestresowany**. W ciągu ostatnich miesięcy był w sumie na dziesięciu rozmowach o pracę i za każdym razem słyszał to samo:

Tomek was really stressed out. All in all, he had attended ten job interviews in the last couple of months, and each time he had heard the same exact words:

"Odezwiemy się do Pana wkrótce."

"We will contact you soon."

Niestety, telefon Tomka milczał, a skrzynka e-mailowa pozostawała pusta. Tomek powoli stracił nadzieję na otrzymanie pracy. Tego dnia postanowił **dać z siebie wszystko** i zrobić jak najlepsze **wrażenie**. Nie miał już nic do stracenia. Wiedział, że jeśli nie dostanie tej pracy, będzie musiał wyprowadzić się do swoich rodziców na wieś.

Unfortunately, the telephone was silent, and the e-mail inbox was empty. Tomek was slowly losing hope. But that day he decided to give his best and make a good impression. After all, he had nothing to lose. He knew that if he didn't get this job, he would have had to move to his parents' house in the countryside.

Do spotkania z **rekruterem** zostało 45 minut. Tomek postanowił usiąść w firmowym bufecie na parterze, wypić espresso i zaplanować przebieg rozmowy. Im dłużej ćwiczył w myślach, tym bardziej się stresował. Pomimo tego, że wiedział co chce powiedzieć, uczucie zdenerwowania nie opuszczało go ani na chwilę. Tomek spojrzał na zegarek – Zostało już tylko pół godziny. Przez chwilę wpatrywał się jeszcze we **wskazówkę** zegara, która **zdawała się** przyspieszać z sekundy na sekundę.

The meeting with the recruiter was to begin in 45 minutes. Tomek decided to sit in the café on the first floor, have some espresso and plan the interview. The longer he practiced, the more stressed he felt. Although he knew what he was going to say, he couldn't get rid of huge discomfort. Tomek looked at his watch. He had only half an hour left. He was looking at the sweep hand that seemed to move faster and faster.

Tomek był tak zestresowany, że nawet nie zauważył, że bufet jest pełen ludzi. *Pewnie pracownicy mają przerwę,* pomyślał. W tej samej chwili do kawiarni weszła elegancko ubrana kobieta, trzymająca w ręku plik dokumentów. Zamówiła kawę i szybko **zorientowała się**, że przy żadnym ze stolików nie ma już miejsca. Rozglądając się po sali, zauważyła, że przy stoliku Tomka jest wolne miejsce.

Tomek was so stressed that he hadn't noticed that the café is full of people. *Perhaps the employees have a lunch break,* he thought. At the same moment, an elegantly dressed woman walked into the café. She was holding a couple of documents. She ordered some coffee and quickly realized that there hadn't been any seats left. Looking around, she saw one seat by Tomek's table.

"Cześć, jestem Karolina. Czy mogę się dosiąść?" zapytała.

"Hi, I'm Karolina. Can I sit here?" she asked.

"Pewnie. Zapraszam. Jestem Tomek."

"Sure, go ahead. I'm Tomek."

"Miło mi. Czy ty u nas pracujesz? Przychodzę tu na przerwę codziennie i widzę cię pierwszy raz."

"Nice to meet you. Do you work here? I have been coming here every day, but I have seen you for the first time."

Tomek przez moment nie wiedział co odpowiedzieć, ale w końcu postanowił powiedzieć prawdę: "Nie pracuję tutaj. Przyszedłem na rozmowę o pracę, która ma odbyć się za pół godziny."

Tomek didn't know what to say, but finally, he decided to tell her the truth: "I don't work here. I came here because I have a job interview that begins in 30 minutes."

Karolina była bardzo miłą osobą. Tomek dowiedział się, że pracuje w firmie już od kilku lat i bardzo lubi swoją pracę ponieważ spotyka w niej wielu ciekawych ludzi. Postanowił opowiedzieć jej o swoim życiu, o ukończeniu studiów i mieszkaniu w Warszawie. Pokazał jej nawet swoje CV, aby powiedziała mu czy ma jakieś **szanse** na dostanie pracy.

Karolina was a really nice person. Tomek found out that she had been working in the company for several years, and she really liked her job since she was meeting new people all the time. He decided to tell her a couple of things about his life, his university graduation, and living in Warsaw. He even showed her his CV so that she could tell him whether he had any chances of getting the job.

"Twoje CV wygląda naprawdę dobrze. Ukończyłeś najlepszy **uniwersytet** w mieście i na dodatek jesteś bardzo utalentowany. Nasza firma szuka ludzi takich jak ty. Mam nadzieję, że dostaniesz tę pracę," stwierdziła Karolina po obejrzeniu **życiorysu** Tomka.

"Your CV looks really cool. You graduated from the top university in the city, and you are so talented. Our company is looking for someone like you. I hope you'll get the job," she said after seeing his **résumé**.

"Byłem już w kilku firmach i za każdym razem mnie **chwalili**. Mimo wszystko, nadal jestem bez pracy. Co jest ze mną nie tak?" odpowiedział Tomek.

"I have visited several companies already, and each time they kept extolling my skills. Regardless, I'm still unemployed. What is wrong with me?" Tomek replied.

"Czasem twój talent i umiejętności potrzebują trochę szczęścia. Nie każdy umie dostrzec mocne strony drugiej osoby **na pierwszy rzut oka**. Czasem to stres **blokuje** naszą prezentację. Postaraj się zapomnieć o stresie. Będę trzymać za ciebie kciuki," dodała Karolina.

"Sometimes, your talent and skills need a little bit of luck. Not everyone can see the strong assets at first sight. Sometimes it's the stress that blocks us from presenting ourselves well. Try to forget about stress. I will keep my fingers crossed," Karolina said.

"Dzięki za wsparcie. Trzymaj się."

"Thanks for your support. Take care."

Po kilku chwilach Tomek zdał sobie sprawę, że rozmowa rozpoczyna się już za kilka minut. Nie chciał się spóźnić, dlatego wziął ostatni **łyk** espresso, schował dokumenty do teczki i pojechał windą na ostatnie piętro.

After a couple of minutes, Tomek realized that the interview started in a moment. He didn't want to be late, so he took the last sip of his espresso, put the documents in his briefcase, and took the elevator to the top floor.

Rozmowa z Karoliną **dodała mu otuchy**. Wiedział, że musi pokonać stres i pokazać się z jak najlepszej strony. Wtem zauważył pokój 505. Tak, to był ten pokój. Już za chwilę będzie w środku.

The conversation with Karolina made him uplifted. He knew that he had to beat stress and make a good impression. He saw the office 505. Yes, this was *the* office. He was about to go in.

Jedna rozmowa dzieli mnie od mojej **wymarzonej pracy**. *Nie mogę tego zepsuć*, pomyślał Tomek. I nagle..

One interview and I get the dream job. I can't ruin it, he thought. And suddenly...

"Pan Tomasz Kowalski. Zapraszamy na rozmowę. Proszę wejść."

"Mr Tomasz Kowalski. Please, come in."

To był ten moment. Tomek wiedział, że nie ma już **drogi ucieczki**. Wszedł do środka. Biuro było duże. Po środku siedziała sekretarka, a po prawej stronie znajdował się pokój, w którym Tomek miała być rozmowa. Tomek podał wszystkie dokumenty sekretarce i **nerwowo** ściągnął kurtkę.

This was his moment. Tomek knew that there wasn't a way of escape. He went in. The office was huge. In the middle, there was a secretary, and on the right, there was the office in which the interview was supposed to take place. Tomek handed the documents over to the secretary, and nervously took off his jacket.

"Pani Karolina czeka na Pana. Czy chciałby Pan napić się kawy?" zapytała **uprzejmie** sekretarka.

"Ms Karolina is waiting for you. Would you like to have some coffee?" the secretary asked politely.

"Nie dziękuję," odpowiedział Tomek szybko.

"No, thanks," Tomek replied quickly.

Karolina? To musi być **zbieg okoliczności**, pomyślał i wszedł do pokoju 505. Po chwili nie mógł uwierzyć swoim oczom. Przy biurku siedziała kobieta, z którą pół godziny temu rozmawiał w kawiarni na parterze.

Karolina? This has to be a coincidence, he thought and entered office 505. After a second, he couldn't believe his eyes. The woman sitting at the desk was the same woman he talked to 30 minutes ago.

"Cześć Tomek. Zaskoczony?" powiedziała Karolina.

"Hi, Tomek! Surprised?" Karolina said.

"Cześć! Nie mogę uwierzyć, że to ty. Wiedziałaś?" zapytał.

"Hi! I can't believe it's you. Did you know?" he asked.

"**Miałam przeczucie** po tym jak pokazałeś mi swoje CV. Wtedy przypomniałam sobie, że takie samo wysłałeś do nas mailem tydzień temu." Odpowiedziała Karolina i dodała:

"I had a hunch. And after you showed me your CV, I knew. The moment I saw it, I recalled that you sent us the exact same thing a week ago," Karolina replied and added:

"Postanowiłam nic ci nie mówić. Chciałam zobaczyć twoją **zaskoczoną** minę."

"I decided not to tell you. I wanted to see your surprised face."

Tomek poczuł, że cały stres nagle go opuścił. Zanim zdążył cokolwiek powiedzieć, Karolina przerwała mu i dodała:

Tomek felt that all the stress was gone. Before he could say anything, Karolina broke in:

"Wszystkiego o tobie dowiedziałam się podczas naszej rozmowy w kawiarni. Nie muszę już nic więcej wiedzieć. Masz tę pracę."

"I learned everything about you during our conversation in the café. I don't have to know anything else. You just got the job."

Tomek nie wierzył w to co usłyszał. Był bardzo szczęśliwy. Dostał pracę, o której marzył, a na dodatek poznał bardzo miłą osobę.

Tomek couldn't believe his ears. He was really happy. He got his dream job and, what is more, he met an amazing person.

"Jutro o 8:00 rozpoczynasz pracę, ale przyjdź na 7:30," powiedziała Karolina.

"You start tomorrow at 8 AM but come at 7:30," Karolina said.

"Dlaczego?" zapytał Tomek.

"Why?" asked Tomek.

"Spotkamy się w kawiarni i przygotuję cię na pierwszy dzień pracy. Opowiem ci o naszej firmie i pokażę ci nasz budynek," odpowiedziała.

"We will meet at the café, and I will prepare you for your first day. I will tell you a couple of things about the company and show you the entire building," she replied.

"Brzmi świetnie! Zatem, do zobaczenia jutro!"

"Sounds great! See you tomorrow then!"

Tomek wyszedł z biura Karoliny z uśmiechem na twarzy. Jego marzenie się spełniło. Na dodatek, zyskał nowego przyjaciela. Po chwili przypomniał sobie słowa Karoliny:

Tomek walked out of Karolina's office with a big smile on his face. His dream just came true. In addition, he just met a new friend. After a while, he recalled Karolina's words:

"Czasem twój talent i umiejętności potrzebują trochę szczęścia."

"Sometimes your talent and your skills need a little bit of luck."

To był jego szczęśliwy dzień. Po dziesięciu rozmowach dostał to, o czym marzył na studiach. Zdał sobie sprawę z tego, że nie można **poddawać się** zbyt szybko i trzeba w siebie wierzyć. Jeśli masz talent, wiedzę i umiejętności, prędzej czy później zostaniesz **doceniony**. Pożegnał się z sekretarką. Wiedział, że ma przed sobą wspaniałą karierę i przyjaźń ze wspaniałą osobą.

This was his lucky day. After attending ten interviews, he finally got what he dreamed about in his university days. He realized that you can't give up too fast, and you have to believe in yourself. If you have talent, skills, and knowledge, they will be appreciated sooner or later. He said goodbye to the secretary. He knew that he had a wonderful career and friendship right ahead.

Streszczenie

Tomek był bardzo zdenerwowany, ponieważ po studiach nie mógł znaleźć pracy. Tego dnia postanowił pójść na ostatnią rozmowę o pracę. Przed rozmową Tomek postanowił pójść do kawiarni, aby się przygotować. Kawiarnia była pełna ludzi i nie było wolnych stolików. Po chwili do kawiarni weszła kobieta—Karolina. Usiadła z Tomkiem. Tomek dowiedział się, że Karolina pracowała w firmie, w której on chciał pracować. Karolina obejrzała jego CV i pożegnała się z nim. Po wejściu do biura gdzie miała odbyć się rozmowa Tomek zauważył Karolinę. Okazało się, że to ona była rekruterem. Tomek dostał pracę. Kobieta i mężczyzna zostali przyjaciółmi.

Summary

Tomek was really nervous because he couldn't find a job after graduating from university. One day he decided to go to the last job interview. Before the interview, Tomek decided to go to a café to prepare. The café was full of people, and there weren't any tables left. After a while, a woman came into the café—Karolina. She decided to take a seat next to Tomek's. Tomek learned that she was working in the company that he wanted to work in. Karolina looked at his résumé and said goodbye to him. After entering the office where the interview was supposed to take place, Tomek saw Karolina. It turned out that she was the recruiter. Tomek got the job. The woman and the man became friends with each other.

Vocabulary

Mglisty – foggy

Światło na ulicy – traffic light

Zestresowany – stressed

Rozmowa kwalifikacyjna – a job interview

Dać z siebie wszystko – to give one's best

Zdawać się – to seem

Wskazówka – a sweep hand

Zorientować się – to realize

Szanse – chances

Uniwersytet – university

Życiorys – résumé/CV

Chwalić - to extoll

Na pierwszy rzut oka - at a first glance

Blokować - to block

Łyk - a sip

Dodać otuchy - to make somebody uplifted

Wymarzona praca - a dream job

Droga ucieczki - a way of escape

Nerwowo - nervously

Uprzejmie - politely

Zbieg okoliczności - a coincidence

Mieć przeczucie - to have a hunch

Zaskoczony - surprised

Poddawać się - to give up

Doceniony - appreciated

Pytania

1. Jak miała na imię kobieta, którą Tomek poznał w kawiarnii?

2. Dlaczego kobieta usiadła obok Tomka?

3. Dlaczego Tomek postanowił przyjść wcześniej na rozmowę i usiąść w kawiarnii?

4. Czy Tomek dostał pracę?

5. Dlaczego kobieta nie powiedział Tomkowi w kawiarni, że to ona była rekruterem?

6. Dlaczego Karolina kazała Tomkowi przyjść wcześniej do pracy kolejnego dnia?

a) Żeby pokazać mu budynek

b) Żeby mógł wyjść wcześniej

c) Żeby skserować jego życiorys

7. Czy Karolinie podobało się CV Tomka?

a) Tak

b) Nie

8. Gdzie mieszkał Tomek?

a) w Warszawie

b) w Poznaniu

c) w Krakowie

9. Jak nazywał się Tomek?

a) Kowalski

b) Nowak

c) Lewandowski

10. Jaki numer miał pokój, w którym Tomek był na rozmowie o pracę?

a) 123

b) 505

c) 303

Questions

1. What was the name of the woman who Tomek met in the café?

2. Why did the woman take a seat next to Tomek?

3. Why did Tomek decide to come earlier and sit at the café before the interview?

4. Did Tomek get the job?

5. Why didn't the woman tell Tomek that she was the recruiter?

6. Why did Karolina want Tomek to come earlier to work the next day?

a) She wanted to show him the building

b) She wanted him to leave earlier

c) She wanted to copy his résumé

7. Did Karolina like Tomek's résumé?

a) Yes

b) No

8. Where did Tomek live?

a) In Warsaw

b) In Poznan

c) In Cracow

9. What was Tomek's last name?

a) Nowak

b) Kowalski

c) Lewandowski

10. What was the number of the office where Tomek had the interview?

a) 123

b) 303

c) 505

Odpowiedzi

1. Karolina

2. Nie było wolnych miejsc przy innych stołach

3. Chciał przygotować się na rozmowę

4. Tak

5. Chciała zobaczyć jego zaskoczoną minę

6. a

7. a

8. a

9. b

10. c

Answers

1. Karolina

2. There weren't any seats left by the other tables

3. He wanted to prepare himself for the interview

4. Yes

5. She wanted to see his surprised face

6. a

7. a

8. a

9. b

10. c

Chapter 2 – Włosy warte miliony [Million-dollar hair]

Sylwia była zwykłą nastolatką. Mieszkała **na przedmieściach** z rodzicami, chodziła do szkoły, miała kilku przyjaciół. Było jednak coś, co odróżniało ją od reszty znajomych ze szkoły—długie, piękne włosy, które **odrastały** bardzo szybko.

Sylvia was a normal teenage girl. She lived in the suburbs with her parents, she was going to school, and she had a few friends. But there was something that made her special—long, beautiful hair that grew really fast.

Po każdej wizycie u fryzjera włosy odrastały **gwałtownie** w ciągu kilku miesięcy. Piękny blond sprawiał, że Sylwia **wyróżniała się** w tłumie. Pomimo tego, że dziewczyna kochała swoje włosy, były one dla niej codziennym utrapieniem. Mycie, suszenie, czesanie—wszystko zajmowało bardzo dużo czasu i wymagało wiele pracy. Nawet zrobienie najprostszej fryzury zdawało się **trwać wieczność**.

After each hairdressing appointment, her hair grew out rapidly within a couple of months. A beautiful blonde color made Sylvia stand out. Although the girl loved her hair, she had faced many struggles because of it. Washing, drying, brushing—everything had taken much time and required a lot of effort. Even making a simple hairstyle seemed to last endlessly.

Pewnego dnia, po powrocie ze szkoły Sylwia spięła włosy w **kok** i zaczęła jeść obiad. Chciała go zjeść jak najszybciej, ponieważ za godzinę miała przyjść do niej przyjaciółka na wspólną naukę do testu z angielskiego. Tymczasem, do domu weszła mama. Sylwia spojrzała na nią i już wiedziała, że coś jest nie tak.

One day, after coming back from school, Sylvia made a simple bun and started to eat her dinner. She wanted to eat it quickly because she was meeting her friend to study with her for an English test in an hour. Meanwhile, her mother came in. Sylvia looked at her, and she knew that something was wrong.

"Hej, Mamo! Co się stało? Wyglądasz dziwnie," zapytała.

"Hi, Mom! What happened? You look different," she asked.

"Cześć, kochanie. Właśnie zwolnili mnie z pracy," odpowiedziała Mama.

"Hi, honey. I have just lost my job," Mom answered.

"Ale... jak? Co zamierzasz zrobić?" Sylwia **wpadła w panikę**. Jej mama zarabiała dobrze. Dzięki jej pracy Sylwia dostawała kieszonkowe i jeździła na obozy wakacyjne.

"But... how? What are you gonna do?" Sylvia panicked. Her mom had had a pretty good salary. Thanks to her job, Sylvia had been receiving pocket money and had been taking part in summer camps.

"Spodziewałam się tego już od jakiegoś czasu. W firmie nie jest dobrze. Przez jakiś czas będziemy musieli **ograniczyć wydatki**. Dopóki nie znajdę nowej pracy będziemy żyć z **pensji** Taty," odpowiedziała Mama.

"I expected this to happen. The company doesn't do well. We have to cut our expenses for a while. We will make a living by Dad's salary until I find a new job," Mom replied.

Sylwia już znała odpowiedź, ale spytała:

Sylvia already knew the answer, yet she asked:

"Czy to oznacza, że nie pojadę w tym roku na obóz?"

"Does this mean that I won't go to the camp this year?"

"Obawiam się że tak, kochanie. Przepraszam."

"I'm afraid so, honey. I'm sorry."

Sylwia była załamana. Cały rok czekała na ten obóz. Chciała znów spotkać się ze swoimi przyjaciółmi, przeżywać przygody i odwiedzać nowe miejsca. Niestety, wiedziała również, że pensja taty nie wystarczy na pokrycie **codziennych wydatków** i wyjazdu.

Sylvia was heartbroken. She had been waiting for the camp for the entire year. She wanted to meet her friends again, experience new adventures, and discover new places. Unfortunately, she knew that her dad's salary was not enough to cover daily expenses and the cost of her camp.

Sylwia szła do swojego pokoju, gdy nagle zadzwonił dzwonek. Przez tę smutną wiadomość całkiem zapomniała o spotkaniu z Anią. Przecież miały się razem uczyć do jutrzejszego testu.

Sylvia was walking into her room when the doorbell rang. Due to the sad news, she had completely forgotten about the meeting with Ania. They wanted to study for tomorrow's test.

"Wyglądasz jakoś dziwnie. Nie możesz skupić się na nauce. Wszystko ok?" zapytała Ania.

" You look different. You can't focus on studying. Is everything okay?" Ania asked.

"Nie jadę w tym roku na obóz. Rodzice nie mają pieniędzy. Mama właśnie straciła pracę," odpowiedziała Sylwia.

"I'm not going to the camp this year. My parents don't have the money. My mom has just lost her job," Sylvia replied.

"Ojej. Przykro mi. Wiesz... Może mogłabyś sama uzbierać te pieniądze?" zasugerowała Ania.

"Oh. I'm sorry for you. You know... maybe you could save the money on your own?" Ania suggested.

"Ale jak? Przecież nie mogę iść do pracy, a sprzedanie kilku ciuchów nic nie da. Potrzebuję kilku tysięcy złotych."

"But how? I can't go to work, and selling a few clothes won't work either. I need several thousand zlotys."

"Wiesz.. widziałam ostatnio ogłoszenie w Internecie. Pewien luksusowy **salon fryzjerski** płaci za ścięcie włosów. Pewnie chcą robić z nich **doczepki.** Szukają włosów takich jak twoje i płacą kilka tysięcy!"

"Well... I saw recently an ad on the Internet. One luxurious hair salon wants to pay for cutting and giving them your hair. Probably they want to make hair extensions. They're looking for hair like yours and they want to pay thousands!"

Sylwia nie mogła uwierzyć własnym uszom. Po spotkaniu za Anią postanowiła jak najszybciej zadzwonić do salonu i umówić się na ścięcie włosów. Fryzjer zaproponował jej pięć tysięcy złotych! Taka kwota z pewnością wystarczyłaby na obóz. Sylwia nie zastanawiała się długo.

Sylvia couldn't believe her ears. After the meeting with Ania, she decided to call the hair salon and make an appointment. The hairdresser offered five thousand zlotys! Such a sum of money would definitely cover the cost of the camp. Sylvia didn't give it a second thought.

Następnego dnia Sylwia postanowiła powiedzieć Ani o rozmowie z fryzjerem.

The next day, Sylvia decided to tell Ania about the conversation with the hairdresser.

"Nie uwierzysz! Umówiłam się na wizytę w tym luksusowym salonie. W przyszłym tygodniu ścinam włosy! Pieniądze dostanę od razu."

"You won't believe! I made an appointment in the luxurious hair salon. Next week I'm having my hair cut! I will get the money straight away."

" A co na to twoi rodzice? Zgodzili się?" zapytała Ania.

"But what about your parents? Did they agree?" Ania asked.

" Powiedzieli tylko, że powinnam ściąć włosy, jeśli mnie to uszczęśliwi," odpowiedziała Sylwia.

"They only said that I should cut my hair if it makes me happy," Sylvia replied.

" Świetnie. Widziałaś ogłoszenie? Dziś idziemy całą klasą na wycieczkę. Odwiedzamy dzieci chore na **raka** w szpitalu, aby zanieść im książki i zabawki. Ja oddaję mój zestaw **przyborów do majsterkowania**."

"Cool. Have you seen the announcement? Today we're going on a short trip with our class. We're visiting children in the hospital that suffer from cancer to give them books and toys. I'm going to give them my DIY tools."

Sylwia całkiem zapomniała. Była tak **pochłonięta** ścięciem włosów, że zapomniała przygotować jakikolwiek prezent. W ostatniej chwili przypomniała sobie, że ma w plecaku książkę, którą skończyła czytać w zeszłym tygodniu. Postanowiła ją oddać.

Sylvia completely forgot about the trip. She was so preoccupied with her hair that she forgot about preparing any present. At the last moment, she recalled that she had a book that she had finished reading last week. She decided to give it as a gift.

Po kilku chwilach klasa Sylwii dotarła na miejsce. Uczniowie przekazali prezenty dzieciom i wysłuchali kilku faktów na temat szpitala.

After a while, Sylvia's class arrived at the hospital. The students gave their gifts and listened to a short history of the hospital.

Podczas wspólnego spędzania czasu z młodymi pacjentami Sylwia zauważyła małą dziewczynkę. Miała na głowie kolorową **chustkę**, która od razu zwróciła uwagę Sylwii.

During the time together with the young patients, Sylvia noticed a small girl. She was wearing a colorful headscarf that drew Sylvia's attention.

" Hej. Jestem Sylwia. Masz na głowie piękną chustę."

"Hi. I'm Sylvia. You're wearing a beautiful headscarf."

"Cześć! Jestem Kasia. Dziękuję. Noszę ją, bo chcę zakryć to czego najbardziej się wstydzę."

"Hi! I'm Kasia. Thanks. I'm wearing it because I want to cover something I'm ashamed of."

" Co masz na myśli?" spytała Sylwia.

"What do you mean?" Sylvia asked.

" Choroba odebrała mi włosy. Kiedyś miałam piękne blond włosy, takie jak ty. Niestety po kilku **zabiegach** wszystkie włosy mi wypadły. Od tego czasu nie patrzę w lustro"

"The illness took away my hair. I used to have blonde, beautiful hair, same as yours. Unfortunately, I lost it after a few treatments. I haven't looked in the mirror since then."

Sylwia była zszokowana. Wyobraziła sobie siebie bez włosów, patrzącą w lustro. Postanowiła podarować Kasi książkę, którą wzięła ze sobą.

Sylvia was shocked. She imagined herself without hair, looking in the mirror. She decided to give Kasia the book she took with herself to the hospital.

" Dziękuję. Kocham tę serię!" powiedziała Kasia.

"Thanks. I love this series," Kasia said.

Po wyjściu ze szpitala Sylwia wiedziała, że książka nie uczyni Kasi szczęśliwą na długo. Całe popołudnie myślała o Kasi i jej włosach.

After leaving the hospital Sylvia knew that the book wouldn't make Kasia happy for so long. She was thinking about Kasia and her hair the whole afternoon.

W końcu nadszedł dzień ścięcia włosów. Sylwia była trochę **poddenerwowana.** Była ciekawa jak wygląda w nowej fryzurze.

Finally, the cutting day came. Sylvia was a little bit nervous. She wanted to know how she looked with the new hairstyle.

"Jesteś gotowa?" zapytał fryzjer.

"Are you ready?" the hairdresser asked.

"Tak!", krzyknęła Sylwia.

"Yes!" Sylvia exclaimed.

Nowa fryzura wyglądała świetnie. Sylwia była z siebie dumna.

The new hairstyle looked amazing. Sylvia was proud of herself.

"Mam pytanie. Czy mogłabym zatrzymać włosy?" spytała Sylwia.

"I have a question. Can I keep my hair?" Sylvia asked.

"Ale...dlaczego? Przecież zapłacimy ci za nie kilka tysięcy." Fryzjer był bardzo zaskoczony.

"But... why? We're going to pay you thousands," the hairdresser was surprised.

" Chciałabym je komuś podarować. Komuś, kto potrzebuje ich bardziej niż **modelki**," odpowiedziała Sylwia.

"I'd like to give it to someone. Someone who needs it more than models," Sylvia replied.

"Hmm... W takim razie weź je. Są przecież twoje."

"Well... Take it then. It's yours."

Sylwia wzięła swoje włosy i od razu pojechała do szpitala. Postanowiła zanieść je do **fundacji**, która zajmuje się robieniem **peruk** dla pacjentów. Nie dostała za nie ani grosza, ale satysfakcja była ogromna.

Sylvia took her hair with her and went to the hospital immediately. She decided to donate it to the charity that makes wigs for cancer patients. She didn't get a penny, yet the feeling of satisfaction she had was huge.

Kilka dni później Sylwia postanowiła odwiedzić Kasię i przynieść jej kolejną książkę. Kiedy Kasia wyszła na korytarz, Sylwia nie mogła uwierzyć własnym oczom. Kasia miała piękne blond włosy! Wyglądała przepięknie. Sylwia była pewna, że podarowanie Kasi nowych włosów było ważniejsze niż obóz. Dziewczyny zaprzyjaźniły się, a Sylwia odwiedzała Kasię codziennie w szpitalu.

After a couple of days, Sylvia decided to visit Kasia and give her another book. When Kasia showed up, Sylvia couldn't believe her eyes. Kasia had beautiful, blonde hair! She looked amazing. Sylvia was sure that giving Kasia new hair was way better than taking part in the summer camp. The girls made really good friends with each other and Sylvia was visiting Kasia in the hospital every day.

Streszczenie

Sylwia była normalną nastolatką. Było jednak coś, co ją wyróżniało - jej piękne długie blond włosy. Pewnego dnia Sylwia wróciła do domu i dowiedziała się, że jej mama straciła pracę. Sylwia była załamana, ponieważ jej mama dobrze zarabiała. Okazało się że przez stratę pracy przez jej mamę Sylwia nie będzie mogła jechać na letni obóz. Sylwię odwiedziła jej najlepsza koleżanka Ania. Sylwia powiedziała jej o tym, że nie pojedzie na obóz. Ania zasugerowała Sylwii ścięcie włosów i sprzedanie ich do luksusowego salonu fryzjerskiego. Sylwia postanowiła to zrobić. Następnego dnia Sylwia powiedziała Ani w szkole, że umówiła się na wizytę. Tego samego dnia klasa Sylwii udała się na odwiedziny do szpitala. Sylwia spotkała tam Kasię - dziewczynkę, która miała raka i nie miała włosów. Dziewczyny zaprzyjaźniły się. Podczas wizyty w salonie fryzjerskim Sylwia zdecydowała się zatrzymać swoje włosy. Postanowiła oddać je do szpitala. Pewnego dnia Sylwia odwiedziła Kasię w szpitalu i zobaczyła, że Kasia miała perukę zrobioną z jej włosów.

Summary

Sylvia was a normal teenage girl. There was something that made her special—her beautiful, long, blonde hair. One day, Sylvia got back home, and her mom told her that she'd lost her job. Sylvia couldn't take part in a summer camp because her mom had lost the job, and the family didn't have enough money. Sylvia was visited by her best friend, Ania. Sylvia told her about the fact that she couldn't go to the summer camp. Ania suggested Sylvia have her hair cut and sell it to a luxurious hair salon. Sylvia decided to do that. The next day, Sylvia told Ania that she had already made a hairdressing appointment. At the same time, Sylvia's class went to a local hospital. Sylvia met Kasia— a girl who had been suffering from cancer and had lost her hair. The girls made friends with each other. During the hairdressing appointment, Sylvia decided to keep her hair. She decided to donate it to the hospital. One day, Sylvia visited Kasia in the hospital, and she saw that the girl was wearing a wig made of Sylvia's hair.

Vocabulary:

Na przedmieściach - in the suburbs

Odrastać - to grow

Gwałtownie - rapidly

Wyróżniać się - to stand out

Trwać wieczność - to last endlessly

Kok - a bun

Wpaść w panikę - to panic

Ograniczyć wydatki - to cut expenses

Pensja - a salary

Codzienne wydatki - daily expenses

Salon fryzjerski - a hair salon

Doczepki - hair extensions

Rak - cancer

Przybory do majsterkowania - DIY tools

Pochłonięty - preoccupied

Chusta - a headscarf

Zabieg - a treatment

Poddenerwowana - nervous

Modelki - models

Fundacja - a charity

Peruka - a wig

Pytania

1. Jak miała na imię przyjaciółka Sylwii ze szkoły?

2. Na co nie było stać Sylwię?

3. Co postanowiła sprzedać Sylwia, aby zarobić pieniądze?

4. Kogo odwiedziła klasa Sylwii?

5. Z kim zaprzyjaźniła się Sylwia w szpitalu?

6. Co zrobiła Sylwia z włosami?

a) Podarowała do szpitala

b) Sprzedała je modelkom

c) Postanowiła ich nie obcinać

7. Jaki prezent dla chorych dzieci postanowiła dać Ania?

a) Książki

b) Narzędzia do majsterkowania

c) Ubrania

8. Co nosiła na głowie Kasia przed otrzymaniem peruki?

a) Czapkę

b) Chustę

c) Kapelusz

9. Dlaczego Kasia nie miała włosów?

a) Straciła je po zabiegu

b) Postanowiła je obciąć

c) Oddała je komuś

Questions

1. What was the name of Sylvia's friend from school?

2. What couldn't Sylvia afford to do?

3. What did Sylvia decide to sell to get the money?

4. Who did Sylvia's class visit?

5. Who did Sylvia make friends with at the hospital?

6. What did Sylvia do with her hair?

a) She donated it to the hospital

b) He sold it to the models

c) She decided not to have it cut

7. What gift did Ania decide to give to the ill children?

a) Books

b) DIY tools

c) Clothes

8. What did Kasia wear before getting a wig?

a) A cap

b) A headscarf

c) A hat

9. Why did Kasia have no hair?

a) She lost it after the treatment

b) She decided to cut it

c) She gave it to someone else

Odpowiedzi

1. Ania

2. Obóz letni

3. Jej włosy

4. Dzieci chore na raka

5. Kasia

6. a

7. b

8. b

9. a

Answers

1. Ania

2. A summer camp

3. Her hair

4. Children that suffered from cancer

5. Kasia

6. a

7. b

8. b

9. a

Chapter 3 – Dobro zawsze powraca [The good always returns]

Gdy Robert w końcu wyszedł z biura, było już bardzo późno. **Spotkanie** z klientem przedłużyło się, ale było tego warte—firma Roberta właśnie podpisała nowy **kontrakt.** Robert nie mógł się doczekać powrotu do domu i kolacji ze swoją żoną. W końcu, było co świętować. Firma radziła sobie bardzo dobrze, a Robert sprawdzał się świetnie jako szef.

It was really late when Robert finally left his office. The meeting with his client took longer than expected, but it was worth it—Robert's company had signed a new contract. Robert was looking forward to coming home and eating dinner with his wife. After all, he wanted to celebrate. His company had been doing very well, and Robert had been a great boss.

Tego wieczora Robert postanowił **pójść pieszo.** Wiedział, że zajmie mu to pół godziny dłużej, ale chciał pozostać przez chwilę **sam na sam** ze swoimi myślami. Widział przed sobą wspaniałą karierę i sukces swojej firmy.

That evening Robert decided to go on foot. He knew that it would take half an hour longer, but he wanted to be left alone with his thoughts for a while. He had a great career and a successful company in front of him.

Przechodząc przez park Robert zauważył człowieka siedzącego na **ławce**. Mężczyzna wyglądał na **załamanego**. Twarz miał schowaną w dłoniach, a **teczka** z papierami leżała otwarta. Robert nie zastanawiał się dłużej – postanowił z nim porozmawiać.

While walking through the park, Robert noticed a man that was sitting on a bench. The man looked broken. He had his face covered with his hands, and his open briefcase lay on the ground. Robert decided to speak to him.

"Przepraszam, wszystko ok? Potrzebuje Pan pomocy?" spytał Robert.

"Excuse me, is everything okay? Do you need help?" Robert asked.

" Dziękuję, nie. Jestem Paweł. I właśnie straciłem wszystko," odpowiedział mężczyzna.

"No, thanks. I'm Paul. And I've just lost everything," the man said.

Robert nie wiedział co powiedzieć. Jego żona czekała już w domu, więc spieszył się, ale postanowił pomóc.

Robert didn't know what to say. His wife had already been waiting for him so he was in a rush, yet he decided to help the man.

"Co się stało?" spytał.

"What happened?" he asked.

"Jestem, a właściwie byłem **szefem** wspaniałej firmy. Niestety, tydzień temu straciliśmy najważniejszego klienta z powodu poważnej **kłótni**. Potem kolejni klienci zaczęli odchodzić... Dziś odszedł od nas ostatni klient. Firma została **rozwiązana**."

"I am, and actually, I was a CEO of an amazing company. Unfortunately, we lost the most important client last week because of a serious argument. After that, the other clients started to leave us. Today, we lost the last client. Our company has been dissolved."

"Przykro mi. Mam nadzieję, że dasz sobie radę," powiedział Robert.

"I'm sorry. I hope you'll figure something out," Robert said.

"Nie mam ani grosza. Zabrali mi **mieszkanie**. Zabrali nawet mój samochód. Miałem straszne **długi**. Wygląda na to, że będę musiał spędzić noc w parku," odpowiedział Paweł.

"I don't have a penny to my name. They took my apartment. They even took my car. I had huge debts. It seems that I have to spend the night in the park," Paul said.

Robert bardzo **współczuł** nowo poznanemu mężczyźnie. Wiedział jak trudno jest się utrzymać **na szczycie**. Jednego dnia jesteś najlepszy, a kolejnego możesz stracić wszystko. Robert postanowił pomóc.

Robert felt really sorry for the newly met man. He knew how difficult it was to stay on top. One day you are the best, and one day you may lose everything. He decided to help Paul.

"Proszę. Weź te pieniądze. Powinno wystarczyć na tydzień w hotelu i jedzenie. Mam nadzieję, że przez ten czas rozwiążesz chociaż część swoich problemów. Masz tutaj mój numer telefonu. Jeśli będziesz w tarapatach, zadzwoń do mnie. Postaram się tobie pomóc."

"Please, take the money. It should be enough for you to book a room in a hotel for a week and buy some food. I hope you'll figure something out in the meantime. Here you have my phone number. If you have any problems, call me. I'll try to help you."

"Dziękuję! Uratowałeś mi życie. Jestem ci winien przysługę," powiedział Paweł.

"Thanks! You saved my life. I owe you a favor," Paul said.

Robert ucieszył się. Wiedział, że taka mała rzecz pomoże Pawłowi **stanąć na nogi**.

Robert was happy. He knew that even such a small thing could help Paul get back on his feet.

"Nie ma za co. Na szczycie nie jest łatwo. Czasem wygrywasz, czasem przegrywasz. Nie poddawaj się. Na pewno coś wykombinujesz," dodał Robert.

"My pleasure. It's always tough at the top. Sometimes you win, sometimes you lose. Don't give up. You'll figure something out," Robert added.

"Dziękuję! Trzymaj się!"

"Thanks! Take care!"

Robert pożegnał się z Pawłem i całą drogę rozmyślał o jego sytuacji. Przypomniał sobie jak zaczynał.

Robert said goodbye to Paul, but he was thinking about his situation all the way home.

Mijały miesiące, a firma Robert świętował kolejne sukcesy. Firma przynosiła ogromne **zyski**. Jednak, od tamtego wieczora w parku Robert nie otrzymał żadnej wiadomości od Pawła. Podejrzewał, że poradził sobie i nie potrzebował już więcej jego pomocy.

Months went by, and Robert celebrated another success. The company made a really good profit. However, Robert hadn't received any message from Paul since that evening. He thought that Paweł did well and didn't need his help any longer.

Pewnego dnia Robert otrzymał telefon od bardzo ważnego klienta:

One day Robert got a call from a very important client:

"Robert, musimy się spotkać i omówić naszą dalszą współpracę."

"Robert, we need to meet and discuss our business."

Robert był zaskoczony, ponieważ sytuacja w firmie była naprawdę dobra. Mimo wszystko, postanowił spotkać się z klientem.

Robert was surprised because the situation in his company was great. Regardless, he decided to meet with his client.

"Dobrze. Spotkajmy się o dwudziestej w restauracji."

"Okay. Let's meet at 8 PM in the restaurant."

Po spotkaniu Robert był **zdruzgotany**. W głowie słyszał tylko słowa klienta:

After the meeting, Robert was devastated. He only heard his client's words:

"Przykro mi. Konkurencja dała nam lepsze **warunki**. Obawiam się, że to koniec naszej współpracy."

"I'm sorry. Your competitors gave us better terms. I'm afraid it's the end of our partnership."

Spodziewał się prawdziwej lawiny. Wiedział, że strata tego klienta sprawi, że inni klienci również zerwą współpracę. Robert obawiał się, że firma wkrótce **upadnie.**

Robert expected a real disaster. He knew that losing this client would make other clients leave his company. Robert was afraid that his company would collapse.

Tak też się stało. W ciągu miesiąca odeszło 90 procent klientów, więc Robert został zmuszony do odejścia. Jego sukces zakończył się **w mgnieniu oka.**

Indeed, all these things happened. Within a month, 90 percent of the clients left, so Robert was forced to back off. His success ended in the blink of an eye.

Kilka dni po zamknięciu firmy Robert załamał się. Nie miał pieniędzy, aby zacząć od nowa, a długi ciągle rosły. Pewnego wieczora otrzymał dziwną wiadomość od **nieznanego** numeru telefonicznego:

After a couple of days, Robert got depressed. He didn't have enough money to start over, and his debt grew really quickly. But one day he got a strange message from an unknown phone number:

"Cześć. Spotkajmy się w parku o dwudziestej pierwszej."

"Hi. Let's meet in the park at 9 PM."

Robert w pierwszej chwili pomyślał, że to jakiś żart. Stwierdził, że zostanie w mieszkaniu. Jednak, po chwili postanowił sprawdzić kim była ta tajemnicza osoba, która chciała się z nim spotkać.

Robert thought that it was a joke. He decided to stay at home. But, after a while, he decided to check who this mysterious person was.

Kiedy Robert przyszedł na miejsce zauważył **elegancko ubranego** mężczyznę siedzącego na ławce. Przyjrzał mu się z oddali. Mężczyzna wyglądał **znajomo...**

When Robert came to the park, he noticed an elegantly dressed man who was sitting on the bench. He looked at him. The man looked familiar...

Robert już wiedział. Zanim zdążył cokolwiek powiedzieć, mężczyzna odezwał się:

Robert already knew. Before he said anything, the man said:

"Cześć, Robert! **Kopę lat!** Przepraszam, że nie odezwałem się do ciebie. Moje życie zmieniło się **całkowicie.**"

"Hi, Robert! It's been ages! I'm sorry I haven't contacted you. My life has changed drastically."

"Paweł. Wow, nie poznałem cię w pierwszej chwili. Co cię tu sprowadza?" spytał Robert.

"Paul. Wow, I didn't recognize you at a first glance. What brings you here?" Robert asked.

"Przeczytałem ostatnio w **gazecie,** że twoja firma upadła. Naprawdę przykro mi z tego powodu," odpowiedział Paweł.

"I've read recently in the newspaper that your company collapsed. I'm really sorry," Paul explained.

Robert poczuł, że ogarnia go wstyd. To on pomógł Pawłowi kilka miesięcy temu, a teraz on sam nie ma ani grosza.

Robert felt really embarrassed. He helped Paul a few months ago, and at this moment, he didn't have a penny to his name.

"Wiesz... dużo myślałem o tamtym wieczorze. Gdyby nie ty, nie **pozbierałbym się**. Kiedy zobaczyłem wiadomość w gazecie postanowiłem, ze muszę coś z tym zrobić. Ktoś taki jak ty nie zasługuje na taki **bałagan**," kontynuował Paweł.

"You know... I've been thinking a lot about that night. But for you, I wouldn't have got myself together. When I saw the info in the newspaper, I decided to do something about it. Someone like you doesn't deserve this mess," Paul continued.

Robert był zaskoczony.

Robert was shocked.

"Jak możesz mi pomóc?" zapytał.

"How can you help me?" he asked.

"Chciałbym, abyś był moim **wspólnikiem**. Przez tamten tydzień udało mi się rozwiązać moje problemy. Moja firma ponownie stanęła na nogi. Koniec końców, wciąż jestem ci winien **przysługę**," odpowiedział Paweł.

"I'd like you to become my partner. During that week, I dealt with my problems. My company bounced back. After all, I still owe you a favor," Paul replied.

Robert nie wiedział co powiedzieć. Zdał sobie sprawę z tego, że jego problemy mogły zniknąć.

Robert didn't know what to say. He realized that his problems could disappear.

"Nie wiem co powiedzieć," odpowiedział Robert.

"I don't know what to say," Robert said.

"Nie mów nic. Przyjdź do mojej firmy jutro rano. Omówimy szczegóły współpracy," odpowiedział Paweł.

"You don't have to. Come to my office tomorrow morning. We'll discuss the details of our partnership," Paul said.

"Dziękuję. Uratowałeś mi życie," dodał Robert.

"Thank you. You saved my life," Robert added.

"Tak jak ty uratowałeś moje. Dobro zawsze powraca."

"Just as you saved mine once. The good always returns."

Streszczenie

Robert był świetnym biznesmenem. Tego dnia udało mu się podpisać ważny kontrakt i postanowił świętować wraz ze swoją żoną. Po wyjściu z biura postanowił pójść na spacer do parku. Kiedy spacerował zauważył w parku mężczyznę, który siedział na ławce. Twarz miał schowaną w dłoniach, a dokumenty leżały na ziemi. Robert podszedł do mężczyzny i postanowił mu pomóc. Okazało się, że tamten mężczyzna miał na imię Paweł i właśnie stracił swoją firmę. Miał długi i wszystko mu zabrali. Robert dał Pawłowi pieniądze aby ten mógł zatrzymać się w hotelu i kupić sobie coś do jedzenia. Od tamtej chwili nie miał kontaktu z Pawłem. Po jakimś czasie firma Roberta straciła ważnego klienta. Po tym zdarzeniu firma Roberta upadła. Robert był załamany. Pewnego dnia dostał wiadomość od nieznanej osoby. Chciała się z nim spotkać w parku. Okazało się że tą osobą był Paweł. Postanowił pomóc Robertowi. Chciał, aby Robert był jego wspólnikiem. Od tamtej pory mężczyźni zostali przyjaciółmi.

Summary

Robert was a great businessman. One day he managed to sign an important contract, and he decided to celebrate with his wife. After leaving his office, he decided to take a walk in the park. While he was walking, he saw a man who was sitting on a bench. He had his face covered with his hands. Some of his documents were lying on the ground. Robert decided to help the man. It turned out that the man, whose name was Paul, had just lost his company. He had huge debts, and everything was taken from him. Robert gave Paul some money so that he could stay at a hotel and buy some food. Since that moment, Robert didn't receive any message from Paul. After some time, Robert's company lost a huge client. Due to that situation, Robert's company collapsed. Robert was devastated. One day he got a text message from an unknown person. The person wanted to meet Robert in the park. It turned out that it was Paul. He decided to help Robert. He wanted Robert to become his business partner. The men made friends with each other.

Vocabulary

Spotkanie – a meeting

Kontrakt – a contract

Pójść pieszo – to go on foot

Sam na sam – alone

Ławka – a bench

Załamany – broken

Teczka – a briefcase

Szef – a CEO (boss)

Kłótnia – an argument

Rozwiązany – dissolved

Mieszkanie – an apartment

Długi – debts

Na szczycie - at the top

Stanąć na nogi - to get back on one's feet

Zyski - profit

Zdruzgotany - devastated

Warunki - terms

Upaść - to collapse

W mgnieniu oka - in the blink of an eye

Nieznany - unknown

Elegancko ubrany - dressed elegantly

Znajomo - familiar

Całkowicie - drastically

Kopę lat! - It's been ages!

Gazeta - a newspaper

Pozbierać się - to get oneself together

Bałagan - mess

Wspólnik - a business partner

Przysługa - a favor

Pytania

1. Co Adam zamierzał zrobić po powrocie do domu?

2. Dlaczego Robert postanowił pójść pieszo?

3. Gdzie Robert spotkał Pawła po raz pierwszy?

4. Dlaczego Paweł nie miał pieniędzy?

5. W jaki sposób Robert pomógł Pawłowi?

6. Gdzie spędził noc Paweł po otrzymaniu pieniędzy od Roberta?

a) w domu Roberta

b) w firmie Roberta

c) w hotelu

7. Dlaczego firma Roberta upadła?

a) Robert prowadził nielegalne interesy

b) Robert stracił klientów

c) Robert nie roszczył się o nią

8. W jaki sposób Paweł pomógł Robertowi?

a) chciał by Robert był jego wspólnikiem

b) dał mu pieniądze

c) kupił firmę Roberta

9. W jaki sposób Paweł dowiedział się o kłopotach Roberta?

a) przeczytał w Internecie

b) od żony Roberta

c) przeczytał w gazecie

Questions

1. What was Robert going to do after going back home?

2. Why did Robert decide to go on foot?

3. Where did Robert meet Paul for the first time?

4. Why did Paul have no money?

5. How did Robert help Paul?

6. Where did Paul spend the night after getting some money from Robert?

a) At Robert's house

b) At Robert's company

c) At a hotel

7. Why did Robert's company collapse?

a) Robert's business was illegal

b) Robert lost his clients

c) Robert didn't care enough about the company

8. How did Paul help Robert?

a) He wanted Robert to become his business partner

b) He gave Robert some money

c) He bought Robert's company

9. How did Paul find out about Robert's problems?

a) He read about it on the Internet

b) From Robert's wife

c) He read about it in the newspaper

Odpowiedzi

1. Świętować z żoną

2. Aby pozostać sam na sam ze swoimi myślami

3. W parku

4. Stracił firmę i miał długi

5. Dał mu pieniądze

6. c

7. b

8. a

9. c

Answers

1. He wanted co celebrate with his wife

2. He wanted to be alone with his thoughts

3. In the park

4. He lost his company and he had debts

5. He gave him some money

6. c

7. b

8. a

9. c

Chapter 4 – Praktyka czyni mistrza [Practice makes perfect]

Ten dzień wreszcie nadszedł. Adam czekał na niego ostatnich kilka lat. Kiedy wszedł do **sali**, ujrzał wszystkich studentów, **wykładowców** i **rektora uczelni**. Rozejrzał się i zobaczył swoich znajomych.

That day finally came. Adam had been waiting for it for the past few years. When he came into the hall, he saw all the students, lecturers, and the college president. He looked around and noticed his friends.

"Adam. Gdzie byłeś? Wszyscy czekają na ciebie. To nasz wielki dzień," spytała jedna z koleżanek.

"Adam. Where have you been? Everybody's waiting for you. It's our big day," one of his friends asked.

Adam był zdenerwowany. Za chwilę miał ukończyć **szkołę muzyczną** i odebrać swój **dyplom**. Był jednym z najlepszych **gitarzystów** na uczelni, ale wiedział że czeka go jeszcze długa droga. Wtem, usłyszał swoje imię i nazwisko:

Adam was nervous. He was to graduate from the music academy and get his diploma in a moment. He was one of the best guitarists, but he knew he would have a long way to go. Suddenly, he heard his name:

"Adam Nowak!"

Dyplom był już w jego rękach. Po zejściu ze sceny **odetchnął z ulgą**. Spoglądając na dokument zdał sobie sprawę z tego, że to już koniec. Od tej chwili będzie musiał radzić sobie sam. Będzie polegał tylko na sobie. Wiedział, że będzie musiał **systematycznie** ćwiczyć, aby dojść do perfekcji. Wiedział też, że będzie tęsknił za swoim ulubionym nauczycielem, panem Zalewskim.

He had his diploma in his hands. After walking down the stage, he could breathe easily. Looking at the diploma, he realized that this was the end. Since that moment, he would have to be on his own. He would have to rely only on himself. He knew that he had to practice regularly in order to reach perfection. He also knew that he would miss his favorite teacher, Mr. Zalewski.

Pan Zalewski był najstarszym nauczycielem na uniwersytecie muzycznym. Wiedział wszystko o każdym instrumencie - był **lutnikiem**. Niektórzy uczniowie twierdzili, że pan Zalewski był dziwny, lecz Adam bardzo go lubił. Uwielbiał chodzić na jego zajęcia, ponieważ pan Zalewski opowiadał z pasją. Po prostu, kochał to, co robił.

Mr. Zalewski was the oldest teacher at the academy. He knew everything about instruments—he was a luthier. Some students thought Mr. Zalewski was weird, but Adam liked him so much. He had enjoyed his classes since Mr. Zalewski was really passionate. He simply loved his job.

Po ceremonii ukończenia Adam postanowił pójść do **gabinetu** profesora i pożegnać się z nim. Kiedy wszedł, zobaczył swojego nauczyciela naprawiającego gitarę. Instrument był cudowny. Adam pierwszy raz w swoim życiu widział takie arcydzieło.

After the graduation ceremony, Adam decided to go to the professor's office and say goodbye to him. When he entered, he saw his teacher fixing a guitar. The instrument was beautiful. Adam had never seen such a masterpiece before.

"Dzień dobry, Panie Zalewski. Przyszedłem się pożegnać. Chciałbym podziękować za te wspaniałe cztery lata. Będę za panem **tęsknił**," powiedział Adam.

"Good afternoon, Mr. Zalewski. I'm going to say goodbye. I'd like to thank you for these amazing four years. I'll miss you," Adam said.

"O, mój ulubiony uczeń, Adam! Siadaj, proszę. Czy chciałbyś napić się kawy? Ten ostatni raz," zasugerował profesor.

"Oh, my favorite student, Adam! Sit down, please. Would you like some tea? Just for the last time," the professor suggested.

"Z przyjemnością!"

"I'd love to!"

Podczas gdy profesor przyrządzał kawę, Adam **nie mógł oderwać wzroku** od gitary.

When the professor was making coffee, Adam couldn't take his eyes off the guitar.

"Prawdziwe arcydzieło. Pochodzi z lat 30 dwudziestego wieku. Właśnie skończyłem ją naprawiać. Podarował mi ją pewien bogaty człowiek," powiedział profesor i dodał,

"Such a masterpiece. It's from the 30s. I've just finished repairing. It was given to me by a really rich man," said the professor and added:

"Byłeś najbardziej utalentowanym studentem, Adamie. Jestem z ciebie dumny. Chciałbym, abyś wziął tę gitarę. Ja jest jem już zbyt stary, aby grać. Moje palce nie chcą współpracować."

"You've been the most talented student, Adam. I'm really proud of you. I'd like you to keep this guitar. I'm too old to play. My fingers don't listen to me."

Adam był zaskoczony. Gitara wyglądała pięknie, ale nie był pewny czy powinien wziąć tak drogi instrument.

Adam was surprised. The guitar looked amazing, but he wasn't sure whether he should take such an expensive instrument.

"Dziękuję, profesorze, ale nie wiem czy powinienem..." odpowiedział Adam.

"Thanks, professor, but I'm not sure I should take it..." Adam said.

"Proszę. Masz wielki talent. Pamiętaj jednak, że talent jest niczym bez praktyki."

"Please. You have a great talent. But remember that talent means nothing without regular practice."

"Co Pan ma na myśli?" zapytał Adam.

"What do you mean?" Adam asked.

"Może wydać ci się to dziwne, może nie uwierzysz.. nieważne. Dostałem tę gitarę od pewnego bogatego muzyka. Był jednym z najlepszych gitarzystów na całym świecie. Gdy spytałem go o jego **umiejętności,** odpowiedział mi, że gitara posiada **specyficzne właściwości.**"

"Maybe you think it's weird, maybe you won't even believe it... nevermind. This guitar was given to me by a really rich musician. He was one of the greatest guitarists in the world. When I asked him about his skill, he said that the guitar has some special properties."

"Jakie właściwości?" Adam był zmieszany.

"What properties?" Adam was confused.

"Osoba, która zacznie na niej grać stanie się najlepszym muzykiem na świecie. Gra nie będzie wymagać wysiłku i ćwiczeń. Spróbuj."

"The person who plays it becomes the best musician in the world. Playing this guitar requires no effort and practice. Try it."

Adam nie wierzył w to, co mówił profesor, ale postanowił spróbować. Po chwili grał jak prawdziwy **profesjonalista!**

Adam didn't believe his professor, yet he decided to try. After a while, he played like a professionalist.

Jak to jest możliwe profesorze? Dopiero ukończyłem szkołę. Potrzeba wielu lat praktyki, aby tak grać," zapytał Adam.

"How is this even possible, professor? I just finished at the academy. It takes years of practice to play like this," Adam asked.

"Istnieją na świecie rzeczy, których nie da się **racjonalnie** wyjaśnić," powiedział pan Zalewski i dodał,

"There are things that you can't explain rationally," said Mr. Zalewski and added,

"Niestety, to nie będzie trwało wiecznie. Gitara straci swoje właściwości po upływie 5 lat od tej chwili. Do tego czasu powinieneś ćwiczyć i ciężko pracować, aby utrzymać swój sukces."

"Unfortunately, it's not going to last forever. The guitar will have its special properties until 5 years from now have gone by. You have to practice and work hard to maintain your success after these 5 years."

Adam podziękował profesorowi za prezent i pożegnał się z nim. Miał przed sobą wspaniałą karierę muzyka. Wychodząc z budynku uniwersytetu miał w głowie słowa profesora:

Adam thanked the professor for the gift and said goodbye. He had great career as a musician ahead. When he was leaving the building, he heard his professor's words in his head:

"Pamiętaj, praktyka, nie talent uczyni z ciebie mistrza. Ćwicz codziennie."

"Remember, talent means nothing without regular practice. Practice every day."

Adam postanowił **rozwinąć swoją karierę** jak najszybciej. Koncertował w **klubach muzycznych**, współpracował ze znanymi muzykami, a nawet nagrał swoją **płytę**. Nigdy nie rozstawał się ze swoją gitarą. Zabierał ją na każdy koncert, na każde nagranie i na każde wydarzenie. Za każdym razem tłumaczył, że gitara jest częścią jego **wizerunku** i nie chce grać na żadnej innej.

Adam decided to develop his career as soon as possible. He performed in many music clubs with some well-known musicians. He even released his own record. He always kept a close eye on his guitar. He took it to every concert, every recording, and every event. Each time he explained that the guitar was a part of his image, and he didn't want to play any other guitar.

Po roku Adam stał się najpopularniejszym gitarzystą w kraju. Jego **trasa koncertowa** obejmowała wszystkie największe miasta. Jego występy robiły ogromne wrażenie. Wracając do domu, jednak, Adam **odkładał** gitarę **na bok**. Stwierdził, że jego talent mu wystarczy.

After a year, Adam became the most popular guitarist in the country. His concert tour included all the biggest cities. His performances were outstanding. However, every time Adam got back home, he put aside his guitar. He thought that his talent was enough.

"To jest **niemożliwe**. Przecież pamiętam wszystkie nuty, chwyty. **Nie ma opcji,** abym zapomniał jak się gra na gitarze po upływie tych 5 lat."

"It's impossible. I remember every note, every chord. There's no way I could ever forget how to play the guitar. Even after these 5 years."

Pewnego dnia Adam otrzymał telefon. Nie mógł uwierzyć w to co usłyszał:

One day, Adam got a call. He couldn't believe what he heard:

"Dzień dobry Panie Nowak. Chcielibyśmy, aby zagrał pan koncert w **filharmonii narodowej**. Czy chciałby pan zagrać?"

"Good morning, Mr. Nowak. We'd like you to play a concert at the National philharmonic. Would you like to play?"

Adam nie wiedział co powiedzieć. To było spełnienie marzeń każdego muzyka! Koncert w filharmonii narodowej był najważniejszą nagrodą.

Adam didn't know what to say. It was a dream come true for every musician! The concert at the National Philharmonic was the best prize he could ever win.

Adam był tak **podekscytowany**, że nie mógł powiedzieć ani słowa. Jedyne co udało musie powiedzieć to, "O... o... oczywiście!"

Adam was so excited that he couldn't say a word. He could only say, "O... of... of course!"

Dzień koncertu w filharmonii w końcu nadszedł. Adam siedział w **garderobie** i **poprawiał swój wygląd**, gdy nagle przypomniał sobie, że dokładnie pięć lat temu ukończył szkołę. Przypomniał sobie swoich znajomych, ceremonię ukończenia i... profesora Zalewskiego.

The day of the concert finally came. Adam was sitting in the dressing room and trying to smarten himself up when he suddenly recalled that he graduated from the music academy exactly five years ago. He remembered his friends, the graduation ceremony and... Professor Zalewski.

Wtem, Adam usłyszał w głowie słowa:

Suddenly, Adam heard a voice in his head:

"Pamiętaj, praktyka, nie talent uczyni z ciebie mistrza. Ćwicz codziennie."

"Remember, talent means nothing without regular practice. Practice every day."

Był zdenerwowany. Za chwilę miał zagrać najważniejszy koncert w swoim życiu.

He was nervous. He was about to give the most important concert of his life.

To nie może być prawda, pomyślał i postanowił zagrać piosenki. Styl gry był ten sam. Pamiętał każdy utwór.

This can't be true, he thought and he decided to play some songs. The style was the same. He remembered each song.

Profesor był troszeczkę dziwny, pomyślał.

The professor was kinda weird, he thought.

W tej samej chwili usłyszał publiczność i **oklaski**. Tak, to był ten moment. Wyszedł na scenę i momentalnie **oślepił go** blask świateł. Po chwili spojrzał na publiczność. Sala była wypełniona po brzegi. W pierwszym rzędzie siedziała jego rodzina, znajomi oraz... pan Zalewski.

At the same moment, he heard the audience clapping. Yes, it was that moment. He entered the stage, and the lights blinded him. After a few seconds, he looked at the audience. The hall was crowded. In the first row, he noticed some familiar faces. There was his family, his friends and... Mr. Zalewski.

Adam usiadł na krześle, położył nuty i zaczął grać. Zagrał utwór ze swojej płyty. Po zagraniu ostatniej nuty Adam spojrzał na publiczność. Nikt nie klaskał. Wszyscy **zamarli**. Po chwili Adam dostrzegł profesora i jego wyraz twarzy. Adam nie mógł w to uwierzyć. Nie usłyszał nawet, że nie umiał już grać.

Adam sat down, placed the note sheets, and started to play. He played a song from his record. Shortly after playing the last note, Adam looked at the audience. No one was clapping. Everyone just froze. Adam looked at the professor, and he noticed the expression on his face. Adam couldn't believe it. He hadn't heard that he couldn't play anymore.

Nie wiedział co ma robić. Spanikował. Odłożył gitarę i uciekł do garderoby. Nie mógł uwierzyć w to co wydarzyło się na scenie. Po chwili usłyszał pukanie do drzwi. To był profesor.

He didn't know what to do. He panicked. He put the guitar aside and escaped to the backstage. He couldn't believe what happened on the stage. After a while, he heard someone knocking at the door.

"Nie ćwiczyłeś prawda?" powiedział profesor.

"You didn't practice, did you?" the professor said.

Adam **przytaknął**.

Adam nodded.

"Za późno. Gitara straciła swoje właściwości, a ty nie ćwiczyłeś przez pięć lat. Musisz zacząć od nowa."

"It's too late. The guitar lost its properties and you didn't practice during these five years. You have to start over."

Adam był zrozpaczony. Jego kariera właśnie **legła w gruzach**. Zapomniał o słowach profesora. Zdał sobie sprawę, że bez wysiłku nie można osiągnąć sukcesu.

Adam was devastated. His career had just collapsed. He had forgotten about the professor's words. He realized that he couldn't be successful without making an effort.

"Przepraszam, profesorze," odpowiedział Adam i dodał, „Powinienem był wiedzieć że praktyka czyni mistrza."

"I'm sorry, professor," Adam said and added, "I should have known that practice makes perfect."

Od tej chwili Adam zaczął ćwiczyć codziennie. Nigdy nie doszedł już do tak wysokiego poziomu, ale powrócił do grania w klubach muzycznych.

Since that moment, Adam started to practice every day. He couldn't reach the highest level, but he eventually got back to performing in music clubs.

Streszczenie

Adam był bardzo utalentowanym studentem. Po ceremonii ukończenia studiów postanowił odwiedzić swojego ulubionego profesora—pana Zalewskiego—w jego biurze. Po wejściu do pokoju pana Zalewskiego Adam zauważył piękną gitarę. Pan Zalewski powiedział Adamowi, że jest to specjalna gitara. Ten który na niej gra nie musi ćwiczyć i staje się najlepszym muzykiem na świecie. Po rozmowie pan Zalewski podarował Adamowi gitarę. Powiedział mu jednak, że gitara zachowa swoje specjalne właściwości tylko przez pięć lat. Do tego czasu Adam musi ciężko pracować i dużo ćwiczyć. Adam nie posłuchał profesora. Stał się najlepszym muzykiem w kraju I grał koncerty. Został poproszony aby zagrać koncert w filharmonii narodowej. Przed koncertem Adam zorientował się, że dokładnie pięć lat temu otrzymał gitarę. Zlekceważył to jednak. Podczas koncertu okazało się, że Adam nie umiał grać. Uciekł ze sceny. Po nieudanym koncercie pan Zalewski przyszedł do garderoby Adama. Był rozczarowany. Powiedział Adamowi, że ma ćwiczyć. Adam nauczył się grać poprzez praktykę.

Summary

Adam was a really gifted student. After the graduation ceremony, he decided to visit his favorite professor—Mr. Zalewski—in his office. After entering Mr. Zalewski's office, Adam noticed a beautiful guitar. Mr. Zalewski told Adam that it was a special guitar. The one who played it could become the best musician in the world and didn't have to practice. After the conversation, Mr. Zalewski gave Adam the guitar as a gift. He told him that the guitar would keep its special features for only five years, so Adam had to practice a lot and work hard anyway.

Adam didn't listen to the professor. He became the best musician in the country and gave a lot of performances. He was asked to give a concert at the National Philharmonic. Before the concert, Adam realized that exactly five years earlier he got the guitar. However, he didn't care. During the concert, it turned out that Adam couldn't play any longer. He escaped from the stage. After an unsuccessful concert, Adam was visited by Mr. Zalewski. The professor was disappointed. He told Adam that he had to practice. Adam learned how to play again through practice.

Vocabulary

Sala – a hall

Wykładowca – a lecturer

Rektor uczelni – a college president

Dyplom – a diploma

Gitarzysta – a guitarist

Odetchnąć z ulgą – to breathe easily

Systematycznie – regularly

Lutnik – a luthier

Gabinet – an office

Tęsknić – to miss

Nie móc oderwać wzroku – you can't take your eyes off something

Umiejętności – skills

Specyficzne właściwości – special properties

Profesjonalista – professionalist

Racjonalnie – rationally

Rozwinąć swoją karierę – to develop one's career

Klub muzyczny – a music club

Płyta – a record

Wizerunek – an image

Trasa koncertowa – a concert tour

Odkładać na bok – set aside

Niemożliwe – impossible

Nie ma opcji – there's no way

Filharmonia narodowa – National Philharmonic

Podekscytowany – excited

Garderoba – backstage

Poprawiać swój wygląd – to smarten oneself up

Oklaski – clapping

Oślepić – to blind

Zamierać – to freeze

Przytaknąć – to nod

Legnąć w gruzach – to collapse

Pytania

1. Kto był ulubionym profesorem Adama?

2. Gdzie poszedł Adam zaraz po ceremonii ukończenia studiów?

3. Co zobaczył Adam zaraz po wejściu do gabinetu profesora?

4. Jaki instrument otrzymał Adam?

5. Jakie specyficzne właściwości posiadała gitara?

6. Co odkrył Adam przed koncertem w filharmonii?

a) Zapomiał zabrać swojej gitary

b) Gitara straciła swoje właściwości

c) Profesora Zalewskiego nie było na sali

7. Co stało się podczas koncertu w filharmonii?

a) Adam nie umiał już pięknie grać

b) Gitara nagle się zepsuła

c) Nikt nie przyszedł na koncert

8. Kto przyszedł do garderoby Adama po nieudanym koncercie?

a) Pan Zalewski

b) Dziewczyna Adama

c) Rodzice Adama

9. Czy Adam zaczął ćwiczyć po nieudanym koncercie?

a) Tak

b) Nie

Questions

1. Who was Adam's favorite professor?

2. Where did Adam go right after the graduation ceremony?

3. What did Adam notice after entering the professor's office?

4. What instrument did Adam get?

5. What special properties did the guitar have?

6. What did Adam discover right before the concert at the Philharmonic?

a) That he had forgotten to take his guitar

b) That the guitar had lost its properties

c) That Mr. Zalewski wasn't inside the Philharmonic

7. What happened at the concert?

a) Adam couldn't play brilliantly any longer

b) The guitar suddenly broke down

c) No one came to the concert

8. What did come to Adam backstage after the unsuccessful concert?

a) Mr. Zalewski

b) Adam's girlfriend

c) Adam's parents

9. Did Adam start to practice after the concert?

a) Yes

b) No

Odpowiedzi

1. Pan Zalewski

2. Do gabinetu profesora Zalewskiego

3. Gitarę

4. Gitarę

5. Ten kto na niej grał zostawał najlepszym muzykiem na świecie i nie musiał ćwiczyć

6. b

7. a

8. a

9. a

Answers

1. Mr. Zalewski

2. To Mr. Zalewski's office

3. A guitar

4. A guitar

5. The one who played it would become the best musician in the world and he\she didn't have to practice

6. b

7. a

8. a

9. a

Chapter 5 – Zaskakujące odkrycie [A suprising discovery]

"Przepraszam. **Nie stać nas na to**" - Joanna miała już dość tych słów. Za każdym razem gdy dzieci lub mąż prosili ją o zakup czegoś, musiała je wypowiedzieć. Rodzina Joanny nie była bogata.

"I'm sorry. We can't afford it" - Joanna was tired of these words. Every time her children had asked her to buy something, she had to tell them. Joanna's family wasn't rich.

Piotr, jej mąż, był zawodowym **kierowcą**. Niestety dwa lata temu stracił swoją pracę z powodu **wypadku**, który spowodował. Od tamtego momentu nie mógł znaleźć pracy. Co więcej, stracił również **prawo jazdy**.

Piotr, her husband, was a professional driver. Unfortunately, two years ago, he lost his job due to an accident he'd caused.

Joanna pracowała jako **sprzątaczka**. Czasem musiała brać **dodatkowe godziny**, aby móc zapłacić **rachunki i czynsz**. Razem z córkami i mężem mieszkała w małym mieszkaniu w Warszawie. Pewnego dnia wraz z rachunkami otrzymała pewien **list**.

Joanna was a cleaning lady. Sometimes she had to work extra hours to pay the bills and rent. She lived in a small apartment in

Warsaw together with her husband and her daughters. One day, she got a letter, along with some bills to pay.

"Mamo, co to jest?" spytała Ania, młodsza córka.

"Mom, what is this?" Ania, her younger daughter, asked.

"To z policji. Boję się otworzyć," odpowiedziała Joanna.

"It's from the police. I'm scared," Joanna replied.

Po chwili Joanna **była w rozsypce**. W liście była informacja o tym, że Joanna **przekroczyła prędkość** i musi zapłacić **mandat**. W **kopercie** było również zdjęcie z **fotoradaru**.

After a while, Joanna was devastated. The letter said that Joanna had exceeded the speed limit and had to pay a speeding ticket. There was also a photo taken by the speed camera inside the envelope.

Joanna wiedziała co to oznacza. Jej rodzina **ledwo wiązała koniec z końcem**, więc zapłacenie 500 zł było dla niej niewykonalne.

Joanna knew what it meant. Her family had struggled to make ends meet, so paying 500 zloty was impossible.

"Będziemy musieli **wziąć pożyczkę**," stwierdził Piotr i dodał „Nie ma innego wyjścia."

"We have to take a bank loan," Piotr said and added, "There's no other way."

Po chwili Joanna zauważyła, że pod stertą kopert jest jeszcze jeden list. Była przerażona.

After a while, Joanna noticed that there was another letter at the bottom of the pile. She got scared.

"Jeśli to jest kolejny mandat lub rachunek, nie wiem co zrobimy," powiedziała.

"If that's another ticket or bill, I don't know what we're going to do," she said.

"Spokojnie. Jeszcze nie wiemy co to jest. Otwórz," uspokoił ją Piotr.

"Easy. We don't know yet. Open it," Piotr tried to calm her.

List był kolejnym **pismem z urzędu**. Czytając tekst, Joanna nie mogła uwierzyć własnym oczom.

It was another official letter. While reading the text, Joanna couldn't believe her eyes.

"I co? I co? Co tam jest?" Piotr i dziewczyny nie mogły się doczekać odpowiedzi.

"What's in there?" Piotr and the girls couldn't wait to know the answer.

"Tutaj jest napisane, że ciocia Helena **zmarła** tydzień temu. Dziwne. Nie miałam z nią kontaktu od dzieciństwa. Miałam pięć lat kiedy wyprowadziła się z Warszawy do Krakowa. Moi rodzice też nie spotkali się z nią," powiedziała Joanna i dodała,

"It says that Aunt Helen died a week ago. That's weird. We haven't been in contact since I was a child. I was five when she moved from Warsaw to Cracow. My parents weren't in contact with her either," Joanna said and added,

"Ciocia mieszkała małym mieszkaniu w Krakowie. W liście jest napisane, że ciocia chciała, abym posprzątała jej mieszkanie i zabrała jej rzeczy, ponieważ właściciel chce je **wynająć** komuś innemu. Mam 30 dni."

"Auntie lived in a small apartment in Cracow. The letter says that she wanted me to clean her apartment and take her stuff since the landlord has to rent it to someone else. I have 30 days."

"Kolejny problem! Co my mamy zrobić z jej rzeczami? Nie możemy zabrać ich do Warszawy; nie mamy miejsca w naszym mieszkaniu," wykrzyknął Piotr.

"Another problem! What are we going to do with her stuff? We can't take it to Warsaw; we don't have enough space in our apartment," Piotr exclaimed.

Joanna nie wiedziała co zrobić. **Miała zbyt dużo na głowie** i zbyt mało pieniędzy, aby zająć się rzeczami ciotki. Pamiętała, ciotka była prawdziwym **zbieraczem** – lubiła **antyki, porcelanę** oraz **obrazy**. W jej mieszkaniu nigdy nie było miejsca. Koniec końców, Joanna postanowiła pojechać wraz z rodziną do Krakowa, aby zająć się rzeczami ciotki.

Joanna didn't know what to do. She had a lot on her plate and almost no money. She couldn't take care of her aunt's stuff. She had a memory of her aunt being a real hoarder—she loved antiques, porcelain, and paintings. She had never had enough space in her apartment. Eventually, Joanna decided to go with her family to Cracow to take care of her aunt's stuff.

Po długiej podróży rodzina w końcu dotarła na miejsce. **Właściciel** mieszkania przekazał Joannie **klucz** i wprowadził całą rodzinę do domu ciotki. Joanna nie mogła uwierzyć w to co zobaczyła.

After a long journey, the family finally reached the destination. The landlord gave Joanna the keys and showed them the apartment. Joanna couldn't believe what she saw.

"Co za bałagan!" wykrzyknęły dziewczyny.

"What a mess!" the girls exclaimed.

Mieszkanie było okropne. **Ściany** były pełne obrazów, półek wypełnionych **figurkami** i książkami, a na podłodze leżały kolorowe **dywany.**

The apartment looked terrible. The walls were covered with paintings, the shelves were full of figurines, and the floor was covered with colorful carpets.

"Co my z tym wszystkim zrobimy?" powiedział Piotr.

"What are we going to do with all this stuff?" said Piotr.

Joanna była załamana. Nie miała pieniędzy na kupienie **magazynu.**

Joanna was broken. She didn't have enough money to buy storage space.

"Musimy się pozbyć tego wszystkiego szybko. Nie mamy czasu. Właściciel powiedział, że mamy tylko 30 dni," powiedziała Joanna.

"We have to get rid of all this stuff quickly. We don't have much time. The landlord said that we have only 30 days," Joanna said.

Rodzina postanowiła zabrać książki, obrazy i figurki i sprzedać je w **antykwariacie.**

The family decided to take books, paintings, and some figurines to sell them at the antique shop.

Po kliku chwilach Joanna ujrzała bardzo dziwny obraz. Pamiętała go kiedy w dzieciństwie odwiedzała ciotkę Helenę. Pamiętała jak ciotka mówiła, że został namalowany przez sławnego artystę.

After a while, Joanna noticed a really weird painting. She remembered it. It was there when she visited her aunt in her childhood. She remembered that it had been painted by a famous artist.

"Poczekajcie. Pamiętam ten obraz. Weźmy go do antykwariatu. Muszę wiedzieć czy jest coś wart," powiedziała Joanna.

"Wait. I remember this painting. Let's take it to the antique shop too. I need to know whether it's worth some money," Joanna said.

Po kilku godzinach Joanna wraz z rodziną skończyli sprzątanie. Mieszkanie wyglądało lepiej, ale wciąż było w nim wiele rzeczy.

After a few hours, Joanna and her family finished cleaning. The apartment looked much better, but there was still too much stuff in it.

"Przyjedziemy za kilka dni. Nie możemy zabrać wszystkiego dzisiaj," powiedział Piotr.

"We'll get back in a few days. We can't take everything today," Piotr said.

Po powrocie do Warszawy Joanna nie mogła przestać myśleć o obrazie, który pamiętała z dzieciństwa. Był naprawdę dziwny – przedstawiał białe **kropki** na czarnym **tle**. Wyglądał okropnie, ale Joanna pamiętała, że był to najważniejszy obraz dla jej ciotki.

After returning to Warsaw, Joanna couldn't stop thinking about the painting that she remembered from her childhood. It was really weird. It showed white dots on the black background. It looked terrible, but Joanna remembered that it had been the most important painting in her aunt's collection.

Następnego dnia Joanna postanowiła udać się do antykwariatu. Gdy pokazała **płótno**, pracownik był zaskoczony.

The next day, Joanna decided to go to the antique shop. When she showed the painting, the dealer got shocked.

"Skąd pani to ma?" zapytał.

"Where did you get this?" he asked.

"To był obraz mojej ciotki. Zmarła tydzień temu," odpowiedziała Joanna.

"It was my aunt's. She died a week ago," Joanna replied.

Pracownik antykwariatu uważnie przyglądał się obrazowi. Joanna była już bardzo **zmieszana**.

The dealer looked at the painting carefully. Joanna was really confused.

"Czy on jest coś wart?" spytała.

"Is it valuable?" she asked.

"Ten obraz to prawdziwe dzieło sztuki. To **autentyk**! Dostanie Pani za niego milion złotych!"

"This painting is a real masterpiece. It's authentic. You'll get a million zlotys for it!"

Joanna nie mogła uwierzyć własnym uszom. Obraz, który tak **nienawidziła** w dzieciństwie mógł rozwiązać jej **problemy finansowe**.

Joanna couldn't believe her ears. The painting that she hated in her childhood could now solve her financial problems.

Kilka dni później Joanna sprzedała obraz za dwa miliony do Muzeum Narodowego. Rodzina postanowiła kupić mieszkanie ciotki Heleny i zachować część rzeczy, która tam pozostała.

After a few days, Joanna sold the painting for two million zlotys to the National Museum.

" Ciotka Helena była prawdziwym **koneserem**. A ja myślałam, że była zwykłym zbieraczem," powiedziała Joanna.

"Aunt Helen was a real connoisseur. And I thought that she was a hoarder," Joanna said.

Od momentu sprzedaży obrazu Joanna nie musiała martwić się o pieniądze. W końcu nie musiała odpowiadać „Przepraszam. Nie stać nas na to."

Since selling the painting, Joanna didn't have to worry about money. She finally didn't have to say "I'm sorry. We can't afford it."

Streszczenie

Joanna wraz z rodziną mieszkała w Warszawie. Byli biedni. Pewnego dnia Joanna otrzymała list. Okazało się, że Joanna przekroczyła limit prędkości i dostała mandat. Joanna była załamana. Nie stać ją było na kolejny niespodziewany wydatek. Po chwili Joanna zauważyła, że pod stosem dokumentów był jeszcze jeden list. Było w nim napisane, że ciotka Joanny zmarła I chciała, aby Joanna posprzątała jej mieszkanie i zabrała jej rzeczy. Joanna z rodziną pojechała do Krakowa, aby zająć się rzeczami ciotki. Podczas sprzątania Joanna zauważyła dziwny obraz. Postanowiła go zabrać do antykwariatu. W antykwariacie Joanna dowiedziała się, że obraz jest wart dużo pieniędzy. Joanna postanowiła go sprzedać. Jej rodzina w końcu nie była biedna.

Summary

Joanna lived in Warsaw with her family. Her family was poor. One day, Joanna got a letter. It said that Joanna had exceeded the speed limit and she'd got a speeding ticket. Joanna was broken. She couldn't afford another unexpected expense. After a while, Joanna saw another letter. It said that her aunt had passed away. The aunt wanted Joanna to clean her apartment and take care of her stuff. Joanna and her family went to Cracow to take care of the aunt's stuff. During the cleaning, Joanna noticed a strange painting. She decided to take the painting to an antique shop. In the antique shop, Joanna learned that the painting was worth a lot of money. She decided to sell it. Her family wasn't poor anymore.

Vocabulary

Nie stać nas na to – we can't afford it

Kierowca – a driver

Wypadek – an accident

Prawo jazdy – a driving licence

Sprzątaczka – a cleaning lady

Dodatkowe godziny - extra hours

Rachunki i czynsz - bills and rent

List - a letter

Być w rozsypce - to be devastated

Przekroczyć prędkość - to exceed the speed limit

Ledwo wiązać koniec z końcem - to struggle to make ends meet

Wziąć pożyczkę - to take a bank loan

Pismo z urzędu - an official letter

Umrzeć - to die

Wynająć - to rent

Mieć zbyt dużo na głowie - to have a lot on one's plate

Zbieracz - a hoarder

Antyki - antiques

Porcelana - porcelain

Obrazy - paintings

Właściciel mieszkania - a landlord

Klucz - a key

Ściany - walls

Figurki - figurines

Dywany - carpets

Magazyn - storage

Antykwariat - an antique shop

Kropki - dots

Tło - background

Płótno - a painting

Zmieszany - confused

Autentyk - authentic

Nienawidzić - to hate

Problem finansowe - financial problems

Koneser - a connoisseur

Pytania

1. Kim z zawodu był mąż Joanny?

2. Dlaczego mąż Joanny stracił pracę?

3. Dlaczego Joanna musiała zapłacić mandat?

4. Co było w drugim liście?

5. Dlaczego Joanna musiała jechać do Krakowa z rodziną?

6. Dlaczego Joanna musiała posprzątać mieszkanie i zabrać rzeczy swojej ciotki?

a) Ponieważ właściciel chciał wynająć mieszkanie komuś innemu

b) Ponieważ wszystkie rzeczy były bardzo cenne

c) Ponieważ rzeczy były zniszczone

7. Co Joanna postanowiła zabrać do antykwariatu?

a) Krzesło

b) Dywan

c) Obraz

8. Czy obraz był wartościowy?

a) Tak

b) Nie

9. Co zrobiła Joanna z obrazem?

a) Oddała go za darmo

b) Powiesiła go na ścianie w swoim domu

c) Sprzedała go

Questions

1. What was the profession of Joanna's husband?

2. Why did Joanna's husband lose his job?

3. Why did Joanna have to pay for the ticket?

4. What was the second letter about?

5. Why did Joanna and her family have to go to Cracow?

6. Why did Joanna have to clean the apartment and take the stuff?

a) Because the landlord wanted to rent it to someone else

b) Because all the things inside were really valuable

c) because all the things inside were broken

7. What did Joanna decide to take to the antique shop?

a) A chair

b) A carpet

c) A painting

8. Was the painting valuable?

a) Yes

b) No

9. What did Joanna do with the painting?

a) She donated it

b) She hung it at her home

c) She sold it

Odpowiedzi

1. Kierowca

2. Spowodował wypadek

3. Przekroczyła limit prędkości

4. Śmierć ciotki

5. Aby zająć się mieszkaniem i rzeczami ciotki

Answers

1. Driver

2. He caused an accident

3. She had exceeded the speed limit

4. Her aunt's death

5. To take care of the aunt's apartment and stuff

6. a

7. c

8. a

9. c

Chapter 6 – Najlepszy przyjaciel [The best friend]

Był zimy poranek. **Liście** i ostatnie **owoce** z drzew zdążyły już opaść. **Mgła** na leśnej polanie była wyjątkowo gęsta.

It was a cold morning. The last leaves and fruits had already fallen from the trees. The fog on the glade was exceptionally thick that day.

Tego dnia Marcin miał dużo pracy. Nadchodziła mroźna zima, a w lesie nie było zbyt wiele jedzenia dla zwierząt. Musiał przygotować **karmniki, paśniki** oraz zostawić trochę warzyw i **karmy dla ptaków**.

That day, Marcin had a lot to do. An extremely cold winter was coming, and there wasn't enough food in the forest to feed the animals. Marcin had to prepare birdhouses and feeders, and leave some vegetables and birdseed.

Marcin od dwudziestu lat robił to co kochał—był **leśniczym**. Wraz ze swoją żoną Natalią **przeprowadzili się** do małego domku w lesie i tam troszczyli się o las i zwierzęta.

Marcin had been a forester for twenty years—and he'd loved his job so much. He and his wife, Natalia, had moved to a small house in the middle of the forest, and they'd taken care of the animals, especially during some cold winters.

Po wysypaniu jedzenia Marcin obserwował jak zwierzęta podchodzą do paśnika. Wiedział, że bez jego pomocy leśne zwierzęta miałyby bardzo ciężko.

After preparing the food, Marcin was watching the animals coming to the feeder. He knew that without his help wild animals couldn't have survived.

Po pracy w lesie Marcin udał się nad **jezioro**. Przez chwilę oglądał ostatnie **stado kaczek odlatujące na południe**, aby przetrwać zimowy czas.

After finishing his work in the forest, Marcin headed towards the lake. He was watching the last flock of ducks heading south to survive the wintertime. "

Chciałbym być teraz w **ciepłych krajach,** pomyślał Marcin. Za każdym razem marzył o tym, aby wyjechać z kraju i spędzić zimę nad **Morzem Śródziemnym**. Ale za każdym razem zostawał. Wiedział, że bez jego pomocy wiele zwierząt zginęłoby z braku jedzenia i zimna – w lasach było coraz mniej pożywienia.

I wish I was in the tropics now, Marcin thought. Every year, he'd dreamt of leaving the country and spending the winter by the Mediterranean Sea. Yet every year, he stayed. He knew that without his help, many wild animals wouldn't have survived the winter due to a lack of food and freezing weather. There had been less and less food in the forests each year.

Wracając do domu, Marcin zauważył w oddali **stado bocianów** zbierających się do lotu.

On his way home, Marcin noticed a flock of storks. They were about to fly out.

Dziwne, pomyślał. *Bociany powinny już dawno odlecieć.*

That's weird, he thought. *The storks should have already been gone.*

Postanowił sprawdzić dlaczego ptaki wciąż pozostawały przy jeziorze. Kiedy podszedł bliżej ptaki odleciały. Nagle... zauważył na plaży bociana, który nie odlatywał.

Marcin decided to check why the storks were still by the lake. When he came closer, the storks flew out. Suddenly... he noticed one stork that couldn't fly.

Marcin zbliżył się do niego, ale ptak dalej pozostawał na miejscu. Postanowił podejść jeszcze bliżej. Gdy Marcin był już dostatecznie blisko, zauważył, że ptak ma **złamane skrzydło.**

Marcin came closer, yet the bird was still staying put. He decided to come even closer. When Marcin was close enough, he noticed that the bird had a broken wing.

"O nie. Ten bocian nie miał zbyt wiele szczęścia. Jeśli nie odleci, **zamarznie na śmierć.**"

"Oh no. This stork wasn't so lucky. If it doesn't fly out, it will freeze to death."

Marcin nie zastanawiał się długo. Postanowił zabrać bociana do swojego domu.

Marcin didn't give it a second thought. He decided to take the stork to his house.

"Co zajęło ci tak długo? Co tam masz?" spytała Natalia, żona Marcina.

"What took you so long? What do you have over there?" asked Natalia, Marcin's wife.

"Po skończonej pracy zauważyłem bociany nad jeziorem. Mam jednego ze złamanym skrzydłem. Musimy mu szybko pomóc, aby mógł odlecieć," odpowiedział Marcin.

"After finishing my work, I noticed a flock of storks. I have a hero one with a broken wing. We have to help him quickly so that he can fly out," Marcin replied.

Marcin i Natalia od razu zaczęli działać. Położyli bociana na stole i opatrzyli jego **rany.**

Marcin and Natalia got down to work immediately. They put the stork on the table and dressed its wounds.

"Miałeś szczęście kolego. Za tydzień będziesz mógł odlecieć na południe. Miejmy nadzieję, że zima nie przyjdzie do tego czasu."

"You were lucky enough, buddy. You will be able to head south in a week. Let's hope winter won't come that fast."

Tydzień minął, ale sytuacja była gorsza niż Marcin zakładał.

The week had gone by, yet the situation was worse than Marcin expected.

"No cóż. Wygląda na to, że spędzisz zimę w naszym domu," powiedział Marcin.

"Well. It seems that you'll have to spend the winter in our house," Marcin said.

Marcin wrócił razem z ptakiem do domu i poprosił Natalię o przygotowanie legowiska dla ptaka.

Marcin returned with the bird to his house and asked Natalia to prepare a place for the bird.

Zima mijała, a bocian **zadomowił się** w leśniczówce. Marcin był bardzo dumny z tego, że znalazł bociana i pomógł mu przetrwać zimę.

Winter was passing, and the bird had already felt at home. Marcin was very proud of the fact that he'd found the stork and helped him survive the winter.

Pewnego poranka, przechadzając się po lesie Marcin usłyszał śpiew ptaków.

One morning, walking through the forest, Marcin heard birds singing.

"Nareszcie!" wykrzyknął. "**Wiosna** przyszła!"

"Finally!" he exclaimed. "The spring has come!"

Marcin pobiegł nad jezioro. Na plaży zauważył stado bocianów, które właśnie wróciły z południa. Postanowił zabrać swojego ptaka z leśniczówki z powrotem do reszty, ponieważ jego skrzydło było już sprawne.

Marcin ran to the lake. On the beach, he noticed a flock of storks that had just returned from the southern countries. He decided to take his bird from the house and return it to the rest of the birds since its wing had already healed.

Wypuszczając ptaka **na plaży** Marcin poczuł smutek. Przez całą zimę zdążył już przyzwyczaić się do jego obecności. Marcin wiedział, że będzie za nim tęsknił. W czasie zimy był to jego dobry przyjaciel.

While letting the bird go on the beach, Marcin felt sad. He'd got used to the bird. Marcin knew that he would miss the bird so much. During the winter, the stork was his best friend.

"Czas cię wypuścić, kolego," powiedział Marcin. „Żegnaj."

"It's time to let you go, buddy," Marcin said. "Goodbye."

Marcin wrócił do domu, ale nadal czuł wielki smutek. Przypomniał sobie jak w czasie zimy razem z żoną i ptakiem spędzali wieczory w domu. Przypomniał sobie jak znalazł bociana na plaży i jak pomógł mu przetrwać.

Marcin returned home. He felt really sad. He remembered that during the winter, he spent all evenings with his wife and the stork. He thought back about finding the stork on the beach and helping him survive.

Mijały miesiące, a Marcin powrócił do swoich codziennych obowiązków. Znów zbliżała się zima. Marcin przygotował karmniki i paśniki. Tego dnia postanowił jednak udać się nad jezioro.

Months went by, and Marcin returned to his daily responsibilities. Another winter was coming. Marcin prepared birdhouses and feeders. That day, he decided to go to the lake.

Niestety, nie było tam już żadnych ptaków.

Unfortunately, there weren't any birds left on the beach.

Musiały już odlecieć na południe, pomyślał. Przez chwilę stał jeszcze na plaży i **patrzył w niebo**.

They should have already headed south, he thought. He stood on the beach for a while and looked at the sky.

Robiło się już bardzo zimno, więc Marcin postanowił wrócić do domu. Zauważył w oddali **światła** w swoim domu. Przez okno widział Natalię przygotowującą jedzenie. Kiedy podszedł do okna, zauważył, że Natalia czyściła **koc**, który zeszłej zimy przygotowali dla bociana.

It was getting really cold, so Marcin decided to return to the house. He noticed lights in his home when he was returning. Through the window, he saw Natalia preparing food. When he came closer to the window, he noticed that Natalia was cleaning the blanket they'd prepared for the stork last winter.

Dziwne, pomyślał. *Ten koc był na strychu. Po co Natalia przyniosła go do kuchni?*

Weird, he thought. *That blanket was in the attic. Why did Natalia bring it to the kitchen?*

Marcin postanowił jak najszybciej to wyjaśnić, jednak po wejściu do domu wszystko było jasne. Marcin zauważył bociana, który leżał na kocu i Natalię przygotowującą jedzenie w kuchni. Był zaskoczony.

Marcin decided to find out as fast as possible. However, after entering the house, everything was clear. Marcin noticed the stork that was lying on the blanket, and Natalia who was preparing food in the kitchen. He was surprised.

"Przygotowywałam jedzenie, gdy nagle zauważyłam go przed domem. Postanowiłam zabrać go do środka. Nie odleciał na południe. Wygląda na to, że chce spędzić zimę z nami," powiedziała Natalia.

"I was preparing some food when I suddenly saw him in front of the house. I decided to take him home. He didn't head south. It seems that he wants to spend the winter with us," Natalia said.

Marcin był wzruszony. Bocian postanowił zostać razem z nim. Od tej pory ptak każdą zimę spędzał w domu Marcina, pomimo tego, że reszta ptaków odlatywała na południe. Marcin z żoną za każdym razem przygotowywali mu miejsce i wyczekiwali jesieni.

Marcin was touched. The stork decided to stay with him. Since that day, the bird spent every winter in the house, although the other birds headed south. Marcin and his wife always prepared a place for him and waited for the autumn.

Streszczenie

Marcin był leśniczym. Mieszkał ze swoją żoną Natalią w małym domku w lesie. Pewnego dnia po skończonej pracy Marcin postanowił udać się nad jezioro. Zauważył tam stado bocianów. Gdy podszedł bliżej zauważył, że jeden bocian miał złamane skrzydło. Marcin postanowił zabrać go domu. Marcin z żoną opatrzyli mu skrzydło. Po pewnym czasie okazało się jednak, że bocian nie mógł odlecieć na południe. Bocian spędził zimę w domu Marcina i Natalii. Po zimie Marcin wypuścił ptaka. Minęły miesiące I nadchodziła kolejna zima. Marcin udał się nad jezioro, ale wszystkie ptaki zdążyły już odlecieć na południe. Po powrocie do domu zauważył, że w jego domu był bocian, któremu pomógł w zeszłym roku. Bocian nie odleciał na południe tylko został na zimę w domu Marcina i Natalii.

Summary

Marcin was a forester. He lived with his wife, Natalia, in a small house in the woods. One day after finishing his work, Marcin decided to go to the lake. He saw a flock of storks. When he came closer, he noticed that one of the storks had a broken wing. Marcin decided to take the bird to his home. Marcin and his wife helped the stork. After some time, it turned out that the stork couldn't head south. The bird spent the winter at Marcin and Natalia's home. After the winter, Marcin let the bird go. A month went by, and another winter was coming. Marcin went to the lake, but all birds had already gone. After returning home, he saw that the stork which he helped survive last winter was at his home. The stork didn't head south and stayed at Marcin and Natalia's home.

Vocabulary

Liście – leaves

Owoce – fruits

Mgła – fog

Karmniki – birdhouses

Paśniki – feeders

Karma dla ptaków – birdseed

Leśniczy - a forester

Przeprowadzić się - to move

Jezioro - a lake

Stado kaczek - a flock of ducks

Odlatywać na południe - to head south

Ciepłe kraje - the tropics

Morze Śródziemne - the Mediterranean Sea

Stado bocianów - a flock of storks

Złamane skrzydło - a broken wing

Zamarznąć na śmierć - to freeze to death

Rany - wounds

Zadomowić się - to feel at home

Wiosna - spring

Na plaży - on the beach

Patrzeć w niebo - to look at the sky

Światła - lights

Koc - a blanket

Pytania

1. Kim był Marcin z zawodu?

2. Z kim Marcin mieszkał w swoim domu?

3. Gdzie był dom Marcina?

4. Co Marcin zauważył na plaży?

5. Dlaczego jeden z bocianów nie odleciał?

a) Nie chciał

b) Bał się

c) Miał złamane skrzydło

6. W jaki sposób Marcin pomógł bocianowi?

a) Zabrał go do paśnika

b) Zabrał go do swojego domu

c) Zbudował mu karmnik

7. Kiedy Marcin postanowił wypuścić bociana?

a) Latem

b) Na początku wiosny

c) Jesienią

8. Co zobaczył Marcin po powrocie do domu?

a) Bociana

b) Pusty dom

c) Swoich rodziców

Questions

1. What was Marcin's profession?

2. Who did Marcin live with?

3. Where was Marcin's house located?

4. What did Marcin notice at the beach?

5. Why didn't one of the storks fly out?

a) It didn't want to

b) It was scared

c) It had a broken wing

6. How did Marcin help the stork?

a) He took it to the feeder

b) He took it to his house

c) He built him a birdhouse

7. When did Marcin decide to let the stork go?

a) During summer

b) At the beginning of spring

c) During fall

8. What did Marcin notice after returning home?

a) The stork

b) An empty house

c) His parents

Odpowiedzi

1. Był leśniczym

2. Z żoną

3. W lesie

4. Bociana

5. c

6. b

7. b

8. a

Answers

1. He was a forester

2. With his wife

3. In the forest

4. A stork

5. c

6. b

7. b

8. a

Chapter 7 – Wszędzie dobrze, ale w domu najlepiej [East or West, home is best]

Magda wyjrzała przez okno. Zobaczyła **pole** pełne **pszenicy** i **kukurydzy**. W oddali znajdował się las do którego uwielbiała chodzić, gdy była dzieckiem. Przypomniała sobie jak w zimie **dokarmiała zwierzęta**, jak latem **zbierała jagody** i jak jesienią **zbierała grzyby**.

Magda looked through the window. She saw a field covered with wheat and corn. In the foreground, there was the forest she enjoyed going to when she was a kid. She looked back on the times she fed wild animals during the winter, collected berries during summer, and gathered mushrooms during fall.

Życie **na wsi** było bardzo spokojne i ciche. Jednak, im starsza Magda była, tym nudniejsze stawało się dla niej mieszkanie w wiosce. W okolicy nie było **nic do roboty**. Nie było kina, nie było restauracji, a nawet nie było sklepu. Magda i jej rodzice musieli robić zakupy w mieście oddalonym o dziesięć kilometrów.

Living in the countryside was peaceful and quiet. However, the older Magda got, the more boring living on a farm was for her. There was nothing to do. There was no cinema, no restaurants. There wasn't even a shop. Magda and her parents had to do the shopping in the city, ten kilometres away from their home.

Dobrze, że jest Internet, pomyślała Magda i włączyła Instagrama.

At least we have the Internet, Magda thought, and she opened Instagram.

Przeglądanie zdjęć na Instagramie było dla Magdy czymś bardzo ciekawym. Uwielbiała oglądać zdjęcia swoich znajomych z miasta i widzieć jak spędzają wolny czas. Zdjęcia z restauracji, zdjęcia z podróży – wszystko to było dla Magdy bardzo **odległe.**

Magda really enjoyed looking at the Instagram pictures. She loved looking at photos of her friends from the city and see how they spent their free time. Pictures from restaurants, pictures from their trips—for Magda, everything looked just unreachable.

Po krótkiej chwili Magda usłyszała **dzwonek do drzw**i. Odłożyła telefon i poszła na dół otworzyć. To był Piotrek, jej chłopak.

After a while, Magda heard the doorbell. He put her phone aside and went downstairs to open the door. It was her boyfriend, Peter.

"Cześć, kochanie. Co u ciebie?" zapytał.

"Hi, honey. How are you?" he asked.

"Dobrze, wejdź. Napijesz się czegoś?" zaproponowała Magda.

"Fine, come in. Would you like something to drink?" Magda suggested.

"Chętnie," odpowiedział.

"I'd love to," he said.

Magda i Piotrek wszystko robili razem. Poznali się już w dzieciństwie, ponieważ Piotrek był jej **sąsiadem.** Później razem chodzili do jednej klasy.

Magda and Peter had always done everything together. They met for the first time as little kids since Peter had been her neighbor. Later, they were in the same class at school.

Po ukończeniu szkoły podstawowej **zostali parą**. Piotrek nie wyjechał na studia, ponieważ postanowił spędzić resztę swojego życia w **gospodarstwie**. Miał nadzieję, że wkrótce **wezmą ślub** i razem będą prowadzić gospodarstwo. Magda chciała iść na studia. Niestety, nie zdała dobrze **egzaminu końcowego** i nie dostała się. Po tym czasie przestała próbować.

After graduating from school, they became a couple. Peter didn't go to university because he decided to spend the rest of his life on the farm. He hoped that one day they would get married and take care of the farm together. Magda wanted to study. Unfortunately, she hadn't got a good score on the state exam, and she hadn't got into the university. After that, she gave up.

Tego dnia Magda czuła się dziwnie. Kochała Piotrka, ale od jakiegoś czasu czuła, że nie mają o czym rozmawiać. Pili kawę w milczeniu. Po krótkiej chwili Piotrek **przerwał milczenie**:

That day Marta felt strange. She loved Peter, yet recently they'd had nothing to talk about. They were drinking coffee, saying nothing. After a while, Peter broke the silence:

"Muszę ci coś powiedzieć."

"I have to tell you something."

"Co takiego?" Magda była zdziwiona.

"What is that?" Magda was surprised.

"Nie pojedziemy w tym roku w **góry**. Muszę tutaj zostać. Mamy dużo pracy w gospodarstwie. Przepraszam, kochanie."

"We aren't going to the mountains this year. I have to stay here. We have too much to do on the farm. I'm sorry, honey."

Magda poczuła się jeszcze gorzej. Miała nadzieję, że choć na chwilę opuści wioskę i zobaczy coś nowego. Czekała na ten wyjazd tak długo... Wiedziała jednak, że Piotrek miał naprawdę dużo pracy. Ostatnio spotykali się coraz rzadziej i spędzali ze sobą coraz mniej czasu.

Magda felt so much worse. She'd hoped that she would leave the village for a while and see something new. She'd been waiting for that trip for a long time. However, she knew that Peter had so much to do. They'd been meeting less and less often, and they'd been spending less and less time together.

Po spotkaniu z Piotrkiem Magda zaczęła rozmyślać nad swoim życiem. Bardzo lubiła swój dom i rodzinę, ale życie na wsi było dla niej **udręką** po ukończeniu szkoły. Nie miała pomysłu na życie i nie wiedziała co chce robić. Wiedziała jedno—nie może tu dłużej zostać.

After meeting Peter, Magda started to think about her life. She loved her home and her family, yet living in the countryside became torture after graduating from school. She didn't know what to do with her life. She knew only one thing—she couldn't stay there any longer.

Pewnego dnia, oglądając Instagrama zobaczyła, że jej koleżanka była na wycieczce w Londynie. Zdjęcie było tak piękne, że Magda przez cały wieczór oglądała zdjęcia miasta i czytała **ciekawostki** na temat Anglii. Otworzyła nawet stronę **linii lotniczych** i udawała, że kupuje bilet.

One day, looking at some Instagram pictures, she saw that her friend was on a trip to London. The picture was so beautiful that it made Magda look at more pictures of the city and read some fun facts about England. She even opened an airline's website and pretended to buy a ticket.

Już miała nacisnąć "Wstecz", gdy nagle... Magda po sekundzie zorientowała się, że zarezerwowała **bilet** z Warszawy do Londynu **w jedną stronę**. To był **impuls**. To było jak spełnienie marzeń. Wiedziała, że nie może dłużej zostać na wsi.

She was about to press the "Back" button when suddenly... After a second, Magda realized that she had just booked a one-way plane ticket from Warsaw to London. It was an impulse. It was like a dream come true. She knew that she couldn't stay in the village any longer.

Nazajutrz Magda postanowiła powiedzieć o tym rodzicom i Piotrkowi.

The next day, Magda decided to tell her parents and Peter about the trip.

"Mamo, tato, pojutrze wylatuję do Londynu!" powiedziała.

"Mom, Dad, I'm going to London the day after tomorrow!" she said.

"Córeczko, jesteś pewna, że chcesz lecieć?" spytała mama.

"My little girl, are you sure you want to go?" her mom asked.

"Tak, muszę to zrobić. Nie mogę tutaj dłużej zostać. Życie na wsi jest zbyt nudne," odpowiedziała Magda.

"Yes, I need to do this. I can't stay here any longer. Living in the countryside is so boring," Magda said.

"Jeśli ten wyjazd sprawi, że będziesz szczęśliwa, to jedź w takim razie," odparł ojciec Magdy.

"If this trip makes you happy, then go," her dad said.

Magda nie mogła uwierzyć za dwa dni miała sama polecieć do Londynu! Trochę się bała. Postanowiła spakować **walizkę** i zabrać najpotrzebniejsze rzeczy. Wiedziała jednak, że przed wyjazdem czekała ją jeszcze jedna, bardzo trudna rozmowa.

Magda couldn't believe she was about to go to London alone in two days! She was scared a bit. She decided to pack her suitcase and take some travel essentials. Yet, she knew that she had to make one more important conversation before the departure.

"Piotrek, musimy porozmawiać."

"Peter, we need to talk."

"O co chodzi?" zapytał Piotrek. Był trochę zmieszany.

"What's going on?" Peter asked. He was confused a bit.

"Piotrek, od pewnego czasu nie jest dobrze. Uważam że powinniśmy to zakończyć."

"Peter, some things between us haven't been well for some time. I think it's time to end this."

"Ale... dlaczego?"

"But... why?"

"Nie chcę spędzić z tobą reszty życia. Życie na wsi jest zbyt nudne. Ja chcę zwiedzać świat, poznawać nowych ludzi. Nie chcę żyć z tobą w gospodarstwie. Po jutrze wylatuję do Londynu," odpowiedziała Magda.

"I don't want to spend the rest of my life with you. Living here is so boring. I want to travel the world, meet new people. I don't want to live with you on the farm. I'm going to London the day after tomorrow," Magda said.

"Czy to oznacza, że **zrywasz ze mną**?" spytał Piotrek.

"Are you breaking up with me?" Peter asked.

"Tak. Myślę, że to koniec. Przepraszam," odpowiedziała Magda.

"Yes. I think that's it. I'm sorry," Magda said.

"Powodzenia, w takim razie." Piotrek był zdruzgotany, jednak wiedział, że musi odpuścić.

"Good luck, then." Peter was devastated. However, he knew that he had to let it go.

W końcu nadszedł dzień wylotu. Magda była bardzo zdenerwowana. Nigdy wcześniej nie latała samolotem. Nigdy wcześniej nie była nawet za granicą. Jednak **ciekawość** była silniejsza niż strach. Magda pożegnała się z rodzicami i udała się w stronę **odprawy**. Po wejściu do samolotu Magda była podekscytowana. Wiedziała, że nie może już wrócić. To była **przełomowa** decyzja.

The day of the departure finally came. Magda was nervous. She had never been on a plane before. She had never been abroad. However, her curiosity was stronger than her fear. Magda said goodbye to her parents and headed towards the check-in gates. After entering the plane, she got excited. She knew that there was no way back. It was her life-changing decision.

Po dotarciu na miejsce Magda była **przytłoczona**, a jednocześnie zachwycona. Nigdy wcześniej nie widziała tak dużego miasta. Wszędzie były restauracje, kluby, setki ludzi. I ona... w samym środku Londynu.

After reaching her destination, Magda was astonished and overwhelmed at the same time. She had never seen such a big city. There were restaurants, clubs, and hundreds of people everywhere. And her... right in the middle of London.

Mijały miesiące. Magda znalazła mieszkanie i pracę. Pracowała jako sprzedawca w supermarkecie. Nie była to wymarzona praca, ale przynajmniej pozwalała na **przetrwanie** w dużym mieście. Praca nie była dla Magdy problemem—całe życie ciężko pracowała w gospodarstwie. Jednak, Magda była bardzo samotna.

Months went by. Magda had already found an apartment and a job. She was working as a shop assistant in a supermarket. It wasn't her dream job, but it could help her survive in the city. Working hard wasn't a problem for Magda—she'd been working hard all her life on the farm. However, Magda was lonely.

W Londynie nie miała żadnych znajomych. Nie miała nawet nikogo, z kim mogłaby porozmawiać o swoich problemach. Czasem rozmawiała z rodzicami przez telefon, jednak czuła że tęskniła za nimi. Pewnego razu rozmawiała nawet z Piotrkiem, ale on jak zwykle, miał dużo pracy i nie miał czasu na długą rozmowę.

She didn't have any friends in London. She didn't have anyone to talk to about her problems. Sometimes she talked with her parents on the phone, but she missed them very much. One day, she even called Peter, but he had a job to do and couldn't talk, as usual.

Pewnego dnia Magda wróciła zmęczona z pracy. W tamtej chwili poczuła rozczarowanie i **samotność**. Miasto było piękne, ale Magdzie brakowało ludzi, których kochała - jej rodziców, a nawet Piotrka.

One day, Magda came home from work really tired. At that moment, she was disappointed and lonely. The city was beautiful, yet she missed the people she loved—her parents and Peter.

*Chyba czas kupić **bilet powrotny**, pomyślała.*

Guess it's time to buy a return ticket, she thought.

Po piętnastu minutach bilet powrotny był już w koszyku. Magda cieszyła się na powrót. Postanowiła powiedzieć rodzicom.

After fifteen minutes, the return ticket was already in her basket on the website. She was happy to finally return home. She decided to tell her parents about it.

Na lotnisku w Warszawie Magda od razu zobaczyła swoich rodziców. Była bardzo szczęśliwa. Bardzo za nimi tęskniła.

At the airport in Warsaw, Magda noticed her parents immediately. She was really happy. She'd missed them so much.

"Mamo, tato, tak się cieszę, że was widzę!" wykrzyknęła.

"Mom, dad, I'm really happy to see you both!" she exclaimed.

"My też się cieszymy, córciu. Ale... tak bardzo chciałaś mieszkać w mieście. Mówiłaś, że życie na wsi jest nudne. Dlaczego postanowiłaś wrócić?" zapytała mama.

"We're happy too, my little girl. But... you wanted to live in the city. You told us that living in the countryside was boring. Why did you decide to return home?" her mother asked.

"Wszędzie dobrze ale w domu najlepiej. Zdałam sobie z tego sprawę, gdy byłam sama w Londynie. Bardzo tęskniłam za wami i za domem," odpowiedziała Magda.

"East, west, home is best. I realized that when I was alone in London. I've missed you and our home so bad," Magda replied.

Po powrocie do domu Magda zobaczyła dom Piotrka. Przypomniało jej się jak bardzo tęskniła za nim podczas pobytu w Londynie.

While returning home, Magda saw Peter's house. She realized how much she'd missed him during the time in London.

"Mamo, myślisz że powinnam iść do niego i go przeprosić?" zapytała Magda.

"Mom, do you think that I should visit him and apologize?" Magda asked.

"Oczywiście. Musisz to zrobić. Jednak jest coś, o czym musisz wiedzieć," odpowiedziała mama.

"Of course. You have to to this. However, there's something you need to know," her mother said.

"Co to takiego?" zapytała Magda.

"What is it?" Magda asked.

"Piotrek jest **zaręczony**," odpowiedziała mama.

"Peter's engaged," her mother said.

"Co?!" Magda była zszokowana.

"What?!" Magda was shocked.

" Po **rozstaniu** Piotrek zaczął chodzić z Anią z sąsiedniej wioski. Zaręczyli się dwa tygodnie temu."

"After your breakup, Peter started to go out with Ania, a girl from another village. They got engaged two weeks ago."

Magda nie wiedziała co powiedzieć. Postanowiła jednak przeprosić Piotrka za wszystko. Chciała, aby zostali chociaż przyjaciółmi. Niestety, jej decyzja miała poważne **konsekwencje**. Wiedziała, że nigdy już nie będzie z Piotrkiem. Jednak, nie **żałowała** wyjazdu. Podczas pobytu w Londynie zdała sobie sprawę z tego, że to ludzie, nie miejsca są **źródłem** szczęścia.

Magda didn't know what to say. She decided to apologize to Peter for everything. She wanted to make friends with him. Unfortunately, her decision had consequences. She knew that she wouldn't be with Peter ever again. However, she didn't regret her trip to London. During the stay in the city, she realized that people, not places, made her happy.

Streszczenie

Magda mieszkała na wsi. Po ukończeniu szkoły poznała Piotrka i para zaczęła chodzić ze sobą. Piotrek nie poszedł na studia, ponieważ chciał spędzić życie na gospodarstwie. Magda również nie poszła na studia, ponieważ się nie dostała. Pewnego dnia Magda oglądała zdjęcia na Instagramie. Była zazdrosna o koleżanki. Po chwili kupiła bilet w jedną stronę do Londynu. Następnego dnia Magda postanowiła powiedzieć o wyjeździe swoim rodzicom. Rodzice zgodzili się. Magda postanowiła zerwać z Piotrkiem. Po kilku dniach Magda wyjechała do Londynu. Minęły miesiące. Magda pracowała w supermarkecie i wynajmowała mieszkanie. Czuła się bardzo samotnie w dużym mieście I nie miała przyjaciół. Postanowiła wrócić do domu. Po powrocie rodzice Magdy ucieszyli się. Magda postanowiła przeprosić Piotrka. Okazało się, że Piotrek był zaręczony. Magda nie żałowała swojej decyzji o powrocie.

Summary

Magda lived in the countryside. After graduating from school, she met Peter. The couple started to go out together. Peter didn't go to a university since he wanted to spend the rest of his life on the farm. Magda didn't go either because she hadn't got a good score on the state exam. One day, Magda was looking at some Instagram pictures. She was jealous of her friends. After a while, she bought a one-way ticket to London. The next day, Magda decided to tell her parents about the trip. They agreed to it. Magda decided to break up with Peter. After a few days, Magda departed to London. A month went by. Magda was working at a supermarket and was renting an apartment. She felt lonely in the big city, and she didn't have any friends. She decided to return home. Her parents were really happy. Magda decided to apologize to Peter. It turned out that he had already been engaged to someone else. Magda didn't regret her decision.

Vocabulary

Pole – a field

Pszenica – wheat

Kukurydza – corn

Dokarmiać zwierzęta – to feed animals

Zbierać jagody – to collect berries

Zbierać grzyby – to gather mushrooms

Na wsi – in the countryside

Nic do roboty – nothing to do

Odległy – unreachable

Dzwonek do drzwi – a doorbell

Sąsiad – a neighbor

Zostać parą – to become a couple

Gospodarstwo – a farm

Wziąć ślub – to get married

Egzamin końcowy – a final exam

Przerwać milczenie – to break the silence

Góry – mountains

Udręka - torture
Ciekawostka - fun facts
Linie lotnicze - airlines
Bilet w jedną stronę - a one-way ticket
Impuls - an impulse
Walizka - suitcase
Zrywać z kimś - to break up with someone
Ciekawość - curiosity
Odprawa - check-in
Przełomowy - life-changing
Przytłoczony - overwhelmed
Bilet powrotny - a return ticket
Zaręczony - engaged
Żałować - to regret
Źródło - a source

Pytania

1. Gdzie mieszkała Magda?
2. Dlaczego Magda nie poszła na studia?
3. Jak miał na imię chłopak Magdy?
4. Dlaczego Piotrek nie poszedł na studia?
5. Jaką aplikację uwielbiała Magda?
6. Gdzie postanowiła wyjechać Magda?
a) Do Rzymu
b) Do Londynu
c) Do Paryża
7. Gdzie pracowała Magda podczas pobytu w Londynie?
a) W sklepie odzieżowym
b) Na poczcie
c) W supermarkecie
8. Dlaczego Magda postanowiła wrócić?
a) Tęskniła za rodzicami i Piotrkiem
b) Jej rodzice umarli
c) Straciła pracę

9. Dlaczego Magda nie wróciła do Piotrka?

a) Piotrek umarł

b) Piotrek był zaręczony z kimś innym

c) Piotrek wyjechał za granicę

10. Czy Magda żałowała swojej decyzji?

a) Tak

b) Nie

Questions

1. Where did Magda live?

2. Why didn't Magda go to the university?

3. What was the name of Magda's boyfriend?

4. Why didn't Peter go to the university?

5. What mobile app did Magda love?

6. Where did Magda fly to?

a) To Rome

b) To London

c) To Paris

7. Where did Magda work at during her stay in London?

a) In a clothing shop

b) At a post office

c) In a supermarket

8. Why did Magda decide to come back?

a) She missed her parents and she missed Peter

b) Her parents passed away

c) She lost her job

9. Why didn't Magda get back to Peter?

a) He passed away

b) Peter was engaged to someone else

c) Peter went abroad

10. Did Magda regret her decision?

a) Yes

b) No

Odpowiedzi

1. Na wsi
2. Nie miała dobrego wyniku na egzaminach końcowych
3. Piotrek
4. Chciał zostać na gospodarstwie
5. Instagram
6. b
7. c
8. a
9. b
10. b

Answers

1. In the countryside
2. She didn't get a good score on her final exam
3. Peter
4. He wanted to stay at his farm
5. Instagram
6. b
7. c
8. a
9. b
10. b

Chapter 8 – Konsekwencje [Consequences]

Sara nie miała tyle szczęścia, co inne dzieci. Jako **noworodek** trafiła do **domu dziecka**. Nie znała swoich rodziców. Nigdy nawet nie próbowała się dowiedzieć kim oni są. Bardzo bała się rozczarowania.

Sara wasn't as lucky as the other kids. As a newborn, she was taken to the orphanage. She didn't know her parents. She didn't try to find out who they were. She was afraid of disappointment.

Sara nie była również **grzecznym** dzieckiem. Właściwie, sprawiała wiele problemów. Wiele razy potrafiła **kłócić się** z innymi dziećmi o **zabawki** czy **miejsce przy stole**.

Sara wasn't a well-behaved kid either. In fact, she always started something. She could start an argument over toys or a seat by a table with the other kids countless times.

Tego dnia Sara obudziła się **zmęczona** i zdenerwowana. Przypomniała sobie jak dwa dni wcześniej **uderzyła** swojego kolegę i została zawieszona. Wiedziała, że to nie była jej **wina**. Tamten chłopak sprowokował ją, robiąc sobie z niej żarty. Sara nie miała żadnych przyjaciół, ale tego było już za wiele. Na dodatek, Pani

Maria, jej opiekunka, zabrała jej wszystkie kieszonkowe przez tę bójkę.

That day, Sara woke up tired and nervous. She remembered that two days before, she hit her friend and got suspended. She knew that it hadn't been her fault. That boy triggered her, making some stupid comments. Sara didn't have many friends, but it was too much for her. In addition, Mrs. Maria, the houseparent, took her pocket money because of that fight.

Bez tych pieniędzy nie będę mogła nic sobie kupić w **galerii***,* pomyślała Sara. Była bardzo smutna, ponieważ za dwa dni wszystkie dzieci z ośrodka miały iść z **opiekunem** do galerii handlowej, aby kupić sobie ubrania.

I won't be able to buy anything in the shopping center because of this fight, Sara thought. She was very sad because in two days, the whole group was supposed to go to the shopping center to buy some clothes.

Nadszedł dzień zakupów. Wszyscy podopieczni udali się do dużej galerii handlowej w centrum miasta. Sara nie miała żadnych pieniędzy, ale postanowiła pojechać. Uwielbiała oglądać te wszystkie piękne ubrania i **biżuterię.** Marzyła o tym, że pewnego dnia kpi sobie tyle rzeczy ile będzie chciała.

The shopping day finally came. All the children went to the big shopping center in the city center. Sara didn't have any money, yet she decided to go. She loved looking at all the clothes and jewelry. She dreamt that, one day, she would buy anything she wanted to.

Sara odłączyła się od grupy zaraz po wejściu do galerii. Bardzo **zazdrościła** swoim koleżankom. Wiedziała, że bez kieszonkowych, które zabrała jej pani Maria nic sobie nie kupi.

Sara left her group shortly after entering the shopping center. She was jealous of her friends. She knew that without the money taken by Mrs. Maria, she wouldn't buy anything.

Po wejściu do jednego ze sklepów z ubraniami Sara zauważyła piękną **sukienkę**. Sukienka była czerwona i miała długie rękawy. Sara postanowiła ją **przymierzyć**.

After going into one of the clothing shops, Sara saw a beautiful dress. It was red and had long sleeves. Sara decided to try it on.

Kiedy Sara zobaczyła siebie w lustrze w tej przepięknej sukience nie mogła uwierzyć. Wyglądała oszałamiająco! Jednak, gdy spojrzała na **cenę** od razu posmutniała. Sukienka kosztowała czterysta złotych. Sara miała w kieszeni tylko kilka monet.

When Sara looked at herself in the mirror, wearing that beautiful dress, she couldn't believe it. She looked absolutely stunning! However, when she looked at the price tag, she felt sad. The dress cost four hundred zlotys. Sara had only a few coins inside her pocket.

Nie chcę jej oddawać, pomyślała.

I don't want to return it, she thought.

Po chwili podeszła do niej **ekspedientka**.

After a while, a shop assistant came up to her.

"Czy kupuje pani tę sukienkę," zapytała ekspedienta. "Wygląda w niej Pani przepięknie," dodała.

"Are you going to buy this dress?" the shop assistant asked. "You look amazing," she added.

Sara poczuła się okropnie. Wiedziała, że musi odłożyć sukienkę.

Sara felt terrible. She knew that she had to return the dress.

"Przymierzę ją jeszcze raz," powiedziała i dodała, "muszę być pewna, że mi pasuje."

"I'll try it on once again," she said and added, "I need to be sure that it fits me well."

Sara weszła do **przymierzalni** jeszcze raz i założyła sukienkę. Tak bardzo nie chciała jej oddawać, że postanowiła przesiedzieć w przymierzalni całą godzinę, aby móc patrzeć jak pięknie wygląda.

Sara entered the fitting room once again and got the dress on. She didn't want to return it so badly that she decided to stay in the fitting room for one hour to see how amazing she looked.

Po jakimś czasie Sara spojrzała na **zegarek.** Było już późno.

After some time, Sara looked at her watch. It was late.

Pani Maria i reszta na pewno już na mnie czekają, pomyślała i zaczęła zdejmować sukienkę.

Mrs. Maria and the other kids are waiting for me, she thought and started to take off the dress.

Po chwili jednak wpadła na pomysł. Przypomniała sobie, że miała w plecaku **nożyczki.**

After a while, she got an idea. She recalled that she'd had a pair of scissors in her backpack.

Hmm... Pani Maria na pewno się nie zorientuje. Zaryzykuję. Nie mogę oddać tej sukienki. Jest zbyt piękna. To nie moja wina, że zabrali mi **kieszonkowe!** *pomyślała Sara.*

Well... Mrs. Maria won't find out. I'll take the risk. I can't return this dress. It's so beautiful. It's not my fault they took my pocket money! Sara thought.

Po kilku minutach sukienka była już w **plecaku** Sary. Dziewczyna wyszła szybko z przymierzalni i **schowała się** za ubraniami, aby ekspedientka jej nie zauważyła. Sara szybko wyszła ze sklepu niezauważona i pobiegła na miejsce zbiórki.

After a few minutes, the dress was inside Sara's backpack. The girl quickly left the fitting room and hid behind some clothes so that the shop assistant couldn't notice her. Sara left the clothing shop unnoticed and ran to the meeting point.

"Spóźniłaś się! Czekamy na ciebie już dziesięć minut!" powiedziała pani Maria.

"You're late! We've been waiting for you for ten minutes!" Mrs. Maria said.

"Przepraszam. Byłam na drugim końcu galerii. Musiałam iść do toalety," odpowiedziała Sara.

"I'm sorry. I was on the other side of the shopping center. I had to go to the toilet," Sara said.

Dziewczyna była zdenerwowana. Bała się, że ekspedientka w sklepie zorientuje się szybką i **złapie** ją zanim jej grupa opuści galerię. Jednak tak się nie stało. Sara wyszła z grupą **niezauważona**.

The girl was nervous. She was afraid of getting caught by the shop assistant before leaving the shopping center. However, it didn't happen. Sara left the building unnoticed with the rest of the group.

Po powrocie do ośrodka Sara postanowiła ukryć sukienkę **pod łóżkiem**. Musiała to zrobić, ponieważ pani Maria szybko odkryłaby, że coś jest nie tak. Sara nie miała przecież żadnych kieszonkowych.

After returning to the orphanage, Sara decided to hide the dress under her bed. She had to do that because Mrs. Maria could see that something was wrong. Sara didn't have any pocket money.

Minęło kilka dni. Sukienka wciąż leżała pod łóżkiem Sary i nikt jej nie odnalazł. Tylko ona wiedziała o tym sekrecie. Jednak, im dłużej sukienka była w jej pokoju, tym bardziej zdenerwowana była Sara. Bała się, że pewnego dnia do ośrodka przyjdzie policja i znajdzie sukienkę. Bała się, że będzie **wyrzucona** z ośrodka i zabrana do **poprawczaka**.

A few days went by. The dress was still lying under Sara's bed and no one had found it. Only Sara knew about the secret. However, the longer the dress was hidden under the bed, the more nervous Sara was getting. She was afraid that, one day, the police will come to the orphanage and find the dress. She was afraid of being expelled and taken to the young detention center.

Ponadto, Sara czuła się źle z powodu **kradzieży** sukienki. Pomyślała o ekspedientce, która będzie musiała zapłacić za to, że sukienka zniknęła ze sklepu.

Moreover, Sara felt bad about stealing the dress from the shop. She thought about the shop assistant who'd had to pay for the missing dress.

Sara postanowiła przyznać się do kradzieży. Zabrała sukienkę i poszła do gabinetu pani Marii.

Sara decided to confess to the theft. She took the dress and went to Mrs. Maria's office.

"Kto tam? Proszę wejść. O... Sara. O co chodzi?" zapytała pani Maria.

"Who's that? Please, come in. Oh... Sara. What's going on?" Mrs. Maria asked.

"Jest coś, o czym musi Pani wiedzieć," odpowiedziała Sara.

"There's something you need to know," Sara said.

"Co się dzieje?" Pani Maria była zaniepokojona.

"What's going on?" Mrs. Maria got worried.

"Tego dnia kiedy byliśmy w galerii... ja.. ja..." Sara nie mogła **złapać oddechu.** Zaczęła płakać.

"That day, when we were in the shopping center... I... I..." Sara couldn't catch a breath. She started to cry.

"Co się stało, kochanie? Powiedz."

"What happened, honey? Tell me."

"Ja... ja... ukradłam sukienkę," odpowiedziała w końcu Sara.

"I... I... I stole a dress," Sara finally answered.

"Jaką sukienkę? Gdzie?"

"What dress? Where?"

"W tym sklepie z sukienkami. Obok kawiarni. Była taka piękna, a ja nie miałam pieniędzy... Przepraszam. Nie powinnam," powiedziała Sara.

"In that dress shop. Next to the restaurant. It was so beautiful, and I didn't have any money... I'm so sorry. I shouldn't have done that," Sara said.

"Och, kochanie. Miejmy nadzieję, że nie jest za późno. Chodź ze mną i weź sukienkę. Musimy to naprawić," odpowiedziała pani Maria.

"Oh, honey. Let's hope it's not too late. Come with me and take the dress. We have to fix it," Mrs. Maria said.

Sara wraz z panią Marią pojechały do galerii handlowej. Sara postanowiła oddać ekspedientce sukienkę. Niestety, sukienka nie miała **metki** więc Sara musiała za nią zapłacić.

Sara and Mrs. Maria went to the shopping center. Sara decided to return the dress to the shop assistant. Unfortunately, the dress didn't have the price tag, so Sara had to pay for it.

"Nie martw się. Ja za nią zapłacę," odpowiedziała pani Maria.

"Don't worry. I'll pay for the dress," Mrs. Maria said.

"Dziękuję Pani," powiedziała Sara.

"Thank you," Sara said.

"Jednak... będziesz musiała ponieść konsekwencje. Codziennie będziesz pomagać w **kuchni** i przygotowywać jedzenie dla reszty podopiecznych w przyszłym miesiącu."

"However, you'll have to face the consequences. You'll be helping in the kitchen and preparing meals for the kids every day next month."

Sara odetchnęła z ulgą. Wiedziała, że będzie musiała ponieść konsekwencje, ale uczucie ulgi było dla niej o wiele lepsze.

Sara was relieved. She knew that she would have to face the consequences, yet the feeling of relief was so much better.

Nigdy więcej tego nie zrobię, pomyślała.

I won't do anything like that again, she thought.

Streszczenie

Sara była sierotą. Nie znała swoich rodziców. Nie chciała ich również poznać ponieważ nie chciała się rozczarować. Sara nie była również grzecznym dzieckiem. Często kłóciła się z innymi dziećmi. Pewnego dnia uderzyła kolegę i została zawieszona. Opiekunka zabrała jej również kieszonkowe. Kolejnego dnia grupa Sary poszła do centrum handlowego, aby kupić ubrania. Sara była smutna, ponieważ nie miała pieniędzy. Postanowiła jednak pójść. W jednym sklepie Sara zobaczyła piękną sukienkę. Postanowiła ją przymierzyć. Okazało się, że Sara wyglądała przepięknie w tej sukience. Niestety, nie miała pieniędzy. Postanowiła ukraść sukienkę. Po powrocie do domu dziecka Sara ukryła sukienkę pod łóżkiem. Po kilku dniach Sara czuła się źle z powodu kradzieży. Postanowiła powiedzieć o wszystkim swojej opiekunce - pani Marii. Pani Maria przebaczyła Sarze. Sara oddała sukienkę do sklepu, jednak musiała za nią zapłacić. Pani Maria zapłaciła za sukienkę.

Summary

Sara was an orphan. She didn't know her parents. She didn't want to meet them since she didn't want to get disappointed. Sara wasn't a well-behaved child. She often had an argument with other children. One day, she hit one child and got suspended. The foster parent took her pocket money. The next day, Sara's group went to a shopping center to buy some clothes. Sara was sad because she didn't have any money. She decided to go anyway. In one shop, Sara saw a beautiful dress. She decided to try it on. Sara looked absolutely stunning in that dress. Unfortunately, she didn't have money. She decided to steal the dress. After returning to the orphanage, she decided to hide the dress under her bed. After a couple of days, Sara felt bad about stealing the dress. She decided to tell her foster parent, Mrs. Maria, everything. Mrs. Maria forgave Sara. Sara returned the dress to the shop, but she had to pay for it. Mrs. Maria paid for the dress.

Vocabulary

Noworodek - a newborn

Dom dziecka - an orphanage

Grzeczny - well-behaved

Zabawki - toys

Miejsce przy stole - a seat by the table

Zmęczony - tired

Uderzyć - to hit

Wina - a fault

Galeria - a shopping center

Biżuteria - jewelry

Zazdrościć - to be jealous

Sukienka - a dress

Przymierzyć - to try on

Cena - a price

Ekspedientka - a shop assistant

Przymierzalnia - a fitting room

Zegarek - a watch

Nożyczki - scissors

Kieszonkowe - pocket money

Plecak - a backpack

Niezauważony - unnoticed

Pod łóżkiem - under the bed

Wyrzucony - expelled

Poprawczak - a young detention center

Złapać oddech - to catch a breath

Metka - a price tag

Kuchnia - kitchen

Pytania

1. Gdzie mieszkała Sara?

2. Dlaczego Sara nie miała przyjaciół?

3. Dlaczego Sara straciła swoje kieszonkowe?

4. Jaką rzecz chciała kupić Sara?

5. Dlaczego Sara nie mogła kupić sukienki?

6. W jaki sposób Sara weszła w posiadanie sukienki?

a) Kupiła ją

b) Ukradła ją

c) Pani Maria kupiła ją Sarze

7. Gdzie Sara ukryła sukienkę?

a) Pod łóżkiem

b) W walizce

c) W szafie

8. Dlaczego Sara postanowiła powiedzieć o wszystkim pani Marii?

a) Czuła się z tym źle

b) Jej koleżanka odkryła jej secret

c) Zgubiła sukienkę

9. Dlaczego Sara musiała zapłacić za sukienkę?

a) Sukienka miała plamy

b) Sukienka nie miała metki

c) Pani Maria jej kazała

Questions

1. Where did Sara live?

2. Why did Sara have no friends?

3. Why did Sara lose her pocket money?

4. What piece of clothing did Sara want to buy?

5. Why was Sara unable to buy the dress?

6. How did Sara come into possession of the dress?

a) She bought it

b) She stole it

c) Mrs. Maria bought her the dress

7. Where did Sara hide the dress?

a) Under the bed

b) In a suitcase

c) In a closet

8. Why did Sara decide to tell Mrs. Maria about everything?

a) She felt bad about it

b) Her friend found her secret

c) She lost the dress

9. Why did Sara have to pay for the dress?

a) The dress had stains

b) The dress didn't have a price tag

c) Mrs. Maria wanted her to pay for it

Odpowiedzi

1. W domu dziecka

2. Często zaczynała kłótnie

3. Została zawieszona z powodu bójki

4. Sukienkę

5. Nie miała pieniędzy

6. b

7. a

8. a

9. b

Answers

1. In the orphanage

2. She often started an argument

3. She got suspended because of a fight

4. A dress

5. She didn't have any money

6. b

7. a

8. a

9. b

Chapter 9 – Zaginione dziecko
[A missing child]

Było już bardzo późno. Mateusz wsiadł do samochodu i pojechał do centrum miasta. Musiał iść do supermarketu, do banku i **wysłać list** na poczcie. Był już spóźniony. Weronika, jego żona już czekała na niego w domu. O dziewiętnastej mieli przyjść **goście**.

It was late. Matthew got inside his car and drove to the city center. He had to go to the supermarket, to the bank, and send a letter to the post office. He was already late. Weronika, his wife, was already waiting for him at home. Guests were coming at 7 PM.

Mateusz **pospiesznie** wszedł do supermarketu. Przechodząc przez **dział z produktami dla dzieci** zauważył kobietę. Była **w ciąży**.

Matthew quickly went inside the supermarket. As he was walking through the children's section, he saw a woman. She was pregnant.

Mateusz poczuł smutek. Od kilku miesięcy starali się z żoną o dziecko. **Bezskutecznie.** Przypomniały mu się słowa lekarza podczas ostatniej wizyty:

Matthew felt very sad. They had tried to have kids for months. Unsuccessfully. He remembered the doctor's words during the last appointment:

"Przykro mi. Nie może mieć pan dzieci. Nie możemy nic zrobić."

"I'm sorry. You can't have kids. We can't do anything about it."

Po tamtej wizycie Mateusz był załamany. Tak bardzo chcieli mieć dziecko. Nie był jeszcze gotowy na **adopcję**. Musiał przemyśleć sobie kilka spraw i przełamać się. Nie było mu łatwo.

Since that appointment, Matthew had been broken. His wife and he wanted to have kids so badly. He wasn't ready for adoption. He had to cope with the problem and figure things out in the first place. It wasn't easy for him.

Mateusz wyszedł z supermarketu i pojechał wysłać list. Podczas stania w kolejce wyjrzał przez okno i zauważył na **chodniku** małą dziewczynkę. Miała na sobie **kolorowy sweter** z **pingwinem**. Wyglądała na zagubioną.

Matthew left the supermarket and went to the post office to send the letter. While standing in line, he looked through the window and noticed a little girl standing on the sidewalk. She was wearing a colorful sweatshirt with a penguin. She seemed lost.

Pewnie czeka na mamę lub tatę, pomyślał.

She's waiting for her mom or dad, he thought.

Jednak nikt nie przychodził. Żaden z **przechodniów** nie zatrzymał się i nie spytał dziewczynki dlaczego tam stoi. Po wyjściu z budynku poczty Mateusz postanowił dowiedzieć się dlaczego dziewczynka stała sama.

But no one was coming. None of the passers-by stopped and asked the girl why she was standing there. After walking out of the post office, Matthew decided to find out why the girl was standing alone.

"Cześć. Jestem Mateusz. Dlaczego stoisz tutaj sama? Gdzie są twoi rodzice?" zapytał.

"Hi. I'm Matthew. Why are you here alone? Where are your parents?" he asked.

Dziewczynka spojrzała się na niego i nic nie odpowiedziała.

The girl looked at him and didn't say anything.

"Czy mogę ci jakoś pomóc? Może razem znajdziemy mamę?" zapytał Mateusz.

"Can I help you? Why don't we find your mom together?" Matthew asked.

"Jestem sama. Zgubiłam rodziców w centrum handlowym i nie wiem gdzie są. Na pewno mnie szukają. A ja przyszłam tutaj i nie wiem co robić," odpowiedziała dziewczynka.

"I'm here alone. I lost my parents at the shopping center, and I don't know where they are. They are looking for me. And I came here, and I don't know what to do," the girl said.

"Jak masz na imię?" zapytał Mateusz.

"What's your name?" Matthew asked.

"Jestem Kasia," odpowiedziała.

"I'm Katie," she said.

"Chodź ze mną. Poszukamy twoich rodziców," powiedział Mateusz.

"Come with me. Let's find your parents," Matthew said.

Jednak dziewczynka zaczęła zachowywać się dziwnie. Nie chciała iść szukać rodziców.

But the girl started to act strange. She didn't want to look for her parents.

"Proszę pana. Moi rodzice na pewno mnie szukają. Może Pan odwiózłby mnie do domu? Tam jest moja **babcia**. Ona zadzwoni do moich rodziców, aby się nie martwili," odpowiedziała Kasia.

"Mister, I'm sure my parents are looking for me right now. Maybe you could drive me home? My grandma is there. She'll call my parents so that they will stop worrying about me," Katie said.

Mateusz był zaskoczony. Było to dla niego bardzo dziwne, ale postanowił zabrać dziewczynkę ze sobą.

Mateusz was surprised. He considered it weird, yet he decided to take the girl with him.

Podczas jazdy samochodem Mateusz postanowił zapytać dziewczynkę gdzie jest jej dom.

While driving, Matthew decided to ask the girl where her house was.

"Gdzie mieszkasz?"

"Where do you live?"

Dziewczynka była zmieszana.

The girl got confused.

"Tam, za miastem. Na ulicy Słonecznej," odpowiedziała.

"There, outside the city. Słoneczna street," she said.

Mateusz był jeszcze bardziej zdziwiony. On też mieszkał z żoną na ulicy Słonecznej! Nigdy wcześniej nie widział tej dziewczynki. Postanowił jednak pojechać. I tak jechał w tamtym kierunku, aby wrócić do domu.

Matthew was even more surprised. His wife and he lived on Słoneczna street! He had never seen the girl before. Still, he decided to go there. After all, he was driving in the same direction to go back home.

Po dojechaniu na ulicę Słoneczną Mateusz postanowił zapytać dziewczynkę o dokładny adres.

After arriving at Słoneczna street, Matthew decided to ask the girl about the exact address.

"Jesteśmy. To gdzie jest twój dom?" zapytał.

"Here we are. So where is your house?" he asked.

"O tam, **na końcu ulicy**," odpowiedziała Kasia.

"There, at the end of the street," Katie said.

Jednak, kiedy Mateusz dotarł na koniec ulicy dziewczynka nie wysiadła z samochodu. Mateusz był już bardzo zmieszany.

However, when they stopped at the end of the street, the girl didn't get out of the car. Matthew was already very confused.

"To gdzie jest twój dom?" zapytał.

"So where is your house?" he asked.

Dziewczynka jednak nic nie odpowiedziała. Siedziała i nic nie mówiła. Naglę ciszę przerwał głos dochodzący z **radia**:

The girl didn't say anything. She was sitting quietly. Suddenly, the silence was broken by a speaker's voice coming from the car radio:

"Uwaga. Podajemy fakty. Dziś rano o godzinie ósmej zaginęła podopieczna z **domu dziecka**. W momencie zaginięcia miała na sobie kolorowy sweter z pingwinem. Jeśli wiesz coś o zaginięciu, zadzwoń pod numer 567 453 098."

"Attention. Here's the news. Today at 8 AM, a child from the orphanage went missing. She was wearing a colorful sweatshirt with a penguin. If you know something, please call 567 453 098."

Mateusz spojrzał najpierw na Kasię, później na jej sweter i nie mógł uwierzyć. To była ona. To ona zniknęła z domu dziecka i wszyscy jej szukają.

Matthew looked at Katie and then at her sweatshirt. He couldn't believe it. It was her. She went missing, and now everybody's looking for her.

"To ty? Ale... dlaczego?" zapytał Mateusz.

"Is it you? But... why?" Matthew asked.

Kasia rozpłakała się. Po chwili zaczęła mówić.

Katie started to cry. After a while, she started speaking.

"Przepraszam proszę pana. Ja nie chciałam uciec. Moi rodzice zginęli w **wypadku samochodowym**. Nie chce wracać do domu dziecka."

"I'm sorry. I didn't want to escape from the orphanage. My parents died in a car accident. I don't want to go back to the orphanage."

Mateusz bardzo współczuł Kasi. Wiedział jednak, że musi ją odwieźć do domu dziecka, bo wszyscy jej szukali.

Matthew felt really sorry for Katie. Yet, he knew that he had to take her to the orphanage since everyone was looking for her.

"Bardzo mi przykro. Muszę jednak zawieźć cię do domu dziecka. Wszyscy cię szukają," powiedział Mateusz.

"I'm really sorry. I have to take you back to the orphanage. Everybody's looking for you," Matthew said.

Kasia rozpłakała się jeszcze bardziej.

Katie started to cry even more.

"Kochanie, obiecuję, że zrobię co w mojej mocy, abyś nie musiała tam mieszkać, dodał Mateusz.

"Honey, I promise I will do my best to get you out of there," Matthew said.

Po odstawieniu dziewczynki do domu dziecka Mateusz był **wzruszony**. Dziewczynka była bardzo miła. Zrobiło mu się jej żal.

After leaving the girl in the orphanage, Matthew was touched. The girl was so nice. He felt really sorry for her.

"Cóż za straszna sytuacja. Kasia miała kochających rodziców, którzy zginęli w wypadku. Ona tak bardzo pragnie mieć rodziców. A my tak bardzo pragniemy dziecka..."

"What a terrible situation. Katie had loving parents and they died in a car accident. She wants to have real parents so badly. And we want to have a child so badly..."

W tamtej chwili Mateusz wiedział, że jest gotowy na adopcję dziecka. Po powrocie do domu opowiedział swojej żonie o całej sytuacji i o Kasi. Weronika **bez wahania** zgodziła się na adopcję.

At that moment, Matthew knew that he was ready for adoption. After returning home, he told his wife about the whole situation and about Katie. Weronika agreed to adoption without hesitation.

W ciągu kilku tygodni Mateusz i Weronika spełnili wszystkie **wymagania** dotyczące adopcji i zabrali Kasię do swojego domu.

In a few weeks, Matthew and Weronika fulfilled all requirements for adoption and took Katie home.

"Widzisz? Teraz naprawdę mieszkasz na ulicy Słonecznej. To twój nowy dom," powiedział Mateusz.

"You see? Now you really live on Słoneczna street. It's your new home," Matthew said.

Dziewczynka była szczęśliwa. Był to dla niej pierwszy szczęśliwy dzień odkąd straciła swoich rodziców.

The girl was happy. It was the first happy day for her since losing her parents.

Mateusz i Weronika byli wspaniałymi rodzicami. Troszczyli się o Kasie jak najlepiej umieli. Kasia również była wspaniałym dzieckiem. Pomimo tego, że ucieczka z domu dziecka nie była dobrą rzeczą, nie żałowała. W końcu odnalazła nowych rodziców i mowy dom.

Matthew and Weronika were great parents. They took care of Katie the best they could. Katie was a great kid. Although escaping from the orphanage wasn't a good thing, she didn't regret that. She finally found new parents and a new home.

Streszczenie

Mateusz mieszkał ze swoją żoną Weroniką na obrzeżach miasta. Para nie mogła mieć dzieci. Pewnego dnia Mateusz pojechał do miasta, aby zrobić zakupy I wysłać list na poczcie. Kiedy Mateusz był na poczcie zauważył małą dziewczynkę, która stała na chodniku. Dziewczynka powiedziała, że się zgubiła I jej rodzice martwią się o nią. Miała na imię Kasia. Poprosiła Mateusza, aby odwiózł ją do domu. Okazało się, że Kasia mieszkała na tej samej ulicy, co Mateusz. Kiedy Mateusz dojechał na miejsce Kasia nie wiedziała gdzie jest jej dom I rozpłakała się. W tym samym czasie Mateusz usłyszał głos z radia mówiący, że mała dziewczynka uciekła z domu dziecka. To była Kasia. Mateusz postanowił odwieźć ją do domu dziecka. Po kilku tygodniach Mateusz I Weronika adoptowali Kasię. Byli wspaniałymi rodzicami, a Kasia była wspaniałym dzieckiem.

Summary

Matthew lived with his wife, Weronika, in the suburbs. The couple wasn't able to have children on their own. One day, Matthew went to the city to do some shopping and send a letter to the post office. While he was at the post office, he saw a little girl who was standing on the sidewalk. The girl told him that she had got lost and her parents were worried about her. Her name was Katie. She asked Matthew to drive her home. It turned out that Katie had been living on the same street as Matthew. When Matthew reached the destination, Katie didn't know where her house was, and she started crying. At the same time, Matthew heard a voice from the car radio that said that a little girl had escaped from an orphanage. It was Katie. Matthew decided to take Katie to the orphanage. After a few weeks, Matthew and Weronika adopted Katie. They were great parents, and Katie was a great child.

Vocabulary

Wysyłać list – to send a letter

Goście – guests

Dział z produtami dla dzieci – children's section

Bezskutecznie – unsuccessfully

Adpocja – an adoption

Chodnik – a sidewalk

Kolorowy sweter – a colorful sweater

Pingwin – a penguin

Przechodzeń – a passer-by

Babcia – a grandma

Na końcu ulicy – at the end of the street

Radio – radio

Dom dziecka – an orphanage

Wypadek samochodowy – a car accident

Wzruszony – touched

Bez wahania – without hesitation

Wymagania – requiremens

Pytania

1. Jak miała na imię żona Mateusza?

2. Dlaczego Mateusz pojechał do miasta?

3. Gdzie Mateusz zauważył Kasię?

4. Co miała na sobie Kasia?

5. W jaki sposób Kasia okłamała Mateusza?

6. W jaki sposób Mateusz dowiedział się prawdy o Kasi?

a) Usłyszał o tym w radio

b) Kasia mu powiedziała

c) Powiedział mu o tym jego żona

7. Jak zginęli rodzice Kasi?

a) Byli chorzy na raka

b) W wypadku samochodowym

c) Popełnili samobójstwo

8. Co zrobił Mateusz zaraz po odkryciu prawdy o Kasi?

a) Odwiózł ją do domu dziecka

b) Ukrył ją w swoim domu

c) Zabrał ją do szpitala

9. Co zrobili Mateusz i Weronika kilka tygodni po spotkaniu Kasi?

a) Zapomnieli o niej

b) Przywieźli jej prezent

c) Adoptowali ją

Questions

1. What was the name of Matthew's wife?
2. Why did Matthew go to the city?
3. Where did Matthew notice Katie?
4. What was Katie wearing?
5. How did Katie lie to Matthew?
6. How did Matthew discover the truth?

a) By hearing the news from the radio

b) Katie told him the truth

c) His wife told him the truth about Katie

7. How did Katie's parents die?

a) They suffered from cancer

b) They had a car accident

c) They committed suicide

8. What did Matthew do immediately after discovering the truth about Katie?

a) He took her to the orphanage

b) He hid her in his house

c) He took her to a hospital

9. What did Matthew and Weronika do a few weeks after meeting Katie?

a) They forgot about Katie

b) They brought Katie a present

c) They adopted Katie

Odpowiedzi

1. Weronika

2. Musiał zrobić zakupy i wysłać list

3. Na poczcie

4. Kolorowy sweter z pingwinem

5. Powiedziała, że mieszkała z rodzicami i babcią

6. a

7. b

8. a

9. c

Answers

1. Weronika

2. He had to do the shopping and send a letter

3. At the post office

4. A colorful sweater with a penguin

5. She said that she had been living with her parents and her grandma

6. a

7. b

8. a

9. c

Chapter 10 – Szczęście w nieszczęściu [Blessing in disguise]

"Chodźcie, zaraz rozpoczyna się wasz ulubiony **teleturniej!**" powiedziała Gosia do swoich rodziców.

"Come on, your favorite quiz show is about to start!" said Gosia to her parents.

"Zobaczcie, dzisiaj **uczestnik** może wygrać aż 10 000 złotych!" Gosia była podekscytowana. Wraz z rodzicami uwielbiała oglądać teleturnieje. Jej rodzice kochali rozwiązywać **krzyżówki** i kupować **zdrapki**.

"Look, today the participant can win even 10,000 złoty!" Gosia was excited. She loved watching quiz shows with her parents. Her parents loved solving puzzles and buying scratch cards.

W czasach dzieciństwa tata zawsze przynosił Gosi losy i zdrapki z supermarketu. Gosia kochała ten **dreszczyk emocji**. Uwielbiała brać udział w różnych **konkursach**. Często wygrywała pieniądze oraz różne rzeczy. Jej rodzice również kochali konkursy. Pewnego razu mama Gosi wygrała samochód na **loterii**. Cała rodzina pamiętała to przez długi czas.

In her childhood, her father always brought Gosia scratch cards from the supermarket. She loved that thrill of excitement. She loved taking part in competitions. She used to win money and other stuff. Her parents loved competitions too. One day, Gosia's mom won a car! The entire family remembered that day for a long time.

Tego dnia jednak rodzina postanowiła obejrzeć ich ulubiony teleturniej.

That day, the family decided to watch their favorite game show.

"Po pierwsze, obiad!" krzyknęła mama i dodała, "Dziś niestety mamy **zupę błyskawiczną**. Nie miałam czasu nic ugotować."

"But first, dinner!" the mom exclaimed and added, "Today, we have only some instant noodles. I didn't have time to cook anything."

"Nic się nie stało mamo. Uwielbiam zupkę błyskawiczną. Kocham ten **smak**," powiedziała Gosia.

"It's okay, Mom. I love instant noodles. I love that flavor," Gosia said.

"Właśnie się zaczyna," powiedział tata.

"It's beginning," her dad said.

Zupa była błyskawiczna i tania, ale bardzo smaczna. Gosia zaczęła oglądać **paczkę**.

Although the soup was fast and cheap, it tasted great. Gosia started to look through the package.

"Widzicie? Tu jest napisane, że można znaleźć **złotą monetę** w środku paczki. Ten kto ją znajdzie może ją zatrzymać. Ponadto, ten kto ją znajdzie wygra milion złotych i wczasy All Inclusive!" powiedziała Gosia trzymając paczkę zupki.

"You see? It says that you can find a gold coin inside the package. The one who finds it can keep it. Moreover, the one who finds it wins a million zlotys and an all-inclusive holiday!" said Gosia, holding the soup packaging.

"A cóż to za dziwny konkurs? Złoto w zupce błyskawicznej?" rodzice Gosi roześmiali się.

"What a weird offer. A gold coin inside instant noodles?" Gosia's parents started to laugh.

"Dziwny. Ale, nieważne. Tutaj nic nie ma," powiedziała Gosia, zaglądając do paczki.

"Weird, but nevermind. There's nothing in here," said Gosia, looking inside the packaging.

Rodzina zabrała się do jedzenia. Po chwili jednak Gosia zaczęła **kaszleć**.

The family started to eat. However, after a moment, Gosia started coughing.

"Co ci się stało kochanie?" powiedziała mama.

"What happened, honey?" the mom said.

Rodzice Gosi byli zaniepokojeni. Dziewczyna zaczęła się **dusić**. Jej twarz zrobiła się czerwona. Gosia **upadła na podłogę**.

Gosia's parents were worried about her. The girl started to choke. Her face got red. She fell on the floor.

"Dzwoń na **pogotowie**!" krzyknęła mama.

"Call the ambulance!" the mom exclaimed.

Podczas gdy ojciec dzwonił na pogotowie, mama Gosi próbowała jej pomóc. Karetka zjawiła się po kilku minutach.

While the father was calling the ambulance, Gosia's mom tried to help her. The ambulance arrived in a few minutes.

"Co się stało?" zapytał sanitariusz.

"What happened?" the paramedic asked.

"Nie mam pojęcia. Nasza córka jadła obiad i nagle zaczęła się dusić. Ma **alergię pokarmową**," powiedziała mama.

"I have no idea. Our daughter was eating dinner, and suddenly she started to choke. She has a food allergy," Gosia's mom said.

"Jest **nieprzytomna**. Musimy jak najszybciej zabrać ją do szpitala," powiedział sanitariusz.

"She's unconscious. We have to take her to the hospital as quickly as possible," the paramedic said.

Karetka zabrała Gosię do szpitala. Rodzice byli bardzo zmartwieni. Gosia cierpiała na alergię pokarmową, ale nigdy wcześniej nie miała takich **objawów**. Czasami dostawała **wysypki** lub bolała ją głowa. Ale nigdy, przenigdy nie dusiła się.

The ambulance took Gosia to the hospital. Her parents were worried. Gosia had been suffering from a food allergy, yet she had never had such symptoms. Sometimes, she got a rash or she had headaches. But she'd never ever been choking so badly.

Rodzice postanowili pojechać do szpitala za karetką. Byli bardzo zdenerwowani. Bali się o swoją córkę. Po kilku godzinach spędzonych w szpitalu w końcu przyszedł do nich lekarz.

The parents decided to follow the ambulance. They were really concerned about their daughter. Thy were scared. After a few hours spent at the hospital, the doctor finally came to them.

"Wasza córka obudziła się. Musieliśmy podać jej **zastrzyk**. Wszystko już jest okej," powiedział lekarz.

"Your daughter has woken up. We had to give her an injection. Now everything's okay," the doctor said.

"Ale co się stało?" spytała mama.

"But what happened?" the mom asked.

"Córka faktycznie ma alergię pokarmową. Ale to nie to było powodem **zachłyśnięcia**," odpowiedział lekarz.

"Indeed, your daughter suffers from a food allergy. But it wasn't the reason for choking," the doctor answered.

"To co się stało w takim razie?" zapytał ojciec Gosi. Rodzice byli zmieszani.

"So what happened, then?" Gosia's dad asked. The parents were confused.

"Znaleźliśmy w jej **przełyku** złotą monetę. Czy wiedzą może państwo jak się tam znalazła?" zapytał lekarz.

"We found a gold coin in her gullet. Do you have any idea how this thing got there?" the doctor asked.

"Nie mogę w to uwierzyć!" krzyknęła mama. "Nie mogę w to uwierzyć!"

"I can't believe it!" the mom exclaimed. "I can't believe it!"

Po kilku minutach rodzice postanowili wejść do sali, gdzie leżała ich córka.

After a few minutes, the parents decided to enter the room where their daughter was resting.

"Cześć, kochanie!" powiedziała mama.

"Hi, honey!" the mom said.

"Mamo, tato... co się stało?" zapytała Gosia. Była bardzo zmęczona. "Czy moja alergia pokarmowa się **pogorszyła**?" dodała.

"Mom, dad... what happened?" Gosia asked. She was really tired. "Has my food allergy gotten worse?" she asked.

"Nie, kochanie. To coś innego," odpowiedział ojciec.

"No, honey. It was something different," her father said.

"Prawdziwe szczęście w nieszczęściu," dodała mama.

"Truly a blessing in disguise," her mom added.

"Nie rozumiem. Co tak naprawdę się stało?" Gosia była zmieszana.

"I don't understand. What really happened?" Gosia was confused.

"Kochanie, w twojej zupie była złota moneta. Nie poczułaś jej i **połknęłaś ją. Utknęła** ci w przełyku. Lekarze już ją wyciągnęli," odpowiedział ojciec.

"Honey, you had a gold coin in your soup. You didn't feel it in your mouth and you swallowed it. It got stuck in your gullet. The doctors have already taken it out," the father said.

Gosia nie mogła w to uwierzyć. To była moneta z loterii.

Gosia couldn't believe it. It was the coin from the lottery.

Po wyjściu ze szpitala Gosia otrzymała monetę. Od razu skontaktowała się z firmą produkującej zupki i pokazała im monetę. Gosia wygrała milion złotych i wczasy! Pomimo tego, że nie była to do końca szczęśliwa wygrana, Gosia była zadowolona. To było prawdziwe szczęście w nieszczęściu.

After leaving the hospital, Gosia got the coin back. She immediately contacted the soup company and showed them the gold coin. Gosia won a million zlotys and holidays! Although it wasn't a lucky win, Gosia was happy. It was truly a blessing in disguise.

Streszczenie

Gosia mieszkała ze swoimi rodzicami. Jej rodzice uwielbiali brać udział w konkursach I kupować zdrapki. Tata zawsze przynosił Gosi zdrapki z supermarketu. Gosia też uwielbiała brać udział w konkursach. Pewnego dnia rodzina oglądała teleturniej. Mama Gosi przygotowała błyskawiczną zupę na obiad. Gosia przeczytała na opakowaniu, że w opakowaniu można znaleźć złotą monetę. Ten kto ją znalazł mógł wygrać milion złotych i wczasy. W opakowaniu jednak nic nie było. Po chwili Gosia zaczęła się dusić. Rodzice zadzwonili na pogotowie I Gosia została zabrana do szpitala. Po kilku godzinach lekarze powiedzieli rodzicom, że znaleźli w przełyku Gosi złotą monetę. Rodzice nie mogli uwierzyć. Powiedzieli o wszystkim Gosi. Gosia zatrzymała monetę I wygrała milion złotych.

Summary

Gosia lived with her parents. Her parents loved taking part in lotteries and buying scratch cards. Her dad had always brought Gosia some scratch cards from a supermarket. Gosia also loved taking part in lotteries. One day, the whole family was watching a game show. Gosia's mom prepared some instant noodles for dinner. Gosia read on the packaging that there could be a gold coin inside. The one who found it won one million zlotys and holidays. There was nothing inside Gosia's packaging. After a while, Gosia started choking. Her parents called an ambulance, and Gosia was taken to the hospital. After a few hours, the doctors told Gosia's parents that there was a gold coin inside Gosia's gullet. Her parents couldn't believe it. They told Gosia about everything. Gosia kept the coin, and she won one million zlotys.

Vocabulary

Teleturniej - a quiz how

Uczestnik - a participant

Krzyżówki - puzzles

Zdrapki - scratch cards

Dreszczyk emocji - the thrill of excitement

Loteria - a lottery

Zupa błyskawiczna - instant noodles

Smak - flavor

Paczka - a packaging

Złota moneta - a golden coin

Kaszleć - to cough

Dusić się - to choke

Upaść na podłoge - to fall on the floor

Pogotowie - an ambulance

Alergia pokarmowa - food allergy

Nieprzytomny - unconscious

Objawy - symptoms

Wysypka - rash

Zastrzyk - an injection

Przełyk - a gullet

Pogorszyć się - to get worse

Połknąć - to swallow

Utknąć - to get stuck

Pytania

1. Jakie hobby miała Gosia?

2. Co przynosił Gosi jej ojciec z supermarketu?

3. Co robiła Gosia I jej rodzice podczas jedzenia obiadu?

4. Co rodzina Gosi miała na obiad?

5. Co stało się z Gosią po zjedzeniu zupy?

a) Wymiotowała

b) Zaczęła się dusić

c) Dostała wysypki

6. Na co chorowała Gosia?

a) Alergię pokarmową

b) Raka

c) Depresję

7. Co znaleźli lekarze w przełyku Gosi?

a) Kamień

b) Złotą monetę

c) Plastikowy guzik

8. Co Gosia zrobiła po wyjściu ze szpitala?

a) Skontaktowała się z firmą produkującą zupki

b) Pojechała do domu

c) Poszła do szkoły

9. Co wygrała Gosia?

a) Samochód

b) Zegarek

c) Pieniądze i wczasy

Questions

1. What was Gosia's hobby?

2. What did Gosia's dad used to bring her from the supermarket?

3. What were Gosia and her parents doing while eating dinner?

4. What did Gosia and her parents have for dinner?

5. What happened with Gosia after eating the soup?

a) She vomited

b) She started to choke

c) She got a rash

6. What was Gosia's illness?

a) Food allergy

b) Cancer

c) Depression

7. What did the doctors find in Gosia's gullet?

a) A stone

b) A golden coin

c) A plastic button

8. What did Gosia win?

a) A car

b) A watch

c) Money and a holiday

Odpowiedzi

1. Udział w konkursach, zdrapki

2. Zdrapki

3. Oglądali teleturniej

4. Zupkę błyskawiczną

5. b

6. a

7. b

8. c

Answers

1. Taking part in competitions and lotteries, scratch cards

2. Scratch cards

3. They were watching a game show

4. Instant noodles

5. b

6. a

7. b

8. c

Chapter 11 – Incognito
[Incognito]

Agnieszka wysłała ostatni e-mail i wyłączyła komputer.

Agnes sent the last email and switched off the computer.

Weekend. Nareszcie. Czas na **odpoczynek,** pomyślała i zamknęła drzwi biura. Był ciepły, **słoneczny** dzień, więc Agnieszka postanowiła nie spieszyć się do domu. W końcu mogła **odetchnąć** po ciężkim tygodniu w pracy.

Weekend. Finally. It's time to relax, she thought and closed the office door. It was a hot summer day, so Agnes decided not to rush home. She could finally get some rest after a long and hard week at work.

Jej biuro było w centrum miasta, dlatego postanowiła przejść się po starym mieście i zjeść jej ulubione **lody.** Siedząc w **restauracyjnym ogródku** usłyszała gitarę i śpiew.

Her office was located in the city center, so she decided to take a walk in the old town and eat her favorite ice cream. As she was sitting in the restaurant garden, she heard someone playing guitar and singing.

To na pewno on, pomyślała.

It has to be him, she thought.

Tak. To był on. **Grajek,** którego słyszała codziennie.

Yes. It was him. The musician she had been hearing every day.

Tego dnia miała dużo czasu. Powoli jadła lody i wsłuchiwała się w muzykę. Muzyk wyglądał **dziwacznie.** Przypominał trochę **bezdomnego.** Miał długą **brodę** i **wąsy,** długie włosy. Był ubrany w stare, **znoszone** dżinsy oraz T-shirt. Po chwili Agnieszka zauważyła **dziury** w jego bluzce.

That day, she had a lot of time. She was eating the ice cream slowly, and she was enjoying the music. The musician looked peculiar. He looked like a homeless man. He had a long beard, mustache, and long hair. He was wearing old, worn-out jeans and a T-shirt. After a while, Agnes noticed holes in his T-shirt.

On jednak **nie przejmował się.** Grał dalej, a jego głos brzmiał jak głos Agnieszki ulubionego artysty z radia.

However, he didn't care. He was playing on, and his voice sounded like the voice of Agnes' favorite artist from the radio.

Po kilku chwilach wokół muzyka zebrał się **tłum ludzi.** Wszyscy słuchali tego tajemniczego gościa i **nagrywali go.**

After a few moments, a crowd gathered around the musician. Everyone was listening to that mysterious man, and everyone was filming him.

Szkoda mi go. Ma taki talent i tak piękny głos. Wygląda na biednego i bezdomnego, pomyślała Agnieszka.

I'm really sorry for him. He's got great talent and a beautiful voice. He looks like a poor and homeless man, Agnes thought.

Kobieta szybko zjadła lody i podeszła do muzyka. Wrzuciła do **gitarowego futerału** kilka monet i postanowiła jeszcze chwilę go posłuchać. Muzyk wyglądał bardzo znajomo...

The woman ate her ice cream quickly and approached the musician. She threw some coins into his guitar case and decided to stay a little longer and listen to him. The musician looked familiar...

*To zwykły **zbieg okoliczności.** To niemożliwe,* pomyślała Agnieszka.

It has to be a pure coincidence. It's impossible, Agnes thought.

Muzyk przypominał jej ulubionego piosenkarza. Agnieszka poczuła się dziwnie. Tylko jej idol posiadał **charakterystyczne, jasnoniebieskie** oczy. Ten muzyk miał takie same.

The musician looked like her favorite artist. Agnes felt strange. Only her idol had so characteristic light blue eyes. That musician's eyes looked exactly the same.

Ale ta broda... i te ubrania... To musi być ktoś inny, pomyślała.

But that beard... and these clothes... It has to be someone else, she thought.

Agnieszka tak długo wsłuchiwała się w koncert, że nie zorientowała się że było już ciemno i późno. Wszyscy ludzie dookoła **rozeszli się.** Została tylko ona i muzyk.

Agnes had listened to the concert for so long that she didn't realize that it had got dark and late. The crowd dispersed. Only her and the musician were still standing there.

"A to był ostatni **utwór** na dziś. Dziękuję bardzo," powiedział muzyk do mikrofonu. Po chwili zaczął pakować swoją gitarę oraz swój sprzęt.

"It was the last song. Thank you very much," the musician said to the microphone. After a while, he started to pack his guitar and his gear.

Agnieszka postanowiła podejść do muzyka i podziękować mu za świetny koncert.

Agnes decided to come closer and thank the musician for a great concert.

"Cześć. Jestem Agnieszka. To był naprawdę świetny koncert. Bardzo lubię słuchać jak grasz," powiedziała.

"Hi. I'm Agnes. It was a really great concert. I really enjoy listening to you," she said.

"Cześć. Dzięki. Miło cię poznać. Jestem Artur," odpowiedział muzyk.

"Hi. Thanks. Nice to meet you. I'm Artur," the musician said.

"Wiesz... pracuję niedaleko stąd. Tam jest moje biuro." Agnieszka wskazała swoim palcem na ulicę. "Codziennie słyszę jak grasz. Naprawdę uwielbiam cię słuchać. Przypominasz mi mojego ulubionego **idola** Filipa Lewandowskiego. Jest świetnym artystą. Mam wszystkie jego **płyty**," dodała Agnieszka.

"You know... I work over there. My office is right there." Agnes pointed with her finger. "Every day I hear you play. I really like listening to your music. You remind me of my idol, Filip Lewandowski. He's a great artist. I have all his records," Agnes said.

"Serio? Też uwielbiam Filipa Zalewskiego. Byłem ostatnio na jego koncercie. Świetnie gra. Mam nadzieję, że kiedyś będę grał tak jak on," odpowiedział Artur.

"Really? I like Filip Lewandowski too. I was at his concert recently. He plays really well. I hope I will play as good as him one day," Artur said.

"Ale ty przecież grasz tak jak on! Masz taki sam głos. Może wyglądasz troszkę inaczej, masz brodę i długie włosy... ale masz takie same oczy. Ten kolor jest bardzo **rzadki**," powiedziała Agnieszka.

"But you already play as good as him! You have the same voice. Maybe you look different, you have a beard and a mustache... but you have the same eyes. That color is very rare," Agnes said.

"Dzięki. Miło mi to słyszeć," odpowiedział Artur.

"Thanks. Nice to hear that," Artur said.

Agnieszka postanowiła zadać **niewygodne** pytanie.

Agnes decided to ask an inconvenient question.

"Przepraszam, że pytam, ale... czy ty jesteś bezdomny? Potrzebujesz pomocy? Widziałam, że ludzie nie wrzucili ci dziś dużo pieniędzy do twojego futerału. Może potrzebujesz czegoś? Nie zrozum mnie źle... Czasem widzę muzyków, którzy grają tylko dlatego, że potrzebują pieniędzy. Chcę tylko pomóc," powiedziała Agnieszka.

"I'm sorry I'm asking but... are you homeless? Do you need help? I saw that people didn't throw much money to your guitar case.

Maybe you need something? Don't get me wrong... Sometimes I see musicians who play only because they need some money. I only want to help," Agnes said.

Artur był zmieszany. Nie wiedział co powiedzieć. Przez chwilę Agnieszka bała się, że **uraziła** muzyka.

Artur was confused. He didn't know what to say. Agnes was afraid that she could hurt the musician.

"Nie... nie jestem bezdomny. Gram, bo kocham muzykę," odpowiedział muzyk.

"No... I'm not homeless. I play because I love music," the musician said.

Agnieszka czuła jednak, że coś było nie tak. Po pytaniu o pieniądze Artur był bardzo zmieszany. Zaczął zachowywać się bardzo dziwnie.

However, Agnes felt that something was wrong. After asking Artur about the money, he got confused. He started to act strange.

"Coś nie tak? Uraziłam cię? Jeśli tak to bardzo przepraszam. Chyba coś jest nie tak," powiedziała Agnieszka.

"Something wrong? Did I hurt you? If so, I'm really sorry. I see something's wrong," Agnes said.

"Nie... wszystko jest ok," odpowiedział muzyk. Po chwili jednak odezwał się jeszcze raz.

"No... everything's okay," the musician said. After a while, he started to speak.

"Wiesz co... **powiem ci prawdę**. Nie jestem Artur. Skłamałem. Przepraszam."

"You know what... I'll tell you the truth. I'm not Arthur. I lied to you. I'm sorry."

Agnieszka nie wiedziała co powiedzieć. Muzyk kontynuował.

Agnes didn't know what to say. The musician continued.

"Udało ci się dostrzec **podobieństwo** do Filipa. Ale tak naprawdę nie jestem do niego podobny. To ja. Filip Lewandowski."

"You've managed to notice the resemblance to Filip. The truth is, I don't look like him. It's me. Filip Lewandowski."

Agnieszka nie mogła uwierzyć.

Agnes couldn't believe it.

"Ale dlaczego? Dlaczego przedstawiłeś się jako Artur? Dlaczego grasz tutaj? I ta broda, długie włosy. Nie rozumiem." Agnieszka nie mogła ukryć zaskoczenia.

"But why? Why did you say you were Artur? Why do you play here? And that beard, long hair. I don't understand." Agnes couldn't hide her surprise.

"To **sztuczna** broda," powiedział muzyk i **odkleił** brodę. Po chwili ściągnął także **perukę.**

"The beard's fake," the musician said and detached the beard. He took off the wig too.

"Nadal nie rozumiem," powiedziała Agnieszka i dodała „Czy to jest jakieś reality show? Czy ja jestem w **ukrytej kamerze**?"

"I still don't understand," said Agnes and added "Is it a reality show? Is there a hidden camera here?"

Filip roześmiał się.

Filip started to laugh.

"Nie. Nic z tych rzeczy. Ja po prostu lubię koncertować incognito. Lubię kiedy ludzie słuchają mnie i **podziwiają** mój talent, nie mój **wygląd**. Dlatego udaję kogoś innego i zakładam perukę i sztuczną brodę. Nie chcę, aby ktoś mnie poznał," odpowiedział.

"No. Nothing like this. I just like performing incognito. I really like when people listen to me and appreciate my talent, not my physical appearance. That's why I pretend to be someone else, and I wear a wig and a fake beard. I don't want to be recognized by anyone," he said.

Agnieszka w końcu zrozumiała. Jednak nadal nie mogła uwierzyć. Rozmawiała ze swoim idolem!

Agnes finally understood, yet she still couldn't believe it. She was talking to her idol!

"Jesteś moim idolem. Uwielbiam cię słuchać. Mam wszystkie twoje płyty," powiedziała.

"You're my idol. I love listening to your music. I have all your records," she said.

"Dziękuję. Jesteś wspaniałą osobą. Doceniasz mój talent. Nie wiedziałaś, że to ja, a mimo to podeszłaś do mnie i powiedziałaś mi, że dałem świetny koncert. Chciałbym, abyś przyjechała na mój kolejny koncert. Tym razem już jako Filip Lewandowski. Oczywiście dostajesz darmowy bilet i miejsce na bekstejdżu," odpowiedział Filip.

"Thank you. You're an amazing person. You appreciate my talent. You didn't know it was me, and still, you approached me, and you said that I'd played an amazing concert. I'd like you to come to my concert. But this time, I will perform as Filip Lewandowski. Of course, you get a free ticket and a place backstage," Filip said.

Agnieszka nie mogła uwierzyć. To było jak spełnienie marzeń. Od tamtego dnia jej idol stał się jej przyjacielem. Agnieszka chodziła na każdy koncert i spędzała czas z Filipem. Zawsze było dla niej miejsce na bekstejdżu.

Agnes couldn't believe it. It was like a dream come true. Since that day, her idol was her best friend. Agnes was at every concert of his and spent time with him. She always had a place backstage.

Streszczenie

Agnieszka pracowała w biurze w centrum miasta. Codziennie słyszała jak ktoś śpiewał i grał na gitarze. Pewnego dnia po skończonej pracy poszła na stare miasto i postanowiła zjeść lody. Po chwili zauważyła muzyka. To był ten sam muzyk, którego codziennie słyszała. Muzyk był bardzo podobny do idola Agnieszki—Filipa Lewandowskiego. Po skończonym koncercie Agnieszka powiedziała muzykowi, że zagrał świetny koncert. Muzyk wyglądał jak bezdomny więc Agnieszka postanowiła mu pomóc. On jednak powiedział, że nie potrzebuje pomocy. Okazało się, że muzyk był Filipem

Lewandowskim i grał incognito. Agnieszka i jej idol stali się przyjaciółmi.

Summary

Agnes worked in an office in the city center. Every day, she heard someone sing and play the guitar. One day after finishing work, Agnes went to the old town and decided to eat ice cream. After a while, she saw a musician. It was the musician she had heard every day. The musician looked exactly like Agnes' idol—Filip Lewandowski. After the performance, Agnes told the musician that he played a really good concert. The musician looked like a homeless man, so Agnes decided to help him. He said that he didn't need any help. It turned out that the musician was Filip Lewandowski, who performed incognito. Agnes and her idol made friends with each other.

Vocabulary

Odpoczynek – relax

Słoneczny – sunny

Odetchnąć – to get some rest

Lody – ice cream

Restauracyjny ogródek – a restaurant garden

Grajek/muzyk – a musician

Dziwacznie – peculiar

Bezdomny – homeless

Broda i wąsy – beard and mustache

Znoszony – worn-out

Dziury – holes

Nie przejmować się – to not care

Tłum ludzi – a crowd

Nagrywać – to film

Gitarowy futerał – a guitar case

Zbieg okoliczności – a coincidence

Charakterystyczny – characteristics

Jasnoniebieski – light blue

Rozejść się – to disperse

Utwór – a song

Idol – an idol

Płyta – a record

Rzadki – rare

Niewygodny – inconvenient

Urazić kogoś – to hurt someone

Powiedzieć prawde – to tell the truth

Podobieństwo – resemblance

Sztuczny – fake

Odkleić – to detach

Peruka – a wig

Ukryta kamera – a hidden camera

Podziwiać – appreciate

Wygląd – physical appearance

Pytania

1. Gdzie pracowała Agnieszka?

2. Co zrobiła Agnieszka po skończonej pracy?

3. Na jakim instrumencie grał muzyk?

4. W co był ubrany muzyk?

5. Jak się nazywał idol Agnieszki?

6. Jaki kolor oczu miał muzyk?

a) Zielone

b) Brązowe

c) Jasnoniebieskie

7. Jakie nieprawdziwe imię miał muzyk?

a) Artur

b) Robert

c) Filip

8. Jak Agnieszka dowiedziała się, że muzyk był jej idolem?

a) Ktoś jej powiedział

b) Muzyk jej powiedział

c) Odkryła to sama

9. Co stało się po odkryciu prawdy?

a) Agnieszka i Filip stali się przyjaciółmi

b) Filip obraził się na Agnieszkę

c) Filip uciekł z kraju

Questions

1. Where did Agnes work?
2. What did Agnes do after finishing her work?
3. What instrument did the musician play?
4. What did the musician wear?
5. What was the name of Agnes' idol?
6. What color were the musician's eyes?

a) Green

b) Brown

c) Light blue

7. What was the musician's fake name?

a) Artur

b) Robert

c) Filip

8. How did Agnes discover that the musician was her idol?

a) Someone told her

b) The musician told her

c) She discovered it on her own

9. What happened after discovering the truth?

a) Agnes and Filip became friends

b) Filip took offence at Agnes

c) Filip escaped from the country

Odpowiedzi

1. W biurze
2. Poszła do restauracji zjeść lody
3. Na gitarze
4. Dżinsy i T-shirt
5. Filip Lewandowski
6. c
7. a

8. b

9. a

Answers

1. At an office

2. She went to the restaurant to eat ice cream

3. Guitar

4. Jeans and a T-shirt

5. Filip Lewandowksi

6. c

7. a

8. b

9. a

Conclusion

Congratulations on making it through to the end of this book. It should have been informative and provided you with all of the tools you need to achieve your language learning goals. Hopefully, you also enjoyed the interesting stories and learned something!

Now, you should feel more secure while reading or even talking. It is recommended that you reread everything, from the beginning, and see if you understand it a little better the second time around.

From this point, you can finally start the real journey, where you will apply your knowledge and express yourself more aptly and naturally and make your Polish shine. Plus, if you ever get stuck, you can always come back to this book at any time for a refresher lesson.

Part 3: Polish Phrase Book

Over 1000 Essential Polish Phrases That Will Be Helpful During Your Trip to Poland

Introduction to the Polish Language

If you are reading this, you have probably made an important, life-changing decision to learn a foreign language. If you are either a native or non-native English speaker, it does not matter—since speaking more than one foreign language is becoming the standard. Apart from advanced or proficient knowledge of English, which is a *lingua franca* nowadays, learning another, especially niche, language may be beneficial. Therefore, your decision to learn Polish will definitely pay off—provided you stay on track. Whatever your motivation is, we will try our best to make your journey enjoyable, fun and challenging.

There have been many changes in teaching and learning foreign languages throughout the centuries, and what is more, each method has been focused on different aspects of a given language. For example, in the fifteenth century, foreign language learners were to master grammar rules in order to produce ideal literary texts. In the 1950s, a great deal of stress was put on repetition and memorization, so students often had to learn long dialogs and language patterns by heart, instead of staying creative. Finally, studies in first and second language acquisition influenced the way of teaching and learning foreign languages across the globe. Today, we know that mastering and integrating language skills (such as reading, listening, writing, speaking) is the fastest and the most efficient way to become proficient. Moreover, introducing new grammar and vocabulary items based on real context is vital. Therefore, this book will teach you the basics of the Polish language, using the most contemporary and most effective methods.

Polish is certainly not one of the most spoken languages in the world—since it is the official language of Poland exclusively. It has around 38 million speakers in Poland, but many immigrants in countries such as the USA, UK, Germany, Norway or Ireland are Polish. The Polish Community Abroad includes, for example, more than one million Poles in the UK and nearly one million in the States. What is also interesting is that many Americans are of Polish origin, due to the mass emigration caused by the difficult political situation in Poland in the eighteenth and nineteenth centuries.

Many native speakers of English consider Polish (along with Chinese, Arabic, and Japanese) as one of the hardest languages to learn, due to its heavy inflectional system and, probably, pronunciation. It may be partially true; however, the beginning is always the toughest part of any language journey. The more you practice, the more automatic your grammar use will become, and the more familiar Polish sounds will become. Besides, speaking one of the hardest languages in the world is quite an achievement. Before immersing yourself in learning, look at a few notes on what you are about to get your hands, brain, and heart on:

Poland has been considered a country since 966 AD (the moment of declaring Christianity as an official religion in Poland), so it is not a "young" country. Despite the strong influence of Latin in the Middle Ages, Poland has managed to preserve its original Slavic language, yet Polish contains many words of Latin etymology. What is noteworthy is that many Polish medieval literary texts are written in the original language, according to the famous quote of Mikołaj Rej—one of the Polish writers:

"Among other nations let it always be known

That the Poles are not geese, have a tongue of their own."

Indeed, Poland has had many brilliant authors, including three Noble laureates (Henryk Sienkiewicz, Czesław Miłosz, and Wisława Szymborska). Furthermore, Joseph Conrad is of Polish origin (his actual name is Józef Teodor Konrad Korzeniowski).

Did You Know That...?

- Polish is a highly inflectional language. It has seven cases, and each of them requires using different suffixes. Many native speakers of English consider this feature as one of the most difficult to acquire.

- Unlike English, Polish has "free" word order. Although there are some popular and generally accepted patterns, we can place words in a simple sentence nearly randomly, and it will be grammatically correct.

- Polish has only three grammatical tenses (present, past, and future). The choice of tenses is very different from that of the English language. In fact, Polish native speakers have many problems with acquiring English tenses.

- Because of the influence of the inflectional system, Polish people add inflections to foreign names. For instance, you can notice different suffixes added to Harry Potter or Spiderman in different cases.

- All Polish women's first names end with the vowel "a", except for the ones with foreign origin.

- Polish shares many grammatical and lexical features with the other Slavic languages, such as Czech or Slovak.

- Unlike English, Polish has grammatical genders (masculine, feminine, and neutral). It means that gender does not correspond with the actual sex. For example, the word *table* in Polish is masculine, and the word *book* is feminine.

As mentioned earlier, Polish is rather a tough language for English speakers, as far as pronunciation is concerned. This is because it contains many complex consonant clusters (such as szcz, dżdż), and what is more, each consonant and vowel should be pronounced. Despite the processes of devoicing and softening that make pronunciation a little bit easier, there is still a great deal of difficulty for English speakers.

Taking into account the reasons above and the ones yet for you to discover, your journey seems to be challenging yet rewarding. Polish is one of the most interesting Slavic languages since it is a blend of Slavic pronunciation (intended rather for the Cyrillic script) and the Roman alphabet. Due to many differences, the rich inflections in Polish will often leave you confused, but at the end of the day, you will be delighted with the process of learning such a different language. Along with learning the language, you will also discover the Polish culture— very close yet a completely different world.

To Begin With...

Knowing some basic differences between your mother tongue and your target language is vital. Thus, before diving straight into the actual learning, let's take a closer look at some features that can be quickly noticed from the very beginning of your journey.

Use of Formal/Informal

As you probably know, English speakers do not have many opportunities, as far as using formal forms of address is concerned. In Polish, however, formality is of great importance. The biggest difference between these languages can be observed in situations that require using the second person singular or plural (*you*). When addressing somebody that is not a friend or relative, Polish speakers use *Pan/Pani* instead of *you* (*Pan* is for men, and *Pani* is for women).

For example, "Could *you* tell me what time it is?" would be "Czy mógłby *Pan* mi powiedzieć która jest godzina?" or "Czy mogłaby *Pani* powiedzieć mi która jest godzina?" What is more, the second person plural involves using a different formal form so that the above sentence would look like this: "Czy mogliby *Państwo* powiedzieć mi która jest godzina?" Interestingly, if you have known someone for a while in Poland, you can suggest "*przejście na ty*" which literally means "*switching to you [form]*".

Use of Masculine/Feminine

As mentioned, the Polish language differs from English significantly in the field of gender, since Polish masculine, feminine or neuter do not correspond with the actual sex. To be more precise, the Polish language has grammatical gender, whereas English has biological gender. What is even more interesting is that Polish speakers use masculine or feminine often when talking about inanimate objects such as pieces of furniture or fruit.

For example, the Polish word *banan* [banana] is masculine, the word *truskawka* [strawberry] is feminine, and the word *mango* [mango] is neutral. Indeed, as presented above, a category has nothing to do with the actual gender, which is one of the most difficult concepts to grasp by non-native Polish language learners.

Use of Singular/Plural

As far as the grammatical number is concerned, Polish singular or plural are usually formed with different endings that correspond with gender. In the Polish plural form, there are only two genders—masculine and non-masculine. By comparison, English plural involves the ending -s with only a few exceptions, whereas Polish plural involves endings such as -y, -i, -e, or -a. To make matters worse, the usage of these endings is not determined by any rules.

For example, the word *dom* [house] is masculine, yet it is an object. Then its plural form *domy* [houses] involves the ending -y. The word *mężczyzna* [man] is masculine and refers to a person. Its plural form *mężczyźni* [men] ends with -i. As you can see, there are more popular patterns, yet no clear principles can be distinguished as far as endings are concerned.

Nouns and Polish Cases

Unfortunately, there are seven (yes, seven!) cases in the Polish language, and they all require using different endings attached to a particular noun. English speakers usually consider a variety of cases as one of the most difficult concepts. In fact, it is not only English non-natives that face many problems while acquiring this concept—since all these problematic suffixes that form Polish cases are hard to remember. However, before being too hard on yourself, please note that using a wrong case does not significantly affect communication. Although mastering the rules can be worthwhile, aiming at perfection can be daunting, especially at the beginning of your journey. Remember: if you apply a wrong suffix, your message will be 99 percent understandable anyway.

Let's take a closer look at the words *książka* [book] and *komputer* [computer] to get familiar with the concept of Polish cases:

Nominative - książ*ka*

Genitive - książ*ki*

Dative - książ*ce*

Accusative - książ*kę*

Ablative - (z) książ*ką*

Locative - (o) książ*ce*

Vocative - książ*ko!*

Nominative - komput*er*

Genitive - komput*era*

Dative - komput*erowi*

Accusative - komput*er*

Ablative - (z) komput*erem*

Locative - (o) komput*erze*

Vocative - komput*erze!*

As you can see, some of the endings look similar, yet no clear rules can be applied as far as the suffixes are concerned. Some of the Polish loanwords (for example *kakao* [cacao], *logo* [logo] or *wideo* [video]) are not to be declined by case and stay in the same form, yet they constitute only a small percentage of the Polish lexicon. It is advisable to learn the cases gradually, in context, and by using associations. If you try to learn all variations of the same word by heart, you will find yourself overwhelmed sooner or later—so don't worry.

Countable and Uncountable Nouns

While the concept of uncountable nouns is a standard in English, it is not that popular in Polish. To be more precise, Polish speakers do not distinguish countable and uncountable things; they apply the singular or plural rather intuitively. Nouns that are uncountable in English (such as information, advice or furniture) can be singular or plural in Polish. Let's take a look at some examples:

"Czy możesz dać mi te informacje?" can be literally translated as "Could you give me these informations?"

"Co oznacza ta informacja?" can be literally translated as "What does this information mean?"

"Czy możesz udzielić mi porady?" can be translated as "Could you give me any advice?"

"Nie chcę twoich rad!" can be literally translated as "I don't want your advices!"

"Jeśli idziesz do sklepu, kup trzy mleka" can be literally translated as "If you go to the grocery store, buy three milks." [you don't have to say *cartons/bottles of milk*, just *milks*]

"Piję kawę z mlekiem" can be translated as "I drink coffee with milk."

"Ten mebel nie podoba mi się" can be translated as "I don't like this furniture."

"Te meble nie podobają mi się" can be literally translated as "I don't like these furnitures." [you don't have to say *pieces of furniture*, just *furnitures*].

Looking at the examples above, you can easily notice that some English uncountable nouns can be pluralized in Polish. Interestingly, Polish speakers have some difficulties with learning uncountable nouns; they very often make mistakes such as *informations, advices, furnitures* or *moneys.*

Proper Nouns

In Polish, proper nouns are also influenced by heavy declension. To be more precise, almost all proper names correspond with gender, number, and case. For instance, some countries (such as *Egipt* [Egypt], *Izrael* [Israel] or *Meksyk* [Mexico]) are masculine, some are feminine (*Kanada* [Canada], *Wielka Brytania* [Great Britain], *Francja* [France]), some are neutral (*Kongo* [Congo], *Chile* [Chile], *Fidżi* [Fiji]), and some are always plural (*Niemcy* [Germany], *Włochy* [Italy], *Stany Zjednoczone* [the United States]). What is even more interesting is that all proper nouns are subordinate to all seven cases, so this means that they can appear with different inflectional endings.

Let's look at one country from each gender category:

Meksyk [Mexico] – masculine noun

Nominative – Meksyk (<u>Meksyk</u> jest pięknym krajem. – Mexico is a beautiful country.)

Genitive – Meksyku (Na mojej mapie nie ma <u>Meksyku</u>. – There's no Mexico on my map.)

Dative – Meksykowi (Przyglądam się pięknemu <u>Meksykowi</u>. – I am looking at beautiful Mexico.)

Accusative – Meksyk (Widzę <u>Meksyk</u> na horyzoncie. – I'm seeing Mexico on the horizon.)

Ablative – (z) Meksykiem (Wraz z <u>Meksykiem</u>, USA leżą w Ameryce Północnej. – Along with Mexico, USA is located in North America.)

Locative – (o) Meksyku (Cały czas myślę o <u>Meksyku</u>. – I'm thinking about Mexico all the time.)

Vocative – Meksyku! (<u>Meksyku</u>, moja ojczyzno! – Mexico, my homeland!)

Francja [France] – feminine noun

Nominative – Francja

Genitive – Francji

Dative – Francji

Accusative – Francję

Ablative – (z) Francją

Locative – (o) Francji

Vocative – Francjo!

Włochy [Italy] – plural noun

Nominative – Włochy

Genitive – Włoch

Dative – Włochom

Accusative – Włochy

Ablative – (z) Włochami

Locative – (o) Włoszech

Vocative – Włochy!

Kongo [Congo] – neutral noun

Nominative – Kongo

Genitive – Konga

Dative – Kongu

Accusative – Kongo

Ablative – (z) Kongiem

Locative – (o) Kongu

Vocative – Kongo!

The cases do not influence some of the proper names (such as Fidżi, Chile). This means that they do not change form and do not require different endings.

Polish Verbs

Verbs in the Polish language are a quite complex phenomenon since different groups require different declensions. This means no one universal pattern could apply to all verbs. Polish verbs correspond with **gender, number, and person**. To show how they work, let's analyze the present forms of *iść* [to go], *mieć* [to have], *być* [to be].

iść [to go]

Ja [I] - idę

Ty [you] - idziesz

On [he] - idzie

Ona [she] - idzie

Ono [it] - idzie

My [we] - idziemy

Wy [you] - idziecie

Oni [they masc.] - idą

One [they fem.] - idą

mieć [to have]

Ja [I] - mam

Ty [you] – masz

On [he] – ma

Ona [she] – ma

Ono [it] – ma

My [we] – mamy

Wy [you] – macie

Oni [they masc.] – mają

One [they fem.] – mają

być [to be]

Ja [I] – jestem

Ty [you] – jesteś

On [he] – jest

Ona [she] – jest

Ono [it] – jest

My [we] – jesteśmy

Wy [you] – jesteście

Oni [they masc.] – są

One [they fem.] – są

Polish contains only two aspects—**perfective** (that indicates completed action) and **imperfective** (that indicates uncompleted action). It is important to note that both aspects do not refer to the past only. You can apply the perfective or imperfective to the future as well.

Let's look at the verb *robić* [do] in the past form:

robić [to do] – imperfective

Ja [I] – robiłem (m.) / robiłam (f.)

Ty [you] – robiłeś (m.) / robiłaś (f.)

On [he] – robił

Ona [she] – robiła

Ono [it] – robiło

My [we] – robiliśmy (m.) / robiłyśmy (f.)

Wy [you] – robiliście (m.) / robiłyście (f.)

Oni [they masc.] – robili

One [they fem.] – robiły

robić [to do] – perfective

Ja [I] – zrobiłem (m.) / zrobiłam (f.)

Ty [you] – zrobiłeś (m.) / zrobiłaś (f.)

On [he] – zrobił

Ona [she] – zrobiła

Ono [it] – zrobiło

My [we] – zrobiliśmy (m.) / zrobiłyśmy (f.)

Wy [you] – zrobiliście (m.) / zrobiłyście (f.)

Oni [they masc.] – zrobili

One [they fem.] – zrobiły

Wczoraj naprawiłem samochód. – I fixed the car yesterday. (The action was completed; the car was fixed)

Wczoraj naprawiałem samochód. – I was fixing the car yesterday. (The car wasn't necessarily finished)

Jutro naprawię samochód. – I will fix the car tomorrow. (This means that I will completely fix the car)

Jutro będę naprawiał samochód. – I will be fixing the car tomorrow. (This means that I may not finish the action tomorrow)

You may compare the imperfective aspect with the English progressive, yet these are different concepts, so don't rely completely on such comparison. It is advisable to learn the use of perfective and imperfective naturally and in context. Learning off by heart will not give you the best results. Thus, these examples and declensions are here only to show you how the Polish verbs work in practice.

Essential Polish Verbs

Być – to be (Jestem Paula. – I am Paula.)

Mieć – to have (Mam kota. – I have a cat)

Iść – to go (Idę do sklepu. – I'm going to the store)

Robić – to do / to make (Robię zakupy. – I'm doing shopping)

Próbować – to try (Próbowałem wiele razy. – I've tried many times)

Pomagać – to help (Pomagam tacie. – I'm helping my dad.)

Grać / bawić się – to play (Lubię bawić się na dworze. – I like playing outside.)

Spacerować – to walk (Lubisz spacerować? – Do you like walking?)

Uczyć się – to learn (W szkole muszę się uczyć. – I have to learn at school.)

Mieszkać – to live (Mieszkam w mieście. – I live in a city.)

Pracować – to work (Pracuję w dużej firmie. – I work in a big company.)

Jeść – to eat (Chodźmy coś zjeść! – Let's go eat something!)

Pić – to drink (Ona wypiła już kawę. – She has already drunk her coffee.)

Pisać – to write (Piszę e-mail. – I'm writing an e-mail.)

Czytać – to read (On czyta książkę. – He's reading a book.)

Liczyć – to count (Mogę na ciebie liczyć? – Can I count on you?)

Rysować – to draw (Uczę się rysować. – I'm learning how to draw.)

Malować – to paint (Oni malują. – They're painting.)

Widzieć – to see (Nie widzę go. – I can't see him.)

Wyglądać / spoglądać - to look (Dobrze wyglądasz! - You look good!)

Oglądać - to watch (Oglądam telewizję - I'm watching TV)

Słyszeć - to hear (Usłyszałem dziwny głos. - I've just heard a strange voice)

Słuchać - to listen (Słuchamy muzyki. - We're listening to music.)

Spać - to sleep (Idę spać. - I'm going to sleep.)

Gotować - to cook (Umiesz gotować? - Can you cook?)

Sprzątać - to clean (Muszę dzisiaj sprzątać mieszkanie. - I have to clean the flat today.)

Podróżować - to travel (Podrózuję do Chin. - I'm traveling to China.)

Jechać - to drive (Jadę do domu. - I'm driving home.)

Latać - to fly (Chciałbyś polecieć do Londynu? - Would you like to fly to London?)

Pływać - to swim (Nie umiem pływać. - I can't swim.)

Biegać - to run (Ona teraz biega. - She's running now.)

Siedzieć - to sit (Usiądźcie. - Sit down.)

Rozpoczynać - to begin (Przedstawienie zaczyna się o 8:00. - The show begins at 8 AM.)

Stać - to stand (Stań tutaj. - Stand here.)

Kłaść - to put (Gdzie mogę położyć tę paczkę? - Where can I put this parcel?)

Wychodzić - to leave (Właśnie wychodziliśmy. - We were just leaving.)

Przychodzić - to come (Przyjdź do mojego biura o 9:00. - Come to my office at 9 AM.)

Śpiewać - to sing (Nie umiem śpiewać. - I can't sing.)

Tańczyć – to dance (Zatańczymy? – Shall we dance?)

Pamiętać – to remember (Pamiętaj o mnie. – Remember about me.)

Zapominać – to forget (Zapomniałem o spotkaniu! – I've just forgotten about the meeting!)

Wybierać – to choose (Wybierz jedną opcję. – Choose one option.)

Zamykać – to close (Zamknij drzwi, proszę. – Close the door, please.)

Otwierać – to open (Czy mógłbyś otworzyć okno? – Could you open the window?)

Tworzyć – to create (Stwórzmy własny projekt! – Let's create our own project!)

Budować – to build (On buduje dom. – He's building a house.)

Pokazywać / przedstawiać – to show (Pokażesz mi? – Can you show me?)

Czuć – to feel (Czuję się dobrze. – I feel good.)

Czuć / wąchać – to smell (Czuję coś dziwnego. – I'm smelling something strange.)

Smakować / próbować – to taste (Spróbuj tej zupy. – Taste this soup.)

Myśleć – to think (Myślę, że... – I think that...)

Rosnąć – to grow (Dzieci rosną bardzo szybko. – Children grow very fast.)

Myć – to wash (Muszę umyć samochód. – I need to wash my car.)

Wierzyć – to believe (Wierzę, że... – I believe that...)

Mówić – to speak (Mów głośniej! – Speak up!)

Powiedzieć – to say (Powiedz coś! – Say something!)

Rozmawiać - to talk (Możemy teraz porozmawiać? - Can we talk now?)

Dawać - to give (Czy mógłbyś mi to dać? - Could you give me this?)

Brać - to take (Muszę wziąć dzień wolnego. - I have to take a day off.)

Pożyczać - to borrow (Pożyczysz mi swój samochód? - Could you borrow me your car?)

Pożyczać - to lend (Pożyczę ci mój samochód. - I will borrow you my car.)

Skakać - to jump (On skacze bardzo wysoko. - He's jumping very high.)

Odejść - to quit (Odchodzę! - I quit!)

Uderzyć - to hit (Mocno mnie uderzyła!- She hit me hard!)

Strzelać - to shoot (Strzelaj! - Shoot!)

Kupować - to buy (Chcę kupić nowy samochód. - I want to buy a new car.)

Sprzedawać - to sell (Muszę sprzedać dom. - I have to sell my house.)

Wymieniać - to exchange (Czy mogę wymienić pieniądze? - Can I exchange my money?)

Wygrywać - to win (Moja drużyna wygrała zawody! - My team won the competition!)

Przegrywać - to lose (moja drużyna przegrała zawody - My team lost the competition.)

Rozumieć - to understand (Rozumiesz? - Do you understand?)

Uczyć - to teach (Uczę w szkole podstawowej. - I teach at primary school.)

Łapać - to catch (Łap piłkę! - Catch the ball!)

Reflexive Verbs

As you probably know, some verbs require using reflexive pronouns, such as *myself, yourself* or *themselves*. These verbs usually require the same person to be the doer of the activity and the object. In Polish, such verbs are created by adding the word "się". You don't need to add different pronouns since the main verb is already inflected. Let's compare Polish *myć się* and English *to wash oneself*, to make it more understandable:

myć się – to wash oneself

Ja myję się – I wash myself

Ty myjesz się – You wash yourself

On myje się – He washes himself

Ona myje się – She washes herself

Ono myje się – It washes itself

My myjemy się – We wash ourselves

Wy myjecie się – You wash yourselves

Oni myją się (masc.) – They wash themselves

One myją się (fem.) – They wash themselves

Looking at the examples, you can easily notice that each version of the Polish verb contains the word *się*. This word is used instead of the English *myself, yourself*, etc. As a matter of fact, the Polish verb doesn't need to be accompanied by a special pronoun—since the information about the doer of the activity is implicit in the main verb (to be more precise, in the inflectional ending). To sum up, you just need to add *się* to the activity in order to create a reflexive verb. Pretty easy, isn't it?

Tenses

The concept of Polish tenses is significantly different from English—since in Polish we can choose only between the past, present or future. When it comes to the present, we can have different situations with the same structure:

Myję zęby każdego dnia. - I brush my teeth every day.

Myję zęby teraz. - I am brushing my teeth now.

Myję zęby od siedmiu lat. - I have brushed my teeth for seven years.

Myję zęby od siedmiu lat - I have been brushing my teeth for seven years.

Robię zadania domowe w weekendy. - I do my homework on weekends.

Robię zadania domowe. - I am doing my homework.

Robię zadania domowe odkąd poszedłem do szkoły - I have been doing my homework since I went to school.

Robię zadania domowe odkąd poszedłem do szkoły - I have done my homework since I went to school.

As you can see above, the Polish language does not contain the distinction between the simple present, the continuous aspect, and the perfect aspect. All concepts are expressed similarly. As far as the past is concerned, you can notice a similar pattern:

Zrobiłem zadanie domowe wczoraj. - *I did* my homework yesterday.

Robiłem zadanie domowe kiedy zadzwonił telefon. - *I was doing* my homework when the telephone rang.

Zrobiłem właśnie zadanie domowe. - *I have just done* my homework.

Nie wiedziałem czemu dostałem 1, ponieważ _zrobiłem_ zadanie domowe. - I didn't know why I got an E because I _had done_ my homework.

You can clearly notice almost the same forms of the verb (the slight changes result from the perfective or imperfective aspect) in Polish sentences, no matter what situation they refer to. Now, let's focus on some examples of situations that are correlated with the future:

Zrobię zadanie domowe. - _I will do_ my homework.

Zrobię zadanie domowe zanim mama przyjedzie. - _I will have done_ my homework by the time my mom comes back.

Free Word Order

Unlike English, that requires a fixed word order in a sentence, the Polish language is not that strict. The abundance of inflectional endings allows Polish speakers the opportunity to put the same words in different combinations. Therefore, the same sentence can be built in multiple ways since there is no requirement for the subject-verb-object pattern.

Let's look at some examples to see how the free word order works:

"I'm going to the cinema with my girlfriend this evening."

– Idę do kina z moją dziewczyną dziś wieczorem. (I'm going to the cinema with my girlfriend this evening).

– Idę do kina dziś wieczorem z moją dziewczyną. (I'm going to the cinema this evening with my girlfriend.)

– Idę dziś wieczorem do kina z moją dziewczyną. (I'm going this evening to the cinema with my girlfriend.)

– Idę z moją dziewczyną do kina dziś wieczorem. (I'm going with my girlfriend to the cinema this evening.)

– Idę dziś wieczorem z moją dziewczyną do kina. (I'm going this evening with my girlfriend to the cinema.)

- Dziś wieczorem do kina idę z moją dziewczyną. (This evening to the cinema I'm going with my girlfriend.)

- Dziś wieczorem z moją dziewczyną idę do kina. (This evening with my girlfriend I'm going to the cinema.)

- Dziś wieczorem idę do kina z moją dziewczyną. (This evening I'm going to the cinema with my girlfriend.)

- Do kina idę dziś wieczorem z moją dziewczyną. (To the cinema I'm going this evening with my girlfriend.)

- Do kina z moją dziewczyną idę dziś wieczorem. (To the cinema with my girlfriend I'm going this evening.)

- Z moją dziewczyną idę dziś wieczorem do kina. (With my girlfriend I'm going this evening to the cinema.)

- Z moją dziewczyną do kina idę dziś wieczorem. (With my girlfriend to the cinema I'm going this evening.)

Although some of the combinations presented above can be used in English, there are grammatically incorrect ones—since they do not follow the subject-verb-object pattern. For example, the sentence *"With my girlfriend I'm going this evening to the cinema."* looks really strange for English speakers. In Polish, all sentences are grammatically correct, yet there are some more popular patterns. It is important to note that some of the combinations are used only in casual, informal speech, and some of them are more popular in writing (sentences that follow the subject-verb-object pattern appear in writing in most cases).

Double Negation

While expressing double negation in English is impossible (or indicative of certain social groups), it is a common standard in Polish. Polish speakers use this structure on a daily basis in speech, and what is even more interesting, in writing.

Let's analyze a few examples, to see how double negation works:

"Nic nie kupiłem" can be literally translated as "I didn't buy nothing."

"Nie ma niczego" can be literally translated as "There isn't nothing."

"Nic nie robię" can be literally translated as "I am not doing nothing."

"Nigdy nie byłem w Chinach" can be literally translated as "I haven't never been to China."

Taking a deeper look at the above examples, you can notice that Polish double negation is expressed by a verb in a negative form along with a pronoun that carries a negative meaning (such as *nic* [nothing], *nigdy* [never]). What is interesting is that the phenomenon of double negation can be found in the other Slavic languages, such as Czech or Russian.

Articles

Use of articles represents another significant difference between English and Polish. Generally, there are neither definite nor indefinite articles in Polish, which is quite interesting. Unfortunately, Polish learners of English face many difficulties while learning the articles—since it is a concept really difficult to grasp. In fact, despite knowing the rules and exceptions, even advanced and proficient Polish speakers of English cannot fully understand articles, and what is more, they usually cannot apply them intuitively.

Personal Pronouns

English appears to contain only a few personal pronouns when compared to Polish. Why? The answer is pretty simple—Polish personal pronouns are inflected by case, gender, and number.

Let's see how it works in practice:

I (Ja) – Me

[Nominative] ja

[Genitive] mnie

[Dative] – mi/mnie

[Accusative] – mnie

[Ablative] – (ze) mną

[Locative] – (o) mnie

[Vocative] – ja!

You (Ty) – You

[Nominative] ty

[Genitive] cię/ciebie

[Dative] – ci/tobie

[Accusative] – cię/ciebie

[Ablative] - (z) tobą

[Locative] - (o) tobie

[Vocative] - ty!

He (On) - Him

[Nominative] on

[Genitive] jego/niego

[Dative] - jemu/mu/niemu

[Accusative] - jego/go/niego

[Ablative] - (z) nim

[Locative] - (o) nim

[Vocative] - on!

She (Ona) - Her

[Nominative] ona

[Genitive] jej/niej

[Dative] - jej/niej

[Accusative] - ją/nią

[Ablative] - (z) nią

[Locative] - (o) niej

[Vocative] - ona!

It (Ono) - Its

[Nominative] ono

[Genitive] jego/go/niego

[Dative] - jemu/mu/niemu

[Accusative] - je/nie

[Ablative] - (z) nim

[Locative] - (o) nim

[Vocative] - ono!

We (My) – Us

[Nominative] my

[Genitive] nas

[Dative] – nam

[Accusative] – nas

[Ablative] – (z) nami

[Locative] – (o) nas

[Vocative] – my!

You (Wy) – You

[Nominative] wy

[Genitive] was

[Dative] – wam

[Accusative] – was

[Ablative] – (z) wami

[Locative] – (o) was

[Vocative] – wy!

They (Oni/One) – Them

[Nominative] oni / one

[Genitive] ich / ich

[Dative] – im / im

[Accusative] – ich / je

[Ablative] – (z) nimi / nimi

[Locative] – (o) nich / nich

[Vocative] – oni! / one!

To sum up, there are many different personal pronouns in the Polish language. However, do not learn the examples above by heart; it won't work. Instead, try to immerse yourself in the language—read, listen and try to speak. The more you use your language in context, the more unintentional is your use of inflections. Every time you need some help with the pronouns, go back to the examples above.

Demonstratives

The Polish principles of using demonstratives are almost similar to the English equivalents because they work to refer to something near or far from the speaker. However, the most important difference involves declination—since Polish demonstrative adjectives correspond with a **number, gender, and case.**

Let's see how they work in practice:

This: (masculine / feminine / neuter)

[Nominative] ten / ta / to

[Genitive] tego / tej / tego

[Dative] - temu / tej / temu

[Accusative] - ten / tę / to

[Ablative] - (z) tym / tą / tym

[Locative] - (o) tym / tej / tym

[Vocative] - ten! / ta! / to!

Those: (masculine / feminine / neuter)

[Nominative] tamten / tamta / tamto

[Genitive] tamtego / tamtej / tamtego

[Dative] - tamtemu / tamtej / tamtemu

[Accusative] – tamten / tamtą / tamto

[Ablative] – (z) tamtym / tamtą / tamtym

[Locative] – (o) tamtym / tamtej / tamtym

[Vocative] – tamten! / tamta! / tamto!

These: (masculine / non-masculine)

[Nominative] – ci / te

[Genitive] – tych / tych

[Dative] – tym / tym

[Accusative] – tych / te

[Ablative] – (z) tymi / tymi

[Locative] – (o) tych / tych

[Vocative] – ci! / te!

Those: (masculine / non-masculine)

[Nominative] – tamci / tamte

[Genitive] – tamtych / tamtych

[Dative] – tamtym / tamtym

[Accusative] – tamtych / tamte

[Ablative] – (z) tamtymi / tamtymi

[Locative] – (o) tamtych / tamtych

[Vocative] – tamci! / tamte!

As you can see above, Polish demonstratives are quite a challenge because they change according to gender and case. What can be clearly noticed from the beginning is that the demonstrative has the prefix *tam-* when referring to something far from the speaker. As in the case of learning Polish cases, it is advisable to learn demonstratives (or any items that require heavy declension) in context and gradually, so as not to become quickly overwhelmed by the amount of the material.

Let's take a look at some examples to see how demonstratives work in practice:

Ten chłopak mi się podoba - I like this guy.

Nie chcę tego jeść! - I don't want to eat that!

Ta koszula nie wygląda dobrze. - This shirt doesn't look good.

Chciałbym kupić tamtą lampę. - I would like to buy that lamp.

Tamten koleś wygląda dziwnie. - That guy looks weird.

Just as in English, we can use demonstratives to refer to a specific period of time. However, there is a slight difference in forming such construction—since Polish usually requires using different cases and prepositions. Here are some examples:

w tym tygodniu - this week (Polish construction requires locative case and preposition w [in]. This structure can be literally translated as [in this week]).

w tym roku - this year (Again, Polish construction requires locative case and preposition w [in]. This structure can be literally translated as [in this year]).

o tej porze roku - at this time of the year (In this case, the English phrase requires using a preposition as well. The Polish structure is the same).

w tym miesiącu - this month (Polish construction requires locative case and preposition w [in], as in the examples above. This structure can be literally translated as [in this month]).

Possessives

As you probably know, English possessives look different, depending on the kind of possessive. In other words, there are possessive adjectives (such as *my, your*) and possessive pronouns (such as *mine, yours*). In contrast to English, Polish possessive adjectives look the same as possessive pronouns, yet unfortunately, they are declined by gender, number, and case. What is important to know is **that Polish possessives change according to the noun of the object possessed and the person it's possessed by** (look at the third person singular [his, her, its], for example). The best way to learn them is to see how they work in actual sentences—since, without the context, learning will not be efficient. At first, let's take a look at **possessives correlated with the singular form of a noun that is possessed:**

my/mine [sing.] (masculine / feminine / neutral)

[Nominative] mój / moja / moje

[Genitive] mojego / mojej / mojego

[Dative] - mojemu / mojej / mojemu

[Accusative] - mój / moją / moje

[Ablative] - (z) moim / moją / moim

[Locative] - (o) moim / mojej / moim

[Vocative] – mój! / moja! / moje!

your/yours [sing.] (masculine / feminine / neutral)

[Nominative] twój / twoja / twoje

[Genitive] twojego / twojej / twojego

[Dative] – twojemu / twojej / twojemu

[Accusative] – twój / twoją / twoje

[Ablative] – (z) twoim / twoją / twoim

[Locative] – (o) twoim / twojej / twoim

[Vocative] – twój! / twoja! / twoje!

our/ours [pl.] (masculine / feminine / neutral)

[Nominative] nasz / nasza / nasze

[Genitive] naszego / naszej / naszego

[Dative] – naszemu / naszej / naszemu

[Accusative] – nasz / naszą / nasze

[Ablative] – (z) naszym / naszą / naszym

[Locative] – (o) naszym / naszej / naszym

[Vocative] – nasz! / nasza! / nasze!

your/yours [pl.] (masculine / feminine / neutral)

[Nominative] wasz / wasza / wasze

[Genitive] waszego / waszej / waszego

[Dative] – waszemu / waszej / waszemu

[Accusative] – wasz / waszą / wasze

[Ablative] – (z) waszym / waszą / waszym

[Locative] – (o) waszym / waszej / waszym

[Vocative] – wasz! / wasza! / wasze!

their/theirs [pl.] (masculine / feminine / neutral)

[Nominative] ich / ich / tych

[Genitive] ich / ich / tych

[Dative] - ich / ich / tych

[Accusative] - ich / ich / tych

[Ablative] - (z) ich / ich / tych

[Locative] - (o) ich / ich / tych

[Vocative] - ich! / ich! / tych!

To sum up, there are a few patterns that can be noticed after taking a closer look at the examples above. Firstly, third person singular and third person plural does not require adding different endings; each form looks the same (*jego, jej, jego, ich*). As far as other persons are concerned, you can easily notice that "the basis" of given possessive changes, yet the endings remain nearly the same (there are only a few exceptions). Thus, all you need to do is learn some patterns instead of memorizing long tables of declensions. What is more, these endings look nearly the same not only in possessives but also in demonstratives, adjectives and other important items that are correlated with the noun. Indeed, Polish may look overwhelming at the beginning; however, some strategies make you learn faster and easier.

Now, let's look at **the possessives that are correlated with the plural form of a noun that is possessed** (we will skip third person singular and third person plural—since, in both situations, possessive forms are the same [*jego, jej, jego, ich*]):

My/mine (masculine / non-masculine)

[Nominative] - moi / moje

[Genitive] - moich / moich

[Dative] - moim / moim

[Accusative] - moich / moje

[Ablative] - (z) moimi / moimi

[Locative] - (o) moich / moich

[Vocative] – moi! / moje!

your/yours (masculine / non-masculine)

[Nominative] – twoi / twoje

[Genitive] – twoich / twoich

[Dative] – twoim / twoim

[Accusative] – twoich / twoje

[Ablative] – (z) twoimi / twoimi

[Locative] – (o) twoich / twoich

[Vocative] – twoi! / twoje!

our/ours (masculine / non-masculine)

[Nominative] – nasi / nasze

[Genitive] – naszych / naszych

[Dative] – naszym / naszym

[Accusative] – naszych / nasze

[Ablative] – (z) naszymi / naszymi

[Locative] – (o) naszych / naszych

[Vocative] – nasi! / nasze!

your/yours (masculine / non-masculine)

[Nominative] – wasi / wasze

[Genitive] – waszych / waszych

[Dative] – waszym / waszym

[Accusative] – waszych / wasze

[Ablative] – (z) waszymi / waszymi

[Locative] – (o) waszych / waszych

[Vocative] – wasi! / wasze!

As you can see above, the same patterns can be observed in the plural form of the possessed noun. All the presented declensions are not to discourage you from learning; they are to make you notice the repeatability and some interesting formulas. The more you practice your target language in a real context, the more automatic your use of the heavy declined items.

Let's take a look at some possessives in sentences:

Mój długopis - my pen (masculine noun, singular)

Ten długopis jest <u>mój</u>. - This pen is mine. (masculine noun, singular)

Twoja torebka - your bag (feminine noun, singular)

Ta torebka jest twoja. - This bag is yours. (feminine noun, singular)

Jego dziecko - his child (neutral noun, singular)

To dziecko jest jego. - This child is his. (neutral noun, singular)

Jej naszyjnik - her necklace (masculine noun, singular)

Ten naszyjnik jest jej. - This necklace is hers. (masculine noun, singular)

Nasz dom - our house (masculine noun, singular)

To jest nasz dom. - This is our house. (masculine noun, singular)

Wasza szafa - your wardrobe (feminine noun, singular)

Ta szafa jest wasza. - This wardrobe is yours. (feminine noun, singular)

Ich samochód - their car (masculine noun, singular)

Ten samochód jest ich. - This car is theirs. (masculine noun, singular)

Now let's take a look at the plural forms of the same nouns:

Moje długopisy - my pens (masculine noun, plural)

Te długopisy są moje. - These pens are mine. (masculine noun, plural)

Twoje torebki - your bags (non-masculine noun, plural)

Te torebki są twoje. – These bags are yours. (non-masculine noun, plural)

Jego dzieci – his children (non-masculine noun, plural)

Te dzieci są jego. – These children are his. (non-masculine noun, plural)

Jej naszyjniki – her necklaces (masculine noun, plural)

Te naszyjniki są jej. – These necklaces are hers. (masculine noun, plural)

Nasze domy – our houses (masculine noun, plural)

To są nasze domy. – These are our houses. (masculine noun, plural)

Wasze szafy – your wardrobes (non-masculine noun, plural)

Te szafy są wasze. – These wardrobes are yours. (non-masculine noun, plural)

Ich samochody – their cars (masculine noun, plural)

Te samochody są ich. – These cars are theirs. (masculine noun, plural)

Adjectives

Polish adjectives, just as the nouns, are declined by gender, number, and case. However, the adjectives depend directly on the noun they describe. In other words, they have the same gender, number and case as the noun they refer to. You don't need to memorize all the complex declensions—they are here only to show you some processes in the target language. It is advisable to create your adjective intuitively and in context, provided you are more or less familiar with the patterns. Otherwise, you will drown in the sea of different endings sooner or later. To see how the process works, let's analyze the adjective *mały* [small] with different nouns:

mały samochód – a small car (masculine noun, singular)

[Nominative] mały samochód

[Genitive] małego samochodu

[Dative] – małemu samochodowi

[Accusative] – mały samochód

[Ablative] – (z) małym samochodem

[Locative] – (o) małym samochodzie

[Vocative] – mały samochodzie!

Mała dziewczynka – a small girl (feminine noun, singular)

[Nominative] mała dziewczynka

[Genitive] małej dziewczynki

[Dative] – małej dziewczynce

[Accusative] – małą dziewczynkę

[Ablative] – (z) małą dziewczynką

[Locative] – (o) małej dziewczynce

[Vocative] – mała dziewczynko!

Małe dziecko – a small child (neutral noun, singular)

[Nominative] małe dziecko

[Genitive] małego dziecka

[Dative] – małemu dziecku

[Accusative] – małe dziecko

[Ablative] – (z) małym dzieckiem

[Locative] – (o) małym dziecku

[Vocative] – małe dziecko!

małe samochody – small cars (masculine noun, plural)

[Nominative] małe samochody

[Genitive] małych samochodów

[Dative] – małym samochodom

[Accusative] – małe samochody

[Ablative] – (z) małymi samochodami

[Locative] – (o) małych samochodach

[Vocative] – małe samochody!

Małe dzieci – small children (non-masculine noun, plural)

[Nominative] małe dzieci

[Genitive] małych dzieci

[Dative] – małym dzieciom

[Accusative] – małe dzieci

[Ablative] – (z) małymi dziećmi

[Locative] – (o) małych dzieciach

[Vocative] – małe dzieci!

Essential Polish Adjectives

Polish adjectives are created on the basis of similar rules. There are comparative adjectives and superlative adjectives and both of them are built differently depending on their length. Of course, there are some exceptions. At first, let's look at short adjectives and their gradation:

Długi (long) - dłuższy (longer) - najdłuższy (the longest)

Krótki (short) - krótszy (shorter) - najkrótszy (the shortest)

Niski (low) - niższy (lower) - najniższy (the lowest)

Chudy (skinny) - chudszy (skinnier) - najchudszy (the skinniest)

Ciepły (warm) - cieplejszy (warmer) - najcieplejszy (the warmest)

Zimny (cold) - zimniejszy (colder) - najzimniejszy (the coldest)

Jasny (light) - jaśniejszy (lighter) - najjaśniejszy (the lightest)

Ciemny (dark) - ciemniejszy (darker) - najciemniejszy (the darkest)

Miły (nice) - milszy (nicer) - najmilszy (the nicest)

Szczęśliwy (happy) - szczęśliwszy (happier) - najszczęśliwszy (the happiest)

Smutny (sad) - smutniejszy (sadder) - najsmutniejszy (the saddest)

Młody (young) - młodszy (younger) - najmłodszy (the youngest)

Stary (old) – starszy (older) – najstarszy (the oldest)

Nowy (new) – nowszy (newer) – najnowszy (the newest)

Śmieszny (funny) – śmieszniejszy (funnier) – najśmieszniejszy (the funniest)

Fajny (cool) – fajniejszy (cooler) – najfajniejszy (the coolest)

Gruby (fat) – grubszy (fatter) – najgrubszy (the fattest)

Ciężki (heavy) – cięższy (heavier) – najcięższy (the heaviest)

Silny (strong) – silniejszy (stronger) – najsilniejszy (the strongest)

Słaby (weak) – słabszy (weaker) – najsłabszy (the weakest)

Późny (late) – późniejszy (later) – najpóźniejszy (the latest)

Wczesny (early) – wcześniejszy (earlier) – najwcześniejszy (the earliest)

Twardy (hard) – twardszy (harder) – najtwardszy (the hardest)

Miękki (soft) – miększy (softer) – najmiększy (the softest)

Tani (cheap) – tańszy (cheaper) – najtańszy (the cheapest)

Biały (white) – bielszy (whiter) – najbielszy (the whitest)

Mądry (smart) – mądrzejszy (smarter) – najmądrzejszy (the smartest)

As you can guess from the examples, Polish comparative adjectives are created by adding the ending *-szy*. Unfortunately, along with adding the suffix, some of the adjectives undergo some major changes in their stems. Superlative adjectives are created by adding the prefix *naj-* to the comparative adjective. The examples below show that some Polish adjectives require different rules of gradation when compared to the English ones:

Drogi (expensive) – droższy (more expensive) – najdroższy (the most expensive)

Piękny (beautiful) – piękniejszy (more beautiful) – najpiękniejszy (the most beautiful)

Ważny (important) - ważniejszy (more important) - najważniejszy (the most important)

Some adjectives in Polish require the so-called descriptive gradation (the equivalent of English more ... the most ...). However, the rules are not the same. Remember that English adjectives are graded in the descriptive way when they have more than two syllables. When it comes to Polish, the descriptive gradation can be used with both short and long adjectives. What is more, some adjectives have regular gradation and the descriptive gradation as well:

Inteligentny (intelligent) - bardziej inteligentny (more intelligent) - najbardziej inteligentny (the most intelligent)

Inteligentny - inteligentniejszy - najinteligentniejszy

Popularny (popular) - popularniejszy (more popular) - najpopularniejszy (the most popular)

Popularny - bardziej popularny - najbardziej popularny

Zielony (green) - bardziej zielony (greener) - najbardziej zielony (the greenest)

Zielony - zieleńszy - najzieleńszy

Now, let's look at some irregular adjectives:

Dobry (good) - lepszy (better) - najlepszy (the best)

Zły (bad) - gorszy (worse) - najgorszy (the worst)

Duży (big) - większy (bigger) - największy (the biggest)

Mały (small) - mniejszy (smaller) - najmniejszy (the smallest)

Wysoki (tall) - wyższy (taller) - najwyższy (the tallest)

Indefinite Adjectives / Nouns

In Polish language, indefinite adjectives refer to quantity most of the time. They are also subordinate to the case, gender, and number. It is important to note that *anything* can be perceived in Polish differently, depending on the context. It can mean *nothing* or *something*:

Coś/nic – anything

Coś – something

Ktoś – someone/somebody

Każdy –every/each

Kiedyś – someday

Dużo – much/a lot of

Wiele – many/a lot of

Czy <u>ktoś</u> zna tę kobietę? – Does <u>someone</u> know this woman?

Nie słyszałem <u>nic</u> nowego ostatnio. – I haven't heard <u>anything</u> new recently. (double negation)

Słyszałeś <u>coś</u> nowego ostatnio? – Have you heard <u>anything</u> new recently?

Każde dziecko powinno chodzić do szkoły. – Every child should go to school.

<u>Nikogo</u> nie było w restauracji. – <u>Nobody</u> was at the restaurant.

Nie mam <u>nic</u> do powiedzenia. – I have got <u>nothing</u> to say. (double negation)

Chodźmy <u>gdzieś</u> na spacer – Let's go for a walk <u>somewhere</u>.

The Alphabet

The Polish alphabet contains 33 letters in total (including nine vowels). As mentioned before, the Polish alphabet is based on the Latin alphabet, yet the pronunciation is of Slavic origin. Therefore, some unique letters cannot be found in English. What is more, the Polish alphabet contains some diagraphs (and even one trigraph). Although the Polish alphabet is of Latin origin, it doesn't contain letters *x*, *v*, and *q*. Let's take a look at the Polish letters and their pronunciation:

POLISH ALPHABET:

Polish letter / English sound / pronunciation example

A a / u / as in fun

Ą ą / on, om / as in long

B b / b / as in bat

C c / ts / as in bits

Ć ć / ch / as in cheek

D d / d / as in dog

E e / e / as in red

Ę ę / en, em / as in dense

F f / f / as in frog

G g / g / as in gap

H h / ch / as in hamster (heavily aspirated)

I i / ee / as in cheek

J j / y / as in yeti

K k / c / as in call

L l / l / as in look

Ł ł / w / as in wall

M m / m / as in mom

N n / n / as in nose

Ń ń / ng (soft) / as in onion

O o / o / as in hot

Ó ó / u / as in push

P p / p / as in push

R r / r / as in Rome (rolled)

S s / s / as in seek

Ś ś / sh (soft) / as in sheep

T t / t / as in top

U u / u / as in push

W w / v / as in vital

Y y / y / as in rhythm

Z z / z / as in zebra

Ź ź / zh / as in Niger (very soft)

Ż ż / zh / as in pleasure (hard)

POLISH DIPHTHONGS

Polish diphthong / English sound / pronunciation example

Ch / ch / as in hamster

Ci / ch / as in cheek

Cz / ch / as in chalk

Dz / dz / as in goods (but with voiced s)

Dzi / dz / as in duke (very soft)

Dź / dz / as in duke (very soft)

Ni / ni / as in onion

Rz / s / as in treasure

Si / sh / as in sheep (soft)

Sz / sh / as in shark (hard)

Szcz / shch / - this is a consonant cluster that is absent in English, however, you try to join the sounds / sh / as in shark and / ch / as in chalk - / shch /

Zi / zh /as in Niger (very soft)

As you can see, Polish pronunciation is quite different from the English version—since some sounds are absent in English. For example, there are diphthongs (strange consonant clusters) that are quite difficult to distinguish from the very beginning. Despite the existence of diphthongs that add some difficulty, the good news is that most Polish sounds are not represented by many different combinations of letters. For example, the English sound [i] can be represented in the script in many ways (*e, ee, i, y* and so on). In Polish, however, the sound [i] is represented only by the letter *i*. Once you learn the Polish alphabet and its pronunciation, your learning will be gradually getting easier and easier.

The most difficult concept to learn is Polish orthography. Although there are some rules, it should be learned by heart. As stated before, most of the Polish letters are represented by only one sound; however, there are some sounds that are represented by more than one letter. Let's take a look at these combinations:

POLISH ORTOGRAPHY

[The sound] - Example 1 / Example 2

[u] – u / ó

[h] (heavily aspirated) - h / ch

[zh] (hard) – ż / rz

[zh] (soft) - ź / zi

[sh] (soft) – ś / si

[ch] (soft) – ć / ci

[ng] (soft) – ń / ni

[om] – ą / om

The rest of the Polish sounds contain only one written representation. To sum up, Polish pronunciation is quite different from the English version, yet if you get familiar with the sounds, you will not have problems with pronunciation. The most difficult things for foreigners are the Polish orthography and the diphthongs. Indeed, Polish diphthongs can make you struggle—since they involve strange consonant clusters that will definitely make your tongue twist. The orthography will be getting more and more familiar, along with your advancement. If you make a spelling mistake, don't worry. Most of the Polish native speakers have many problems with the orthography, for it is a really difficult concept. Try to learn the Polish pronunciation gradually—listen to the Polish language and try to associate the sound with a particular letter /word. Learning in context is the best way!

Polish Numbers (1-100)

1- jeden

2- dwa

3- trzy

4- cztery

5- pięć

6- sześć

7- siedem

8- osiem

9- dziewięć

10- dziesięć

11- jedenaście

12- dwanaście

13- trzynaście

14- czternaście

15- piętnaście

16- szesnaście

17- siedemnaście

18- osiemnaście

19- dziewiętnaście

20- dwadzieścia

30- trzydzieści

40- czterdzieści

50- pięćdziesiąt

60- sześćdziesiąt

70- siedemdziesiąt

80- osiemdziesiąt

90- dziewięćdziesiąt

100- sto

The rule of creating Polish numbers is similar to the English one. You just read what you see from left to right. However, polish numbers are some of the toughest words to pronounce, so don't get discouraged. Let's see how it works in practice:

23 – dwadzieścia trzy (twenty-three)

56 – pięćdziesiąt sześć (fifty-six)

78 – siedemdziesiąt osiem (seventy-eight)

33 – trzydzieści trzy (thirty-three)

99 – dziewięćdziesiąt dziewięć (ninety-nine)

These are just Polish numbers. When it comes to the numerals, they are more complex—

since they are declined by gender, number, and case. For now, let's just skip the numerals.

Greetings and Basic Everyday Expressions

Polish basic everyday expressions are similar to the English ones with only one exception—Polish people do not use an equivalent of the English *good afternoon*. Let's take a look at some of the general greetings:

Dzień dobry! – Good morning / Good afternoon!

Dobry wieczór! – Good evening! (rather formal)

Do widzenia! – Goodbye!

Dzień dobry Pani – Good morning Mrs./Ms.*

Dzień dobry Panu/Panie – Good morning Mr.*

Cześć! – Hello / Hi!*

Cześć! – Bye! (informal)*

*Cultural note: When you don't know someone, or you address a much older person, always use *dzień dobry* instead of *cześć*. When you are at work, it is advisable to say *dzień dobry / do widzenia (Pani / Panie)* instead of *cześć* (*cześć* is rather an informal form of address), unless you get to know your colleagues better. Also, students at school/university never say *cześć* to their teachers, and teachers do not use *cześć* when addressing to their students. If you want to address a teacher, always use *dzień dobry* and be polite, no matter how long you know the teacher.

Dobranoc! - Good night!

Tak - Yes

Nie - No

Może... - I guess... / Maybe

Smacznego! - Enjoy your meal! / Bon appetit!

Na zdrowie! - Bless you!

Na zdrowie! - Cheers! (when making a toast)

Przepraszam - I am sorry / Excuse me

Dziękuję - Thank you

Nie ma za co - You're welcome

Proszę - Please

Proszę - Here / Here you are/ Here you go / There you go

Szczęść Boże! - God bless you! (Polish people rarely use *dzień dobry / dobry wieczór* when addressing to priests, nuns, monks, etc. Instead, they use *Szczęść Boże* [God bless you] or *Niech Będzie Pochwalony Jezus Chrystus* [Praised be Jesus Christ]).

Co tam? / Co u ciebie? - How are you? / How do you do?*

***Cultural note:** It is important to note that expressions such as *how are you / how do you do* are perceived differently in Poland since Polish people use them rarely. Generally, asking such questions is not a standard pattern. If you ask a Polish person *how do you do?* don't expect something like *I'm fine / I'm okay / I'm doing great.* Instead, a Polish person will tell you a couple of things about the job/school/family life, etc. So, Polish *co tam / co u ciebie?* is slightly different from the English *how are you?.*

There are also some colloquial expressions that are mostly used by younger generations. It is good to know a couple of informal greetings as well, so take a look at some of them:

Siema! – Hey!

Elo! – Yo! (a very informal form of addressing your close friends)

Jak leci? – What's up?

Trzymaj się! – Take care!

Na razie! – Bye! (informal)

Dzięki! – Thanks!

Spoko! / Ok! / Okej! – Okay! / No problem! (Polish people say *okay* very often)

Sory / Sorki – Sorry (again, Polish younger generations often say *sorry* instead of *przepraszam*)

Introducing Each Other and Initial Conversation

Dzień dobry! Nazywam się... – Good morning! My name is...

Cześć! Jestem... – Hi! / Hello! I am ... (more informal)

Jak się nazywasz? – What's your name?

To jest mój przyjaciel ... – This is my friend ....

Skąd pochodzisz? – Where are you from?

Jestem z Polski. – I am from Poland.

Jestem z Anglii. – I am from England.

Gdzie mieszkasz? – Where do you live?

Mieszkam w Warszawie. – I live in Warsaw.

Mieszkam w Londynie. – I live in London.

Ile masz lat? – How old are you?

Mam 23 lata. – I am 23 years old.

Jestem studentem (m.) / studentką (f.) – I am a student.

Pracuję w ... – I work at / in ...

Miło mi cię poznać. – Nice to meet you!

Mówisz po angielsku? - Do you speak English?

Mówię po angielsku. - I speak English.

Nie mówię dobrze po angielsku. - I don't speak English very well.

A ty? - And you? / How about you?

Ja też. - Me too.

Ja też nie. - Me neither.

Czy mogę ci jakoś pomóc? - How can I help you?

Nie, dziękuję. - No, thank you.

Myślę, że tak. - I think so.

Myślę, że nie. - I don't think so.

Oczywiście. - Of course. / Sure.

Nie ma problemu. - No problem.

Czy mógłbyś / mogłabyś przeliterować? - Could you spell it?

Czy mógłbyś / mogłabyś powtórzyć? - Could you repeat?

Nie rozumiem. - I don't understand.

Powodzenia! - Good luck!

Dobry pomysł! - Good idea!

Myślę, że to dobry pomysł. - I think it's a good idea.

Niech pomyślę... - Let me think...

Poczekaj chwilę. - Wait a moment.

Przepraszam. - Excuse me / I'm sorry

Przepraszam. Muszę już iść. - I'm sorry. I have to go.

Przepraszam za spóźnienie. - Sorry for being late.

Przepraszam, która jest godzina? - Excuse me, whet time is it?

Przepraszam, gdzie jest ...? - Excuse me, where is ...?

Czy mógłbyś / mogłabyś pokazać mi gdzie jest ...? – Could you show me where ... is?

Czy mógłbyś / mogłabyś pokazać na mapie? – Could you show me on the map?

Days of the Week, Months, Date

When it comes to the Polish names of days of the week / months /etc., they significantly differ from the English ones. Let's take a look:

Months:

Styczeń – January

Luty – February

Marzec – March

Kwiecień – April

Maj – May

Czerwiec – June

Lipiec – July

Sierpień – August

Wrzesień – September

Październik – October

Listopad – November

Grudzień – December

Days of the week:

Poniedziałek – Monday

Wtorek – Tuesday

Środa – Wednesday

Czwartek – Thursday

Piątek – Friday

Sobota – Saturday

Niedziela – Sunday

Seasons:

Wiosna – Spring

Lato – Summer

Jesień – Autumn / Fall

Zima - Winter

The format of the Polish date is as follows: "01.01.2019". Usually, the date starts from the day and ends with the year. It is important to note that you have to use a numeral, not a number, if you read the date (similar to the English pattern). As mentioned, Polish numerals and nouns (months too) are declined by gender, number, and case. However, the good news is that all months are masculine, so the endings are quite similar to one another.

Public Holidays

In Poland, most of the public holidays are similar to English equivalents, but there are a few differences. Let's take a closer look at the most important holidays in Poland, starting from 31st December:

Sylwester [31st December] – New Year's Eve – this is how Polish people say New Year's Eve. However, Sylwester is a male name that has its name day on 31st December.

Nowy rok [1st January] – New year – a statutory holiday in Poland

Święto Trzech Króli [6th January] – Epiphany / Three Kings' Day – Christian feast day that celebrates the revelation of God in his Son as a human in Jesus Christ. It is also a statutory holiday in Poland. However, it was declared a statutory holiday only a couple of years ago.

Środa Popielcowa [movable feast] – Ash Wednesday – although it is not a statutory holiday, it is a very important day for Poles since it symbolizes the beginning of Lent. On this day, Poles go to church and priests sprinkle people's heads with ash.

Wielka Sobota [movable] – Holy Saturday / Easter Eve – on this day, people take Easter baskets to the church to bless the food inside them (usually some meat, bread, salt, pepper, eggs, fruit, and cake)

Wielkanoc [movable] – Easter – on Easter Sunday, Polish people have special Easter breakfast (they usually eat the blessed food from the basket plus some dishes prepared at home)

Lany Poniedziałek [movable] – Easter Monday – it is a statutory holiday.

Święto Pracy [1ˢᵗ May] – Labor Day – this is a statutory holiday, yet it is no longer celebrated. During the 1970s and 1980s, people organized marches to symbolize the importance of labor. Today, however, people just spend this day casually at home or organize a barbecue or a short trip—since the celebration of this holiday (marches, etc.) is of communist origin.

Święto Konstytucji [3ʳᵈ May] – Constitution Day – this is a statutory holiday that marks the date of signing the Polish Constitution (3ʳᵈ May 1791). People usually hang Polish flags and spend this day with family.

Boże Ciało – [movable, but always on Thursday] – Corpus Christi – on this day, people celebrate the **real presence** of the body and blood of **Jesus Christ**, the **Son of God**, in the elements of the **Eucharist**. It is a statutory holiday in Poland.

Święto Wojska Polskiego [15ᵗʰ August] – Polish Army Holiday – it is also a church holiday connected with the mother of Jesus Christ, which the Poles call Mary Queen of Poland. It is a statutory holiday.

Wszystkich Świętych [1ˢᵗ November] – All Saints' Day – it is a statutory holiday. On this day, Polish people go to church and to the cemetery to visit the resting places of members of their families and friends.

Święto Niepodległości [11ᵗʰ November] – Independence Day – it is a statutory holiday that marks the date of winning the independence in 1918 after 123 years of occupation. On this day, Polish people usually hang flags and spend time with their families; however, Independence Day is not celebrated as strongly as in the States.

Wigilia [24th December] – Christmas Eve – this is the most important day of Polish Christmas. On this day, Polish people have Christmas supper, and they exchange presents after supper. There is also a special mass at midnight in each Polish church called *pasterka* that symbolizes the birth of Jesus Christ.

Pierwszy dzień świąt [25th December] – Christmas Day – it is a statutory holiday. Polish people usually spend this day with family or visit relatives.

Drugi dzień świąt [26th December] – Boxing Day – it is a statutory holiday, but Polish people do not have any traditions connected to it. They just spend time with their families at home.

Holiday Greetings

Wesołych Świąt Bożego Narodzenia! – Merry Christmas!

Wesołych Świąt Wielkanocnych! – Happy Easter!

Wesołych Świąt! – Happy holidays!

Szczęśliwego nowego roku! – Happy New Year!

Wszystkiego najlepszego! – All the best!

Wszystkiego najlepszego z okazji urodzin! – Happy birthday!

Wszystkiego najlepszego z okazji imienin! – Happy nameday!*

Cultural note: Celebrating name day is quite popular in Poland, especially among the older generations. In some families, the tradition of celebrating name day is still cultivated. When a person has their name day, the whole family gathers together and organizes a party / a special dinner.

Telling the Time

The most important thing to remember is that Polish people tell the time differently. Unlike English speaking countries, Poland follows the 24-hour format; thus you will less often hear a Polish person say something similar to AM or PM. In fact, Polish people may tell the time following the 24-hour format or the 12-hour format.

The second difference is that polish hours are declined by gender and case, so you cannot simply say *jest pięć*. Instead, you have to say *jest piąta*. The good news is that all hours are feminine, so the endings look quite similar.

The 24-hour format is as follows:

1:00 AM – 1:00 – pierwsza

2:00 AM – 2:00 - druga

3:00 AM – 3:00 - trzecia

4:00 AM – 4:00 - czwarta

5:00 AM – 5:00 - piąta

6:00 AM – 6:00 - szósta

7:00 AM – 7:00 - siódma

8:00 AM – 8:00 - ósma

9:00 AM – 9:00 - dziewiąta

10:00 AM – 10:00 - dziesiąta

11:00 AM – 11:00 - jedenasta

12:00 AM - 12:00 - dwunasta

1:00 PM - 13:00 - trzynasta

2:00 PM - 14:00 - czternasta

3:00 PM – 15:00 - piętnasta

4:00 PM – 16:00 - szesnasta

5:00 PM – 17:00 - siedemnasta

6:00 PM – 18:00 - osiemnasta

7:00 PM – 19:00 - dziewiętnasta

8:00 PM – 20:00 - dwudziesta

9:00 PM – 21:00 – dwudziesta pierwsza

10:00 PM – 22:00 – dwudziesta druga

11:00 PM – 23:00 – dwudziesta trzecia

12:00 PM 24:00 – dwudziesta czwarta / północ [midnight]

Która jest godzina? – What time is it?

Jest ... – It's ...

5:00 AM – 5:00 rano [5 in the morning] / 5:00 or piąta

5:00 PM – 5:00 po południu [5 in the afternoon] / 17:00 or siedemnasta

9:00 AM – 9:00 rano [9 in the morning] / 9:00 or dziewiąta

9:00 PM – 9:00 wieczorem [9 in the evening] / 21:00 or dwudziesta pierwsza

4:30 AM – wpół do piątej [half past four] / czwarta trzydzieści [four thirty]

6:15 PM – piętnaście po szóstej / osiemnasta piętnaście [six fifteen]

11:50 PM – za dziesięć dwunasta [ten to twelve] / dwudziesta trzecia pięćdziesiąt [eleven fifty]

As you can see, Polish people follow the 24-hour format as well as the 12-hour format, depending on the context. In the 12-hour format, they usually add expressions such as *rano* [in the morning], *po południu* [in the afternoon] or *wieczorem* [in the evening] to indicate the time of day. It is important to know that the 24-hour format is used more in formal situations and usually appears on train/bus schedules, programs, etc. The 12-hour format is used more in informal interactions.

At the Airport

After long hours spent on the plane, you have finally landed in Poland. The airport is the first place you will probably see on your trip to Poland, so why not start from the beginning?

In Poland, there are only eleven airports you can choose from, but you will probably choose Warsaw, Kraków, Poznań, Gdańsk or Wrocław as your first destination. It is important to note that Polish airports are rather small compared to the English or American ones, so you probably won't get lost. What is more, most of the information at airports is provided in both languages, and the staff speaks very good English. Nevertheless, knowing the most important vocabulary will certainly boost your confidence.

Lotnisko - an airport

Samolot - a plane

Lot - a flight

Bagaż - a luggage

Bagaż rejestrowany - a hold baggage

Bagaż podręczny - a hand baggage

Parking - a car park/parking

Strefa wolnocłowa - a duty-free zone

Wolny od cła - duty-free

Towary - goods

Toaleta - a toilet

Odprawa - check-in

Strażnik / ochroniarz - a security guard

Bilet - a ticket

Paszport - a passport

Kontrola paszportowa - passport control

Dowód osobisty - an identity card/ID card

Wejście na pokład - boarding

Lądowanie - landing

Opóźniony - delayed

Odloty - departures

Przyloty - arrivals

Hala odlotów - a departure lounge

Lądowanie awaryjne - an emergency landing

Międzylądowanie - a layover / intermediate landing

Pas bezpieczeństwa - a seat belt

Czy mogę zobaczyć Pana / Pani paszport? - May I see your passport, please?

Czy mogę zobaczyć Pana / Pani dowód osobisty? - May I see your ID, please?

Czy mogę zobaczyć Pana / Pani bilet? - May I see your ticket, please?

Przepraszam, gdzie jest strefa wolnocłowa? - Excuse me, where is duty-free zone?

Przepraszam, gdzie jest hala odlotów? - Excuse me, where is departure lounge?

Zgubiłem / Zgubiłam mój bagaż. - I've lost my luggage.

Czy mogę to zabrać jako bagaż podręczny? - Can I take this along as hand luggage?

Przykro mi, nie może Pan / Pani tego zabrać. - I'm sorry, you can't take this.

Tak, oczywiście. - Yes, of course.

Chcę zabrać swój bagaż. - I want to take my luggage.

Proszę zapiąć pasy bezpieczeństwa. - Please, fasten your seat belts.

Prosimy nie zostawiać bagażu bez nadzoru. - Please, don't leave your luggage unattended.

Train Station/Bus Station

If you live in Europe, there is a possibility you will get to Poland by train or bus. Polish railway infrastructure is pretty good—in Poland you can get everywhere by train. Also, all the biggest railway stations have been renovated in recent years, so they look nice and modern. Each station is connected to a shopping center with restaurants, information desks, etc. You will be surprised by how good the train/bus stations are in Poland!

Dworzec kolejowy – a train station/railway station

Dworzec autobusowy – a bus station/coach station

Kasa biletowa – a ticket office

Pociąg – a train

Autobus – a bus

Bilet na pociąg / bilet kolejowy – a railway ticket

Bilet na autobus / bilet autobusowy – a bus ticket

Bilety krajowe* – domestic tickets

Bilety Intercity* – Intercity tickets

Keep in mind: there are two ways you can buy a railway ticket in Poland. You can buy either a domestic ticket or an Intercity ticket.

Domestic tickets usually involve short journeys within a certain region, whereas Intercity tickets involve longer journeys. Intercity trains look different from the regular trains—they have special compartments that can be shared only by six-eight people. If you buy an Intercity ticket, you have your own seat on the train (you can see the number of the compartment and the number of your seat on your ticket). If you buy a domestic ticket and choose the Intercity train, you will have to buy another ticket or even pay a special fine!

Peron – a platform

Tory kolejowe – a railway track/railroad track

Kierowca autobusu – a bus driver

Konduktor – a guard / a conductor (the word *konduktor* is used only with regard to trains)

Wagon – a carriage/car

Przedział – a compartment

Wagon sypialny – a sleeper / a sleeping carriage

Wagon restauracyjny / WARS – a diner / a restaurant car

Miejsce – a seat

Walizka – a suitcase

Plecak – a backpack

Torebka – a purse

Opóźniony – delayed

Przesiadka – a change / a stopover

Przystanek autobusowy – a bus stop

Rozkład jazdy – a train schedule / a bus schedule

Trasa pociągu – a train path

Bilet normalny – a full price ticket

Bilet ulgowy – a reduced-fare ticket

Bilet studencki – a student ticket (If you have your student ID with you, you can buy a student ticket which is a half-price ticket)

Czy mogę zobaczyć Pana / Pani bilet? – May I see your ticket, please?

Czy mogę zobaczyć Pana / Pani legitymację? – May I see your student ID, please?

Pociąg jest opóźniony. – The train is delayed.

Poproszę jeden bilet do Warszawy. – One ticket to Warsaw, please.

Poproszę jeden bilet studencki do Krakowa. – One student ticket to Kraków, please.

Przepraszam, czy ten pociąg jedzie do Poznania? – Excuse me, does this train go to Poznań?

Przepraszam, o której odjeżdża pociąg do Wrocławia? – Excuse me, what time does the train to Wrocław leave?

Pociąg do Wrocławia odjeżdża o dziewiątej dwadzieścia. – The train to Wrocław leaves at nine twenty.

Przepraszam, gdzie jest wagon sypialny? – Excuse me, where is the sleeping carriage?

Przepraszam, o której godzinie odjeżdża autobus do Szczecina? – Excuse me, what time does the bus to Szczecin leave?

Autobus do Szczecina odjeżdża za dziesięć minut. – The bus to Szczecin leaves in ten minutes.

On the Road

If you decide to go to Poland by car, there are a couple of things that you need to know. Firstly, because Poland is a member of the Schengen Agreement, its borders are open. It means that if you cross the Polish border, you are not a subject to border control. You can just drive casually, and you will probably not notice that you are in a different country. Secondly, it is your duty to have your daytime running lamps switched on round-the-clock. If the police notice that you don't, they may give you a ticket. Thirdly, there aren't many motorways in Poland (only four), yet there are plenty of express roads that look the same, so don't be scared. In fact, the Polish road infrastructure has improved significantly in recent years; you will certainly be surprised how good it is. Finally, there are speed limits that you must adhere to:

- Max. 50 km/h in a built-up area
- Max. 90 km/h in a non-built-up area
- Max. 120 km/h on express roads
- Max. 140 km/h on motorways
- Max. 20 km/h in home zones

Keep in mind that many speed cameras may take a picture of your car if you exceed the speed limit. Anyway, let's take a look at some vocabulary that might help you survive on the Polish roads:

On The Road

Znak drogowy – a road sign

Znak ostrzegawczy – a warning sign

Znak zakazu – a prohibition sigh

Znak nakazu – a mandatory sign

Znaki poziome – road surface markings

Ścieżka rowerowa – a bike path

Przejście dla pieszych – a pedestrian crossing

Lustro drogowe – a street mirror

Skrzyżowanie / krzyżówka – an intersection / a junction

Rondo – a roundabout/a traffic circle

Wiadukt – a flyover

Przejazd kolejowy – a railroad crossing / a railway crossing

Most – a bridge

Parking – a parking/a car park

Bilet parkingowy – a parking ticket

Kwit parkingowy – a parking voucher

Zjazd z autostrady – an exit ramp

Pas awaryjny – an emergency lane

MOP (miejsce obsługi podróżnych) – motorway service area

Tunel – a tunnel

Przeprawa promowa – a ferry crossing

Limit prędkości – a speed limit

Korek – a traffic jam

Wypadek samochodowy / wypadek na drodze – a car accident

Fotoradar – a street camera

Bramki na autostradzie – motorway gates*

*Keep in mind: If you want to use Polish motorways, you have to drive through a special gate and pay some money. The fees are not high, but sometimes the gates can cause huge traffic jams.

In Your Car:

Pasażer – a passenger

Kierowca – a driver

Samochód – a car

Samochód ciężarowy – a lorry / a truck

Motocykl – a motorbike

Samochód elektryczny – an electric car

Kierownica – a steering wheel

Siedzenia – seats

Pasy bezpieczeństwa – seat belts

Pedał gazu – an accelarator

Hamulec – a brake

Hamulec ręczny – a handbrake / an emergency brake

Skrzynia biegów – a gearbox / a transmission

Sprzęgło – a clutch

Lusterko boczne – a wing mirror

Lusterko wsteczne – a rearview mirror

Wycieraczki – wipers

Światła do jazdy dziennej / światła krótkie – daytime running lamps

Światła drogowe / światła długie – full beam / driving beam

Światła przeciwmgielne – fog lamps

Kierunkowskaz – an indicator / a turn signal

Opona – a tyre

Koło zapasowe – a spare wheel

Bagażnik – a boot/a trunk

Gaśnica – a fire extinguisher

Trójkąt ostrzegawczy – a warning triangle

Linka holownicza – a towrope

Apteczka samochodowa – a car emergency kit

Lewarek / podnośnik – a jack

Prawo jazdy – a driving licence

Dówód rejestracyjny – a registration document

Ubezpieczenie OC – a liablity insurance

Wypożyczać samochód – to rent a car

Wypożyczalnia samochodów – a car hire / a car rental

Regulamin – rules and regulations

Bak – a petrol tank

Olej silnikowy – a motor oil

Płyn do spryskiwaczy – windshield washer fluid / a screenwash

Silnik – an engine/a motor

Dzień dobry, chciałbym / chciałabym wypożyczyć samochód – Hello, I would like to rent a car.

Czy mogę zobaczyć Pani / Pana prawo jazdy? – May I see your driving licence?

Czy mogę zobaczyć dowód rejestracyjny i ubezpieczenie? – May I see the registration document and the car insurance?

Czy może mi Pan / pani pokazać gdzie jest koło zapasowe? – Could you show me where the spare wheel is?

Skręć w prawo na skrzyżowaniu. - Turn right at the next intersecton.

Skręć w lewo na skrzyżowaniu. - Turn left at the next intersection.

Przepraszam, czy mógłby mi Pan / mogłaby Pani pomóc mi z kołem zapasowym? - Excuse me, could you help me with the spare wheel?

Przepraszam, gdzie jest wjazd na autostradę? - Excuse me, how can I get to the motorway?

At the Petrol Station

If you decide either to go to Poland by car or to rent a car, you will need to fuel up sooner or later. Many petrol stations in Poland offer relatively low prices compared to different European countries (such as Germany). If you have an electric car, you may have some problems—since chargers are not that popular and can be found only in big cities or on the motorways. Interestingly, most of the Polish petrol stations offer decent warm meals (e.g., hot-dogs, burgers, tortillas) and some good-quality coffee, so you don't have to go to McDonald's or KFC to eat something on the go. The most popular petrol stations are *Orlen, Lotos, Shell, BP,* and *CircleK.*

Paliwo – fuel

Benzyna – petrol / gasoline

Benzyna bezołowiowa – unleaded petrol / lead-free petrol

Benzyna ołowiowa – leaded petrol

Ropa / ON – petroleum

Dystrybutor paliwa – petrol pump / gas pump

Myjnia samochodowa – car wash

Myjnia bezdotykowa – touch-free / touchless car wash

Dzień dobry, w czym mogę pomóc? – Hello, how can I help you?

Chciałbym / Chciałabym benzynę 95 za 100 złotych. – I would like 95 petrol for 100 złoty.*

*Keep in mind: When you want to fuel up, you can either do it yourself or call the station attendant (on some stations, employees always come out to help you). When the employee comes, you need to say what type of fuel you want and how much (in money). Of course, you can say how many liters you want, yet the popular conversational pattern requires saying the amount of money you want to pay rather than the actual amount of the fuel.

Dzień dobry, chciałbym zapłacić za benzynę. – Hello, I would like to pay for my fuel.

To będzie 100 zł. – That will be 100 zł.

Poproszę jeszcze hot-doga oraz kawę z mlekiem. – I would also like a hot-dog and white coffee.

Dobrze, to będzie 106 zł. – Okay, that will be 106 zł.

Asking for Directions

Being in another country, you will certainly be faced with the problem of getting lost in a big city. Instead of relying exclusively on Google Maps or other fancy apps, why not ask a stranger about the directions? Such small talk is a good opportunity to test your speaking skills and foreign language knowledge. Here are the essential expressions you need to know:

Idź prosto - Go straight

Skręć w prawo - Turn right

Skręć w lewo - Turn left

Po prawej stronie - on the right

Po lewej stronie - on the left

Obok - next to

Za - behind

Na rogu ulicy - on the corner of the street

Po drugiej stronie ulicy - across the street

Na końcu ulicy - at the end of the street

W pobliżu / blisko - near

Naprzeciwko / przed - opposite / in front of

Pomiędzy / między - between

Knowing directions is key, and strangers that you meet on the street will not only give you basic guidelines but also provide you with some specific reference points. Let's look at them:

Ulica - street

Droga - road

Sygnalizacja świetlna- traffic lights

Skrzyżowanie - crossroads / junction

Znak drogowy - road sign

Drogowskaz - signpost

Przejście podziemne - underpass

Przejście dla pieszych - pedestrian crossing

Chodnik - pavement / sidewalk

Ścieżka rowerowa - bike path / cycle path

Accommodation

The inseparable part of each trip is the accommodation. The good news is that you can choose from many options available on the tourist market. Nowadays, you can stay not only at an expensive hotel but also at a youth hostel, a guesthouse, or a private apartment. Due to the globalization, open borders and the fast development of the Internet, booking has become much easier. In Poland, there are many options you can choose from. In some bigger cities, you can stay at a hostel or a hotel, whereas in the countryside you can rent a whole bungalow or stay at a holiday farm. When compared to other European countries, prices for a decent piece of accommodation are relatively low. So, if you are still not sure about your trip to Poland, don't hesitate—go!

Kinds of Accommodation:

Hotel – a hotel

Hostel / schronisko – a youth hostel

Pensjonat – a pension

Domek / bungalow – a bungalow

Kurort / ośrodek wypoczynkowy – a resort

Kurort nadmorski – a beach resort

Przyczepa kempingowa / kemping – a caravan

Obozowisko / pole kempingowe – a campsite

Motel – a motel

Hotel pięciogwiazdkowy – a five-star hotel

Mieszkanie prywatne – a private flat

Apartament – a suite

Schronisko turystczne – a rest house

Schronisko górskie – a mountain chalet

Namiot – a tent

At a Hotel:

Recepcja – a reception

Hol – a lobby

Restauracja hotelowa – a hotel restaurant

Bar hotelowy – a hotel bar

Pokój – a room

Klucz – a key

Pokój jednoosobowy – a single room

Pokój dwuosobowy – a double room

Obsługa hotelowa – room service

Parking dla gości – parking space for guests

Piętro / poziom – a floor / a level

Winda – a lift / an elevator

Schody – stairs

Balkon – a balcony

Taras – a terrace/a patio

Pokój z aneksem kuchennym – a room with a kitchenette

Rezerwować – to book / to make a reservation

Zameldowanie - check-in

Wymeldowanie - check-out

Pełne wyżywienie - full board

Niepełne wyżywienie - half board

Śniadanie - breakfast

Lunch - lunch

Obiadokolacja - dinner

Przekąski - snacks

In Your Room:

Klimatyzacja – air conditioning

Ogrzewanie – heating

Klucz – a key

Łóżko – a bed

Łóżko jednoosobowe – a twin bed

Łóżko dwuosobowe / łoże małżeńskie – a queen bed

Łóżko piętrowe – a bunk bed

Garderoba / szafa na ubrania – a wardrobe / a closet

Stolik nocny – a bedside table

Telewizor – a TV

Darmowe WiFi – Free WiFi

Hasło do WiFi – WiFi password

Okno – a window

Łazienka – a bathroom

Wanna – a bathtub

Prysznic – a shower

Sejf – a safe deposit box / a safe

Suszarka do włosów – a hairdryer

Czajnik bezprzewodowy – an electric kettle

Lodówka – a fridge

Dzień dobry, mam rezerwację dla dwóch osób. – Hello, I have a reservation for two people.

Dzień dobry. Mam rezerwację na nazwisko ... – Hello, I have a reservation. It's under the name...

Czy mają Państwo jakieś wolne pokoje? – Do you have any rooms available?

Czy przyjmują Państwo również zwierzęta? – Are pets allowed?

Czy ręczniki i pościele są wliczone w cenę? – Are sheets and towels included?

O której godzinie jest śniadanie? – What time do you serve breakfast?

O której godzinie jest obiadokolacja? – What time do you serve dinner?

Co jest w cenie zakwaterowania? – What's included in the cost of accommodation?

Czy może Pan/Pani przeliterować nazwisko? – Could you spell your last name, please?

Pókój jest na trzecim piętrze. – Your room is on the third floor.

Czy w tym pokoju jest klimatyzacja? – Does this room have air-conditioning?

Klimatyzacja w moim pokoju nie działa. – The air-conditioning in my room is out of order.

Przepraszam, jakie jest hasło do WiFi? – Excuse me, could you tell me the WiFi password?

Chciałbym / Chciałabym dokonać rezerwacji. – I would like to make a reservation.

Proszę, oto klucz do pokoju. – Here is your key.

Proszę zostawić brudne ręczniki na podłodze. – Please, leave the dirty towels on the floor.

Chciałbym / chciałabym się wymeldować. – I would like to check-out, please.

Chciałbym /chciałabym dostać inny pokój. – I would like a different room.

Bardzo nam się podobało. – We really enjoyed our stay here.

Doing the Shopping

On your trip to Poland, you will certainly have to buy some necessary stuff such as food, tickets, medicine or toiletries. Keep in mind that not all Polish shops offer their services in English, so knowing some basic expressions will definitely help you survive.

Sklep – a shop

Sklep spożywczy – a grocery store

Sklep odzieżowy – a clothing shop

Skep obuwniczy – a shoe shop

Piekarnia – a bakery / baker's

Cukiernia – a confectionery

Księgarnia – a bookshop

Stacja benzynowa – a petrol station / a gas station

Apteka – a pharmacy

Drogeria – a drugstore / chemist

Kiosk – a paper shop / newsagent's/kiosk

Supermarket – a supermarket

Sklep samoobsługowy – a self-service shop

Sklep sportowy – a sports shop

Sklep monopolowy – a liquor store / off-licence

Sklep mięsny – a butcher's shop / meat market

Sklep z narzędziami – a hardware shop

Sklep wielobranżowy – a general store

Sklep z upominkami – a gift shop

Sklep z pamiątkami – a souvenir shop

Sklep wolnocłowy – a duty-free shop

Pieniądze – money

Gotówka – cash

Karta płatnicza – payment card/credit card (In Polish stores people usually say *karta* [card])

Reszta / drobne – change

Banknot – a bank note / banknote

Terminal płatniczy – a payment terminal

Paragon – a receipt

Wózek – a shopping cart / shopping basket

Produkt – a product

Kasa – a checkout

Wyprzedaż – sale

Promocja – a special offer

Karta podarunkowa – a gift card

Zwrot – a return

Przepraszam, ile to kosztuje? – Excuse me, how much does it cost?

Czy mogę zapłacić gotówką? – Can I pay with cash?

Czy chciałby Pan / chciałaby Pani zapłacić kartą czy gotówką? – Would you like to pay with cash or with a credit card?

Czy mogę prosić o paragon? – Can I have a receipt, please?

Czy ma Pan / Pani jakieś drobne? – Have you got any change?*

*Keep in mind: It's quite common that cashiers in Poland ask about change. If you buy only one thing and you give a bank note, you might be asked to provide some change.

Proszę wprowadzić PIN. – Enter your PIN code, please.

Dziś polecamy ... – I recommend buying ... today.

Ok, wezmę to. – Okay, I'll take it.

Nie, dziękuję. – No, thanks.

Czy mogę użyć mojej karty podarunkowej? – Can I use my gift card?

Czy mogę zwrócić ten produkt? – Can I return this product?

At the Supermarket

Polish supermarkets are quite common; you can find at least one even in a small town. When it comes to the bigger cities, there are lots of supermarkets everywhere; however, they are not as big as the American ones. One of the most popular Polish supermarkets is Biedronka [the Ladybird]. You will also find some foreign supermarkets such as Tesco, Lidl, Kaufland, Intermarche, and Carrefour. There are also some smaller franchises you will find in every city, for example, Żabka [the Frog], Stokrotka [the Daisy], Małpka [the Monkey], Polo Market. Names of Polish supermarkets are so cute, aren't they?

Wejście – entrance

Wyjście – exit

Kasa – a checkout

Kasa samoobsługowa – a self-service checkout

Torebka plastikowa – a plastic bag

Torba na zakupy - a shopping bag

Waga - scales

Alejka - an aisle

Artykuły spożywcze - groceries

Artykuły codziennego użytku - convenience goods

Artykuły toaletowe - toiletries

Artykuły biurowe - office suppliers/stationery

Pieczywo - bakery

Mięso - meat

Produkty mleczne - dairy products

Owoce - fruits

Warzywa - vegetables

Jajka - eggs

Słodycze - sweets / candy

Napoje - beverages

Alkohol - alcohol

Karma dla kota - cat food

Karma dla psa - dog food

Przyprawy - spices

Mrożonki - frozen food

Dania gotowe - convenience food / ready meals

Lody - ice cream

Chemia gospodarcza - household chemicals

Artykuły przecenione - sale items

Książki - books

Przepraszam, gdzie znajdę owoce? - Excuse me, where can I find fruit?

Tak, w sekcji artykułów spożywczych - Yes, they are in the produce section.

Czy chciałby Pan / chciałaby pani torbę? - Would you like a plastic bag?

Ten produkt jest obecnie wyprzedany. - This item is currently out of stock.

Czy ten produkt jest w promocji? - Is this product on sale?

Chciałbym / Chciałabym zapłacić gotówką. - I would like to pay with cash.

Chciałbym / Chciałabym zapłacić kartą. - I would like to pay with a credit card.

Proszę, oto reszta. - Here's your change.

Czy jest Pan / Pani członkiem naszego klubu? - Are you a member of our loyalty program?

Food and Drink

Food and drink are one of the most important issues on your trip to a foreign country. Whether you are going to eat out or cook at a hostel/apartment, you will have to know some basic vocabulary. Here are the most essential words:

Dairy Products – produkty mleczne:

Mleko - milk

Śmietana - cream

Ser żółty - cheese

Twarożek - cottage cheese

Jogurt - youghurt

Masło - butter

Margaryna - margarine

Maślanka - buttermilk

Bakery – pieczywo:

Chleb - bread

Chleb pszenny - wheat bread

Świeży chleb - fresh bread

Chleb żytni - rye bread

Chleb tostowy - toast bread

Bułka - bread roll

Bagietka - baguette

Pączki - donuts

Ciastka - biscuits/cookies

Vegetables – warzywa:

Ziemniak - potato

Pomidor - tomato

Ogórek - cucumber

Papryka czerwona - red pepper

Cebula - onion

Kapusta - cabbage

Sałata - lettuce

Marchewka - carrot

Brokuł - broccoli

Kalafior - cauliflower

Fasola - beans

Czosnek - garlic

Dynia - pumpkin

Szpinak - spinach

Pietruszka - parsley

Soja - soy

Seler - celery

Jarmuż - kale

Burak - beet / beetroot

Batat - sweet potato

Fruits – owoce:

Banan - banana

Jabłko - apple

Pomarańcza - orange

Grejfrut - grapefruit

Cytryna - lemon

Gruszka - pear

Brzoskwinia - peach

Kokos - coconut

Ananas - pineapple

Śliwka - plum

Arbuz - watermelon

Truskawka - strawberry

Malina - raspberry

Jagoda - blueberry

Wiśnia - cherry

Awokado - avocado

Orzech włoski - a walnut

Meat – mięso:

Kiełbasa - sausage

Bekon - bacon

Kurczak - chicken

Drób - poultry

Wołowina – beef

Wieprzowina – pork

Baranina – lamb

Szynka – ham

Mięso mielone – minced meat

Kabanos – a kabanos sausage (a snack stick sausage)

Salami – salami

Sweets/Candy – słodycze:

Czekolada – chocolate

Ciastka – cookies / biscuits

Cukierki czekoladowe – bonbons

Delicje – jaffa cakes

Batonik – chocolate bar

Żelki – jelly beans/gummy bears

Deser – dessert

Galaretka – jelly

Wafelek – wafer

Lody – ice cream

Lizak – lollipop

Krówka – fudge

Landrynki – hard candy

Beverages – napoje:

Woda w butelce – bottled water

Woda mineralna – mineral water

Woda gazowana – sparkling water

Cola - cola

Napoje gazowane - fizzy drinks

Sok pomarańczowy - orange juice

Sok jabłkowy - apple juice

Koktajl owocowy - fruit cocktail / smoothie

Kawa - coffee

Kawa rozpuszczalna - instant coffe

Kawa czarna - black coffee

Kawa z mlekiem - white coffee

Herbata - tea

Gorąca czekolada - hot chocolate

Piwo - beer

Wódka - vodka

Czerwone wino - red wine

Białe wino - white wine

Whisky - whiskey

Other Groceries:

Jajka - eggs

Mąka - flour

Sól - salt

Pieprz - pepper

Cukier - sugar

Cukier brązowy - cane sugar

Ryż - rice

Olej - oil

Oliwa z oliwek - olive oil

Przyprawy – spices

Miód – honey

Płatki kukurydziane – corn flakes

Płatki śniadaniowe – cereal

Healthy/Vegan Products:

Mleko sojowe – soy milk

Jogurt sojowy / kokosowy – soy / coconut yogurt

Mleko ryżowe / migdałowe – Rice / almond milk

Tofu – tofu

Hummus – hummus

Bezglutenowy – gluten-free

Soczewica – lentils

Płatki owsiane – oat flakes

Orzechy – nuts

Nasiona – seeds

At the Restaurant

When you visit a different country you probably want to try its cuisine. The best way to do this is to visit restaurants and cafés. Even though most of the staff will probably speak fluent English, it is nice to, at least, say "Thank you!" in the foreign language when visiting a restaurant. And if you go to less known places, don't be surprised when your waiter won't understand English! After all, knowing some basic vocabulary used at a restaurant will make you more confident during your trip to Poland.

Menu – menu

Śniadanie – breakfast

Lunch – lunch

Obiad – dinner

Kolacja – supper

Przystawki – starters / appetizers

Danie główne – main course / main dish

Zimne napoje – cold drinks

Gorące napoje – hot drinks

Kelner – waiter

Kelnerka - waitress

Szef kuchni - chef

Rachunek - bill

Rezerwacja - reservation

Danie dnia - today's special / dish of the day

Zarezerwować stolik - to book a table

Zapłacić gotówką - to pay with cash

Zapłacić kartą - to pay with a credit card

Złożyć zamówienie - to place the order

Napiwek - a tip*

*Cultural note: Leaving huge tips or leaving tips at all is not a very common thing in Poland. If you don't leave a tip, it is absolutely fine.

Dzień dobry, chciałbym / chciałabym zarezerwować stolik dla ... osób. - Good morning, I would like to book a table for ... people.

Dobry wieczór, mam rezerwację dla dwóch osób. - Good evening, I have a reservation for two people.

Dzień dobry, czy mogę przyjąć zamówienie? - Good morning, can I take your order?

Chciałbym/Chaciałabym ... - I would like...

Czy mógłby / mogłaby mi Pan / Pani polecić coś do jedzenia? - Could you recommend something to eat?

Czy mógłby / mogłaby mi Pan / Pani polecić coś do jedzenia? - Could you recommend something to drink?

Czy chciałby/ chciałaby Pan / Pani coś do picia? - Would you like something to drink?

Przepraszam, czy mogę dostać menu? - Excuse me, can I have a menu, please?

Jakie jest dzisiejsze danie dnia? - What dish is today's special?

Chciałbym / chciałabym zapłacić kartą. - I would like to pay with a credit card.

Chciałbym / chciałabym zapłacić gotówką. - I would like to pay with cash.

Chciałbym / Chciałabym zapłacić. - I would like to pay.*

*Cultural note: The service in Polish restaurants looks slightly different; don't expect your waiter to come to you every five minutes and check if everything is okay with the meal. If you want to pay, you just need to call the waiter and say that you want your bill.

Polish Cuisine

If you visit Poland, you definitely need to try Polish cuisine. It does not matter if you go to a grocery shop, or a restaurant, you will certainly find fresh produce that comes from local suppliers. Moreover, some dishes are indicative of a certain region. For instance, *pyry z gzikiem* [potatoes with quark] can be found in Upper Poland. Let's take a look at some popular dishes from Polish cuisine:

Kotlet schabowy – a breaded **pork** cutlet; made of **pork tenderloin** (with the bone or without), or of **pork chop**.

Pierogi – Polish dumplings; they come with different fillings (e. g. cheese, jam, fruits, meat, cabbage, mushrooms).

Bigos – very spicy stew based on **sauerkraut** and meat.

Gołąbki – cabbage leaves filled with spiced minced meat and rice.

Kiełbasa – a Polish sausage, yet it differs significantly from the English equivalent. It comes in different versions (e. g. fresh, smoked) and is made of different types of meat (pork, lamb, veal, game, beef, etc.).

Kapusta kiszona – sauerkraut.

Ogórek konserwowy – a pickled cucumber which is rather sweet and vinegary in taste Sałatka warzywna **(sałatka jarzynowa)** – vegetable salad, a traditional Polish side dish based on cooked vegetables (potato, carrot, parsley root, celery root) with eggs, pickled cucumbers, and mayonnaise.

Żurek - very traditional Polish sour rye soup that contains eggs, Polish sausage, diced potatoes, diced carrots, meat, and mushrooms.

Pyry z gzikiem (Upper Poland) - potatoes (pyry) served with gzik (**quark** with **sour cream**, onion, and chives).

Bryndza **(Lesser Poland)** - sheep milk cheese.

Oscypek **(Tatra Mountains)** - hard, salty cheese from non-pasteurized **sheep milk** which is smoked over a fire. Very often served with some cranberry jam.

Cepeliny **(Podlasie)** - big and long potato dumplings filled with meat.

Kluski śląskie **(Silesia)** - round dumplings made of potatoes that are served with gravy.

These are the traditional dishes, yet there are many new Polish dishes worth trying. For example, if you are into street food, try *zapiekanka* - a short baguette topped with ham, mushrooms, tomato sauce, different vegetables, and mayonnaise. *Zapiekanka* comes in different varieties and sizes. Apart from traditional cuisine, many restaurants offer food from all around the world (Italian, Chinese, Indian, etc.) So don't expect only restaurants that serve *pierogi* and *żurek*. Moreover, if you are on a plant-based diet, you will be surprised how many vegan restaurants can be found in Poland. In fact, Warsaw is in the top ten of European cities with the biggest amount of vegan and vegetarian restaurants.

At the Drugstore/Perfumery

There are many drugstores in Poland; however, they are not that big. The most popular are *Rossmann* (German), *Natura, Hebe, SuperPharm, Douglas.* There are also small drugstores owned by local entrepreneurs.

Podstawowe kosmetyki – Basic Toiletries:

Żel pod prysznic – shower gel

Szampon do włosów – shampoo

Odżywka do włosów – hair conditioner

Dezodorant – deodorant

Mydło – soap

Krem do rąk – hand cream

Balsam do ciała – body lotion

Szczoteczka do zębów – toothbrush

Pasta do zębów - toothpaste

Maszynka do golenia – razor

Płyn po goleniu – aftershave

Pianka do golenia – shaving cream

Papier toaletowy – toilet paper

Chusteczki higieniczne – tissues / wipes

Podpaski – period pads

Tampony – tampons

Lakier do paznokci – nail polish

Zmywacz do paznokci – nail polish remover

Płyn micelarny – micellar water

Płatki kosmetyczne / waciki – cotton pads

Gąbka – sponge

Perfume - perfume

Produkty do makijażu – Make-up Products:

Podkład – foundation

Cień do powiek – eyeshadow

Kredka do oczu – eye pencil

Eyeliner – eyeliner

Szminka / pomadka – lipstick

Tusz do rzęs / maskara – mascara

Korektor – concealer

Bronzer / róż – bronzer / blush

Produkty do sprzątania – Cleaning Products:

Środek wielofunkcyjny – all-purpose cleaner

Proszek do prania – washing powder

Szczoteczka do czyszczenia – cleaning brush

Ściereczka do naczyń – dish towel

Płyn do mycia naczyń – dish soap

Płyn do mycia szyb – window cleaner

Gąbka - sponge

Produkty dla dzieci - Products for Babies

Pieluchy jednorazowe / pampersy - disposable diapers

Smoczek - comforter

Mleko dla niemowląt - baby milk / baby formula

Chusteczki dla niemowląt - baby wipes

Dzień dobry, czy macie proszek do prania? - Hello, do you have washing powder?

Niestety, nie mamy proszku do prania. - I'm sorry, we don't have washing powder.

Tak, znajdzie go Pan / Pani w dziale produktów do sprzątania. - Yes, you can find it in the cleaning products section.

Czy ta pomadka posiada też inne odcienie? - Does this lipstick come with different shades?

Czy ten kolor mi pasuje? - Does this shade fit me well?

Czy chciałaby pani wypróbować ten produkt? - Would you like to try a sample?

Czy mógłbym/mogłabym wypróbować ten produkt? - Can I try a sample of this product?

Czy chciałaby Pani / chciałby Pan plastikową torebkę? - Would you like a plastic bag?

Body Parts

Głowa - Head

Twarz - face

Włosy - hair

Uszy - ears (ucho - ear)

Oczy - eyes (oko - eye)

Nos - nose

Usta - mouth

Język - tongue

Zęby - teeth (ząb - tooth)

Szyja - neck

Gardło - throat

Czoło - forehead

Rzęsy - eyelashes (rzęsa - eyelash)

Brwi - eyebrows (brew - eyebrow)

Policzki - cheeks (policzek - cheek)

Górne części ciała – Upper body

Klatka piersiowa – chest

Plecy – back

Dłoń – hand

Ręka – arm (when you say *ręka*, you mean the whole upper limb – arm and hand together)

Ramię – arm (only an arm)

Łokieć – elbow

Palce – fingers (palec – finger)

Nadgarstek – wrist

Brzuch – stomach

Piersi – breasts

Dolne części ciała – Lower body

Biodra – hips (biodro – hip)

Pośladki – bottom

Nogi – legs (noga – leg)

Stopy – feet (stopa – foot)

Palce u nóg – toes (palec u nogi – toe)

Kolana – knees (kolano – knee)

Pięty – heels (pięta – heel)

Kostka – ankle

Uda – thighs (udo – thigh)

Łydki – calves (łydka – calf)

Kości i organy wewnętrzne – Bones and Internal Organs

Żebra – ribs (żebro – rib)

Czaszka – skull

Żołądek – stomach

Serce - heart

Płuca - lungs (płuco - lung)

Wątroba - liver

Nerki - kidneys

Naczynia krwionośne - blood vessels

Mięśnie - muscles (mięsień - muscle)

At the Doctor's

Even though we wish you good luck, accidents might happen. When you have an accident or start to feel bad, don't hesitate to go to the doctor. Although we hope that you won't have to go to this page during your trip to Poland, it is always better to know at least some body parts or basic expressions. After all, when the doctor doesn't speak English, you need to keep your descriptions as precise as possible.

Polish health care (Narodowy Fundusz Zdrowia - NFZ) is state provided. This means that if you work in Poland, your employer pays your health insurance and you have free access to hospitals and health centers. Nevertheless, the accessibility of health care contributes to huge waiting lines and a really long waiting time for your medical appointment. When it comes to foreigners, health care is directly connected to your health insurance. Thus, always remember your insurance before you decide to go abroad. For now, let's take a look at some vocabulary and basic expressions:

At the Hospital/Health Center:

Szpital – hospital

Ośrodek zdrowia – health center

Poczekalnia – waiting room

Izba przyjęć – casualty department

Szpitalny Oddział Ratunkowy (SOR) – emergency department

Karetka pogotowia / ambulans – ambulance

Karta pacjenta – medical history (chart)

Oddział chirurgiczny – surgical ward

Oddział intensywnej terapii – intensive care unit

Gabinet zabiegowy – doctor's office / treatment room

At the Doctor's Office:

Doktor / lekarz – doctor

Objawy – symptoms (objaw – symptom)

Choroby przewlekłe – chronic diseases

Choroba – disease / illness

Dolegliwość – condition

Zastrzyk – injection

Szczepionka – vaccine

Recepta – prescription

Badanie krwi – a blood test

Badanie USG – ultrasonography / USG

Prześwietlenie / rentgen – X-ray

Mieć prześwietlenie – to have an X-ray

Gips – cast / plaster cast

Ubezpieczenie zdrowotne – health insurance

Ubezpieczony / ubezpieczona – insured

Zwolnienie lekarskie – sick note

Stetoskop – stethoscope

Waga – scale

Igła – needle

Conditions:

Ból głowy – headache

Ból brzucha – stomachache

Ból zęba – toothache

Boleć – to hurt

Ból – ache / pain

Gorączka – fever / temperature

Kaszel – cough

Katar – runny nose

Ból gardła – sore throat

Przeziębienie – cold

Grypa – the flu / influenza

Grypa żołądkowa – gastric flu

Złamana ręka - broken arm

Złamana noga - broken leg

Skręcona kostka - twisted ankle

Spuchnięta kostka - swollen ankle

Siniaki - bruises

Bóle w klatce piersiowej - chest pains

Wymiotować - vomit

Nudności / mdłości - nausea

Biegunka / rozwolnienie - diarrhea

Wysypka - rash

Cukrzyca - diabetes

Uczulony na - allergic to

Ciśnienie krwi - blood pressure

Zatrucie pokarmowe - food poisoning

Boli mnie głowa. - I have a headache.

Boli mnie brzuch. - I have a stomachache.

Mam wysoką gorączkę. - I have a high temperature.

Choruję na cukrzycę. - I have diabetes.

Boli mnie. - I am in pain.

Jestem uczulony / uczulona na laktozę. - I am allergic to lactose.

Jestem przeziębiony / przeziębiona. - I have a cold.

Mam kaszel i katar. - I have a runny nose and a terrible cough.

Złamałem / złamałam nogę. - I have broken my leg.

Złamałem / złamałam rękę. - I have broken my arm.

Skręciłem / skręciłam kostkę. - I have twisted my ankle.

Miałem / miałam wypadek. - I have had an accident.

Chyba mam grypę. – I think I have the flu.

Mam wysokie ciśnienie. – I have high blood pressure.

Wymiotowałem / wymiotowałam cały dzień. – I have been vomiting all day long.

Mam biegunkę. – I have diarrhea.

Kręci mi się w głowie – I feel dizzy.

Medical Advice:

Proszę usiąść. – Please, have a seat.

Co Panu / Pani dolega? – What's the matter?

Czy ma Pan / Pani ubezpieczenie? – Do you have health insurance?

Czy bierze Pan / Pani jakieś leki? – Are you on any medication?

Czy pali Pan / Pani papierosy? – Do you smoke cigarettes?

Czy może Pan / Pani opisać objawy? – Could you describe the symptoms?

Od jak dawna ma Pan / Pani te objawy? – How long have you had these symptoms?

Zmierzę Panu / Pani temperature. – I am going to check your temperature.

Proszę się rozebrać. / Proszę zdjąć ubranie. – Take your clothes off, please.

Proszę otworzyć usta – Open your mouth, please.

Musi Pan / pani zostać w łózku. – You have to stay in bed.

Operacja jest jedyną opcją. – Operation seems to be the only option.

Musi Pan / pani zostać w szpitalu. – You need to stay in the hospital.

Oto recepta. - Here's your prescription.

Proszę brać ten lek dwa razy dziennie. - You need to take this medicine twice a day.

Wyniki testu są pozytywne. - The results of the test are positive.

Muszę przepisać antybiotyk. - I need to prescribe an antibiotic.

At the Chemist's

It is important to know that, in Poland, there are many different kinds of medicines available without a prescription. Sometimes you can even buy some serious painkillers without having to go to the doctor. You can easily buy pain pills, sleeping pills, headache tablets and many more. Despite the fact that Poland offers easy access to some drugs, it is advisable to have at least a first aid kit because safety is a number one issue you need to consider while going on a trip. Anyway, let's take a look at some popular medicine:

Tabletki na ból głowy - headache tablets

Lekarstwo na przeziębienie - cold remedy

Tabletki przeciw chorobie lokomocyjnej - motion sickness pills

Tabletki nasenne - sleeping pills

Lekarstwo na trawienie - stomach powder / indigestion remedy

Syrop na kaszel - cough syrup

Krople do oczu - eye drops

Krople do nosa - nose drops / nasal drops

Krople żołądkowe - stomach drops

Lek przeciwgorączkowy - antipyretic drug

Bandaż / opatrunek – dressing

Woda utleniona – hydrogen peroxide

Rękawiczki medyczne – medical gloves

Leki antydepresyjne – antidepressants

Leki przeciwgorączkowe – antipyretics

Antybiotyki – antibiotics

Leki uspokajające – tranquilizers

Buying Clothes and Shoes

In Poland, you will find many small clothing shops and shoe shops, as well as some bigger franchises such as H&M and Zara. Usually, the well-known stores can be found in shopping malls in some bigger cities. When it comes to shopping centers, they are quite popular in Poland. One of the biggest shopping malls in Europe can be found in Poznań (the mall is called *Posnania*). Let's take a look at some vocabulary:

Basic Pieces of Clothing:

Bluzka z krótkim rękawem / T-shirt – T-shirt

Koszula – shirt

Bluzka – blouse

Sweter – sweater

Bluza – sweatshirt

Podkoszulek – undershirt

Kurtka / marynarka / żakiet – jacket

Płaszcz – coat

Kamizelka – waistcoat

Garnitur – suit

Spodnie – trousers

Dżinsy / Jeansy – jeans

Spódniczka – skirt

Sukienka – dress

Sukienka mini – mini dress

Sukienka midi – midi dress

Długa sukienka / suknia – long dress

Bielizna – Underwear:

Majtki – pants

Stanik / biustonosz – bra

Skarpetki – socks

Bokserki – boxershorts

Rajstopy – tights

Podkolanówki – tube socks / knee-socks

Kalesony – underdrawers

Odzież zimowa – Winter Clothes:

Szal – scarf

Rękawiczki – gloves

Czapka zimowa – winter hat

Komin – infinity scarf

Kurtka zimowa – winter jacket

Kominiarka narciarska – ski mask

Gogle narciarskie – ski goggles

Spodnie narciarskie – ski pants

Kurtka narciarska – ski jacket

Odzież letnia – Summer Clothes:

Szorty / krótkie spodnie – shorts

Strój kąpielowy – swimsuit

Jednoczęściowy strój kąpielowy – one-piece swimsuit

Dwuczęściowy strój kąpielowy – two-piece swimsuit

Pareo – pareo / pareau (wrap-around skirt)

Kapelusz przeciwsłoneczny – sun hat

Buty – Shoes:

Trampki / Adidasy – gym shoes / sneakers

Sandały – sandals

Kozaki – moon boots / winter shoes

Mokasyny – moccasin

Buty na obcasie – high-heeled shoes / high heels

Buty na koturnie – wedge heels

Półbuty – casual shoes

Buty do wspinaczki – climbing boots

Buty do tańca – dancing shoes

Kapcie – slippers

Klapki / japonki – flip-flops

Balerinki / płaskie buty – flat shoes

Dodatki – Accessories:

Okulary – glasses

Okulary przeciwsłoneczne – sunglasses

Torebka – bag

Torba na zakupy – shopping bag

Czapka z daszkiem – cap

Kapelusz – hat

Pasek – belt

Zegarek – watch

Szelki – braces / suspenders

Krawat – tie

Mucha – bow tie

Portfel – wallet

Kopertówka – clutch bag

Plecak – backpack

Torba na laptopa – laptop bag

Chustka – handkerchief

Biżuteria – Jewelerry:

Kolczyki – earrings

Naszynik – necklace

Bransoletka – bracelet / wristband

Bransoletka z wisiorkiem – charm bracelet

Wisiorek – pendant

Broszka – brooch / pin

Spinki do mankietów – links

Kolczyk do nosa – nose ring

Kolczyk na języku – tongue stud

Kolory – Colors:

Biały – white

Czarny – black

Niebieski – blue

Granatowy – navy

Szary – gray

Czerwony – red

Zielony – green

Żółty – yellow

Pomarańczowy – orange

Fioletowy – violet / Purple

Różowy – pink

Brązowy – brown

Beżowy – beige

Kremowy – creamy

Złoty – gold

Srebrny – silver

Kolorowy – colorful

Bezbarwny – colorless

Przeźroczysty – transparent

Wzory – Patterns:

W paski / pasiasty – striped

W kratę – checkered

W kwiaty – floral

W kropki / w grochy / w groszki – spotted / dotted

Cekinowy – sequin

Koronkowy – lacy / lacey

Lśniący / świecący – shiny

Brokatowy / błyszczący – glittery

Matowy – matt / dull

Materiał – Fabric:

Skórzany – leather

Dżinsowy – denim

Sztuczna skóra / skaja – artificial leather

Wełniany – woolen

Bawełniany – cotton

Miękki – soft

Szorstki – coarse

Jedwabny – silken

Satynowy – satin

W sklepie – At the Store:

Przymierzalnia – fitting room / dressing room

Przymierzać coś – to try something on

Wieszak na ubrania – clothing rack

Kolekcja zimowa / wiosenna – winter / spring collection

Modny – fashionable / trendy

Wystawa – display

Okazja – bargain

Cena okazyjna – bargain price

Karta podarunkowa / karta upominkowa – gift card

Reklamacja - consumer complaint

Zwrot - return

Zwrot pieniędzy - refund

Rozmiar - size

Dzień dobry, czy mogę to przymierzyć? - Hello, can I try this on?

Przepraszam, gdzie jest przymierzalnia? - Excuse me, where is the fitting room?

Chciałbym / chciałabym przymierzyć te buty. - I would like to try on these shoes.

Chciałbym / chciałabym zobaczyć tę bluzkę z wystawy. - I would like to see that shirt you have on display.

Jaki rozmiar Pan / Pani nosi? - What size do you take?

Noszę rozmiar 36. - I take a size 36.

Czy mógłby Pan / mogłaby Pani pomóc mi zapiąć ten zamek? - Could you help me with this zip?

Nie jestem pewnien / pewna czy te buty pasują do tych spodni. - I am not sure if these shoes match these trousers.

Ta bluzka mi nie pasuje. Rękawy są za długie. - This T-shirt doesn't suit me well. The sleeves are too long.

Przepraszam, ale te buty są dla mnie zbyt drogie. - I'm sorry, but these shoes are too expensive for me.

Może to Pan/Pani zapakować to jako prezent? - Could you gift wrap it for me?

Czy są większe rozmiary? - Do you have it in a bigger size?

Czy są mniejsze rozmiary? - Do you have it in a smaller size?

Czy macie tę rzecz również w kolorze czarnym? - Do you have it in black?

Z jakiego materiału są te buty? – What fabric are these shoes made of?

Czy mogę dostać większy rozmiar tych butów? – Can I have a bigger size of these shoes?

Ile kosztują te spodnie? – How much do these trousers cost?

Books and Stationery

If you are a bookworm, you will probably want to buy at least one book in Polish, despite how advanced your knowledge is of the Polish language. If you are not into books, you will probably search for at least a decent guidebook or a city plan. It is important to know that there are many bookshops in Polish cities. At every shopping center, there is at least one bookshop that offers not only books but also stationery, board games, and souvenirs. The most famous bookshop in Poland is *Empik*.

Books:

Książka – book

Powieść – novel

Literatura piękna – fiction

Literatura faktu – non-fiction

Literatura dziecięca – children's literature

Przewodnik turystyczny / przewodnik – guidebook

Mapa – map

Plan miasta – a town map – city plan

Bajki dla dzieci – storybooks

Stationery:

Zeszyt / notatnik - notebook

Długopis - pencil

Ołówek - pen

Kredki - colored pencils

Flamaster / pisak - marker pen

Gumka do mazania - rubber / eraser

Temperówka - pencil sharpener

Spinacz do papieru - paper clip

Teczka - file / folder

Taśma klejąca - sticky tape

Przepraszam, czy mógłby Pan / mogłaby Pani powiedzieć mi gdzie jest dział z książkami dla dzieci? - Excuse me, could you tell me where the children's literature section is?

Który przewodnik Pan / Pani poleca? - Which guidebook do you recommend?

Czy mógłby Pan / czy mogłaby Pani pokazać mi gdzie są przewodniki i mapy? - Could you show me where the guidebooks and maps are?

Dzień dobry, chciałbym / chciałabym kupić mapę. - Hello, I would like to buy a map.

Przepraszam, czy kupię tutaj zeszyt? - Excuse me, do you sell notebooks?

Czy mógłby Pan / mogłaby Pani doradzić który plan miasta powinienem / powinnam wziąć? - Could you tell me which city plan should I take?

Czy macie zniżki na książki? - Do you have a discount on books?

Czy dostanę tutaj przewodnik po angielsku? - Do you sell English guidebooks?

Chciałbym / chciałabym kupić ten przewodnik. - I would like to buy this guidebook.

Tourist Information Center/Sightseeing

If you go on a trip to Poland, a tourist information center is one of the places that you should visit on your first day. Keep in mind that Internet sources may contain only some basic information about the place you want to visit or they may not be reliable. A local guide, however, may provide you not only with some detailed guidance but also with the latest news about what is going on in the area. In each bigger city, there is at least one tourist center that is usually available from 9:00 am to 5:00 pm. The staff may give you free guidelines, answer all your questions and offer some trips organized by the local travel agencies. If you don't speak Polish very well, don't worry—the staff will probably speak very good English. Nevertheless, using your target language in real situations is always a good opportunity to face some linguistic challenges and to learn something new. Here is some essential vocabulary:

Centrum informacji turystycznej – tourist center

Punkt informacji turystycznej – tourist information center

Przewodnik – guide

Przewodnik turystyczny – guidebook

Mapa – map

Plan miasta – city plan

Biuro podróży – travel agency

Rezydent turystyczny – holiday representative

Wycieczka – trip

Wycieczka jednodniowa – day trip

Wycieczka autokarowa – coach trip

Zwiedzanie – tour

Zwiedzanie z przewodnikiem – guided tour

Zwiedzać – to do sightseeing

Wycieczka zorganizowana – organized trip

Zwiedzanie miasta – city tour

Opłata za wstęp – entrance fee

Miejsce zbiórki – assembling point

Czas wolny – free time

Places To Visit In A Town:

Stare miasto – Old town

Kamienice zabytkowe – old tenement buildings

Pomnik – monument

Ratusz – town hall

Ratusz Staromiejski – Old Town Hall

Budynek zabytkowy – heritage building

Pomnik zabytkowy – ancient monument

Budynek sejmu – parliament building

Muzeum – museum

Muzeum nauki – science museum

Muzeum historyczne – history museum

Muzeum narodowe – national museum

Muzeum wojskowe – military and war museum

Muzeum na powietrzu – open-air museum

Galeria sztuki – art gallery

Wystawa – exhibition

Park – park

Most – bridge

Promenada – promenade

Deptak – pedestrian zone / pedestrian street

Kościół – church

Bazylika – basilica

Dzień dobry, chciałbym / chciałabym wziąć udział w tej wycieczce. – Hello, I would like to take part in this trip.

Czy mógłby Pan / mogłaby Pani polecić mi ciekawe miejsca do zobaczenia? – Could you recommend me some places to visit here?

Czy mógłby Pan / mogłaby Pani polecić mi ciekawe miejsca, które można zwiedzić za darmo? – Could you recommend me some places that are for free?

Czy mogę tutaj robić zdjęcia? – Can I take pictures here?

Robienie zdjęć jest tutaj niedozwolone. – Taking pictures is not allowed here.

W tym museum robienie zdjęć z lampą błyskową jest zabronione. – Flash photography is not allowed in this museum.

Co warto tutaj zobaczyć? – What places are worth seeing here?

Jakie restauracje Pani / Pan poleca? – What restaurants do you recommend?

Czy ta wycieczka wymaga dużo chodzenia? – Does this trip require a lot of walking?

Czy mógłby Pan / mogłaby Pani pokazać ten punkt na mojej mapie? – Could you show me this point on my map?

Czy mogę rozmawiać z rezydentem turystycznym? – Can I speak with the holiday representative?

Co muszę zabrać ze sobą? – What do I need to take with me?

Ile mamy wolnego czasu? – How much free time do we have?

Czy tutaj płaci się za wstęp? – Is there an entrance fee here?

Jakie wycieczki jednodniowe mają Państwo w ofercie? – What kinds of day trips do you offer?

Czy ta wycieczka jest z przewodnikiem? – Is that a guided tour?

Chciałbym / chciałabym zrezygnować z tej wycieczki. – I would like to cancel my participation in this trip.

Wycieczka była świetna, dziękuję! – The trip was awesome, thank you!

If you are going to visit one of the biggest Polish cities, you may consider either sightseeing on your own or taking part in a guided tour. There are many options available; all you need to do is to go to the tourist center or a local travel agency and ask about their offer. If you don't feel confident enough with your Polish, you can always choose the option with an English-speaking guide. A guided tour may be the best option if you want to learn some history. Exploring on your own will give you some freedom and enable you to visit some less-known places in the area.

At the Bank/Exchange Office

Although most of the transactions nowadays are made using Internet resources, some activities can be done only in the actual building of the bank. Many different banks in Poland offer ATMs and CDM machines around the clock.

As far as exchange offices are concerned, you will find them in airports, shopping centers, on and near the Polish borders, and in the town centers.

At the Bank:

Bank – bank

Wypłata pieniędzy – cash withdrawal

Wypłacać – withdraw

Gotówka – cash

Karta kredytowa – credit card

Karta zbliżeniowa – tap-and-go card / proximity card

Pieniądze – money

Czek – cheque

Wpłata – deposit

Wpłacać – to deposit

Konto bankowe – bank account

Konto oszczędnościowe – savings account

Oszczędności – savings

Przelew bankowy – bank transfer

Przelew krajowy – domestic transfer

Debet – debit / overdraft

Bankomat – ATM / cash machine

Wpłatomat – CDM / cash deposit machine

Potwierdzenie zapłaty – payment confirmation

Transakcja finansowa – financial transaction

Historia transakcji – transaction history

Kredyt – credit / loan

Kredyt studencki – student loan

Kredyt hipoteczny – mortgage

Kredyt konsumpcyjny – consumer credit

Pożyczka – loan

Dług – debt

Rata – installment

Odsetki – interest

Lokata – deposit / investment

Stopa procentowa – interest rate

Podatek – tax

Podatek dochodowy – income tax

Podatek VAT – VAT / value-added tax

Faktura – invoice

Umowa – agreement / contract

Dzień dobry, chciałbym / chciałbym otworzyć konto bankowe. - Hello, I would like to open a new bank account.

Dzień dobry, oczywiście. Potrzebuję Pana / pani dowód osobisty. - Hello, of course. I need your ID.

Chciałby Pan / chciałaby Pani otworzyć zwykłe konto bankowe czy konto oszczędnościowe? - Would you like to open a regular bank account or a savings account?

Dzień dobry, chciałbym / chciałabym wpłacić pieniądze na moje konto. - Hello, I would like to deposit some cash.

Dzień dobry chciałbym / chciałabym wypłacić pieniądze z mojego konta. - Hello, I would like to withraw some cash from my account.

Ile pieniędzy chciałby Pan / chciałaby Pani wpłacić? -How much money would you like to deposit?

Ile pieniędzy chciałby Pan / chciałaby Pani wypłacić? - How much money would you like to withdraw?

Dzień dobry, chciałbym / chciałabym wziąć kredyt konsumpcyjny. - Hello, I would like to take consumer credit.

Przepraszam, gdzie jest najbliższy bankomat? - Excuse me, where is the nearest ATM machine?

Dzień dobry, mam problem z moją kartą bankową. - Hello, I have a problem with my payment card.

Dzień dobry, co dokładnie się dzieje? - Hello, what exactly is happening with the card?

Bankomat nie akceptuje mojej karty. - The ATM doesn't accept my card.

Bankomat połknął moją kartę. - The ATM machine swallowed my card.

Bankomat nie chce wydać mi gotówki. - The ATM machine doesn't want to withdraw my money.

Dzień dobry, chciałbym / chciałaby otworzyć konto oszczędnościowe - Hello, I would like to open a savings account.

At the Exchange Office:

Although Poland is a member of the European Union (EU), it does have its own currency—Polish złoty. Most of the European countries have already accepted the universal currency—the Euro.

Kantor wymiany walut - currency exchange / exchange office

Waluta - currency

Kurs wymiany walut - exchange rate

Bieżący kurs - current rate of exchange

Waluta krajowa - national currency

Wymienić - exchange

Kupić - buy

Sprzedać - sell

Przewalutować - convert a currency

Złoty Polski - Polish zloty

Euro - Euro

Funt brytyjski - British pound

Dolar amerykański - US dollar

Hrywna ukraińska - Ukrainian hryvnia

Korona czeska - Czech koruna

Korona norweska - Norwegian krone

Korona szwedzka - Swedish krone

Forint węgierski - Hungarian forint

Dolar kanadyjski - Canadian dollar

Dolar australijski - Australian dollar

Jen japoński – Japanese yen

Rubel rosyjski – Russian rouble

Rupia indyjska – Indian rupee

Real brazylijski – Brazilian real

Lira turecka – Turkish lira

Kryptowaluta – a cryptocurrency

Bitcoin – Bitcoin

Dzień dobry, chciałbym / chciałabym wymienić moje pieniądze. – Hello, I would like to exchange my money.

Dzień dobry, jaki jest kurs dolara? – What is the US dollar's exchange rate?

Przepraszam, gdzie znajdę kantor wymiany walut? – Excuse me, where can I find the exchange office?

Dzień dobry, chciałbym wymienić moje dolary na złote. – Hello, I would like to exchange my dollars to Polish zloty.

Dzień dobry, ile dolarów chciałby Pan / chciałaby Pani wymienić? – Hello, how much dollars would you like to exchange?

Chciałbym / chciałabym wymienić 500 dolarów. – I would like to exchange 500 US dollars.

Oczywiście, bieżący kurs wymiany to 3,76. – Of course, the current exchange rate today is 3,76.

Przepraszam, czy mogę tutaj wymienić jen japoński na Polski złoty? – Excuse me, can I exchange here Japanese yen to Polish zloty?

Niestety, nie posiadamy jenów japońskich. – I'm sorry, we don't have Japanese yen.

Dzień dobry, czy mogę tutaj wymienić kryptowaluty? – Hello, can I exchange cryptocurrencies here?

Dzień dobry, niestety nie akceptujemy kryptowalut. – Hello. I am sorry, we don't accept cryptocurrencies here.

Dzień dobry, akceptujemy tylko Bitcoin. – Hello, we accept only Bitcoin.

Entertainment

A good trip consists of sightseeing and some entertainment. If you go on a trip on your own, it is up to you how you spend your time. Thus, keep in mind that Polish cities offer plenty of opportunities to enjoy in your free time. Moreover, the nightlife is amazing.

At the Cinema

Cinemas are quite popular in Poland. Cities such as Warsaw, Cracow or Poznan contain at least ten different cinemas, and some smaller cities offer at least one. The tickets usually are more expensive on weekends, so if you want to choose the cheapest way, go to the cinema on Wednesday or Thursday. Sometimes, tickets on weekends can cost twice as much!

Kino - cinema

Film - film / movie

Film akcji - action film

Thriller - thriller

Komedia romantyczna - romantic comedy

Komedia - comedy

Horror - horror film

Film historyczny - historical film

Film przygodowy - adventure film

Film science fiction - science-fiction film

Musical / film muzyczny - musical

Sala kinowa - screening room

Miejsce - seat

Rząd - row

Ekran - screen

Bar przekąskowy - snack bar

Popcorn - popcorn

Zimne napoje - cold beverages

Bilet do kina - cinema ticket

Dzień dobry, poproszę dwa blilety. - Hello, two movie tickets, please.

Jaki film chciałby Pan / chciałaby Pani obejrzeć? - Which film would you like to see?

Chciałbym / chciałabym obejrzeć ten film. - I would like to see this film.

Proszę wybrać swoje miejsce. - Please, choose your seat.

Czy te dwa miejsca są wolne? - Are these two seats free?

Przykro mi, te miejsca nie są już wolne. - I'm sorry, these two are not available.

Czy mogę zabrać jedzenie i napoje na salę? - Can I take food and drink to the screening room?

Może Pan / Pani zabrać tylko jedzenie i picie zakupione w naszym barze. - You can take the food and beverages from our snack bar.

Przepraszam, gdzie jest bar z przekąskami? - Excuse me, where is the snack bar?

Dzień dobry, chciałbym / chciałabym kupić dwa duże popcorny. – Hello, I would like to buy two large popcorns.

Dobrze, czy coś do picia? – Okay, would you like something to drink?

Poproszę dwie duże cole. – Two large cokes, please.

Przepraszam, gdzie jest sala numer 8? – Excuse me, where is room number 8?

Prosimy o wyłączenie telefonów. – Please, switch off your phones.

Nagrywanie filmów jest zabronione. – Recording is not allowed.

At the Theater/Opera

Although theaters are not that popular when compared to previous decades, you can still enjoy some places that are worth visiting. Theaters in Poland can be found in cities such as Warsaw, Krakow, etc.

Teatr – theater

Teatr muzyczny – musical theatre

Sztuka – play

Spektakl / przedstawienie – performance

Występować – perform

Aktor / aktorka – actor

Główna rola – lead / major role

Balet – ballet

Balet klasyczny – classical balet

Kurtyna – curtain

Rekwizyt – prop / stage prop

Scena – stage

Opera – opera

Opera - opera house

Operetka - operetta

Musical - musical

Chór - choir

tancerz / tancerka - dancer

śpiewak operowy - opera singer (masculine)

śpiewaczka operowa - opera singer (feminine)

Dzień dobry, czy są jeszcze bilety na tę sztukę? - Hello, are tickets for this play still available?

Dzień dobry, zostało jeszcze kilka biletów. - Hello, there are only a few tickets left.

Chciałbym / chciałabym trzy bilety na tę sztukę. - I would like to buy three tickets for this play.

Oczywiście, proszę wybrać miejsca. - Of course, please, choose your seats.

Które miejsca są dostępne? - Which seats are free?

Wolne miejsca są tylko w ostatnim rzędzie. - The only free seats are in the last row.

Sztuka rozpoczyna się o godzinie 19:00. - The play starts at 7 PM.

Dzień dobry, chciałbym / chciałabym kupić cztery bilety na tę operę. - Hello, I would like to buy four tickets for this opera.

Oczywiście, czy chciałby Pan / chciałaby Pani miejsce normalne czy w sekcji VIP? - Of course, would you like to book regular seats or seats in the VIP section?

Chciałbym / chciałabym zarezerwować normalne miejsca. - I would like to book regular seats.

O której godzinie rozpoczyna się opera? - What time does the opera start?

Opera rozpoczyna się o godzinie 20:00. – The opera starts at 8 PM.

Nightlife

If you decide to stay in a big city, you will have the opportunity to enjoy the nightlife. There are plenty of night clubs, pubs and good parties in each city in Poland. Moreover, parties do not finish at 2:00 AM or 3:00 AM. Polish night clubs are usually open till morning, that is 6:00 AM or even 7:00 AM. In Poland, you can party all night long.

Nocne życie – nightlife

Klub nocny / klub – night club

Klub muzyczny – music club

Bar / pub – bar / pub

Dyskoteka – disco

Barman – barman / bartender

Barmanka – barmaid / bartender

Parkiet – dance floor

Tańczyć – dance

Muzyka – music

Karaoke – karaoke

Śpiewać – sing

Imprezować – party

Spędzać czas z przyjaciółmi – spend time with friends

Zespół muzyczny – music group

DJ / didżej – DJ / club DJ

Drink / koktajl – cocktail

Loża VIP – VIP lounge

Ochroniarze – security guards

Cześć, chciałbym / chciałabym zamówić dwa koktajle. - Hi, I would like to buy two cocktails.

Oczywiście, jakie drinki? - Of course, which drinks?

Poproszę dwa z owocami. - I would like two drinks with some fruit.

Oczywiście. Czy mam dorzucić kostki lodu? - Of course. Would you like some ice cubes?

Tak, poproszę. - Yes, please.

Cześć, czy mogę prosić o kartę napojów? - Hi, can I have a cocktail menu?

Cześć, oto karta napojów. - Hi, here is the cocktail menu.

Przepraszam, o której startuje impreza? - Excuse me, what time does the party start?

Dobry wieczór, chciałbym / chciałabym zamówić lożę VIP dla 9 osób. - Hello, I would like to book a VIP lounge this night for nine people.

Oczywiście, to będzie 200 zł. - Of course, that will be 200 zł.

At the Swimming Pool/SPA

Sightseeing that requires long hours of walking and eating street food may be tiring. Thus, going swimming or relaxing in a sauna may be the best idea at the end of a day full of different activities. If you decide to stay for a couple of days or even a week, consider dedicating one whole day to relaxing and resting.

Basen / pływalnia - swimming pool

Akwapark / aquapark - water park

Pływać - swim

Basen kryty - indoor swimming pool

Basen odkryty - outdoor swimming pool

Ręcznik kąpielowy – bath towel

Kółko do pływania – swim ring

Deska do pływania – swimming board

Pływaczki – armbands

Ratownik – life guard

Strój kąpielowy – swimsuit

Przebieralnia – changing room

Przebieralnia damska – women's changing room

Przebieralnia męska – men's changing room

Sauna – sauna

Uzdrowisko / spa – spa

Ośrodek odnowy biologicznej – health spa

Masaż – massage

Masaż twarzy – face massage

Zabieg – treatment

Jacuzzi – hot tub / jacuzzi

Dzień dobry, chciałbym / chciałabym kupić dwa bilety na basen. – Hello, I would like to buy two swimming pool tickets.

Oczywiście, dwa bilety normalne? – Of course, two normal tickets?

Jeden bilet normalny i jeden bilet studencki. – One normal ticket and one student ticket.

Czy mogę zobaczyć Pana / Pani legitymację studencką? – May I see your student ID?

Ok, to będzie razem 25 złotych. – Okay, that will be 25 zł.

Przepraszam, gdzie jest damska przebieralnia? – Excuse me, where is the women's changing room?

Czy mogę zabrać tę deskę do pływania? - Can I take this swimming board?

Oczywiście, może Pan / Pani zabrać deskę, ale musi ją Pan / Pani zwrócić ratownikowi przy wyjściu. - Of course, you can take the swimming board but you need to return it to the lifeguard when you decide to leave.

Czy korzystanie z sauny jest wliczone w cenę? - Is the sauna included?

Niestety, sauna wymaga kupienia osobnego biletu. - Unfortunately, using the sauna requires buying a different ticket.

Ile kosztuje korzystanie z sauny? - How much is it for the sauna?

Jedna minuta kosztuje 50 groszy. - One minute spent in the sauna costs 50 groszy.

Ile kosztuje zabieg manicure? - How much is it for the manicure?

Manicure kosztuje 30 zotych. - The manicure costs 30 złotych.

Czy na basenie jest jacuzzi? - Is there a jacuzzi in the swimming pool?

Czy dzieci mogą korzystać z dużego basenu? - Can children swim in the big pool?

Niestey, tylko dorośli mogą pływać w dużym basenie. - I'm sorry, only adults can swim in the big pool.

Going to the Gym

Due to the popularization of a healthy lifestyle, going to the gym even on vacation has become a standard nowadays. If you are a fit lifestyle lover and you don't want to skip your workout while going on holidays, you can, of course, choose the gym that is available at the place of your stay. A healthy lifestyle has become really trendy in Poland; thus, in some cities, there are many options you can choose from.

Siłownia – gym

Karnet na siłownię – gym membership

Trening – workout

Trening kondycyjny – circuit training

Trening siłowy – strength training

Ćwiczenia – exercises

Z przerwami – intervals

Bieżnia stacjonarna / bieżnia – treadmill

Orbitrek – elliptical trainer / cross-trainer

Rower stacjonarny – exercise bicycle

Przyrząd do ćwiczeń siłowych – weight machine

Trening cardio – cardio workout

Podnoszenie ciężarów – weightlifting

Aerobik – aerobics

Mata do ćwiczeń – workout mat

Brzuszki – sit-ups

Przysiady – squats

Pompki – press-ups / push-ups

Hula hop – hula hoop

Skakanka – skipping rope

Ćwiczenia gimnastyczne – keep fit exercises

Strój na siłownię – gym clothes

Leginssy na siłownię – gym leggings

Dzień dobry, chciałbym / chciałabym kupić jeden bilet na siłownię. – Hello, I would like to buy one gym ticket.

Dzień dobry, czy chciałby Pan / chciałaby Pani kupić karnet na siłownię? – Hello, would you like to buy our gym membership?

Nie, dziękuję. - No, thanks.

Jakie urządzenia znajdują się na siłowni? - What machines does your gym have?

Mamy bieżnie, rowerki stacjonarne, przyrządy do ćwiczeń siłowych i wiele innych. - We have treadmills, exercise bicycles, weight machines, and many more.

Czy wasza siłownia ma zniżki dla studentów? - Does your gym offer discounts for students?

Tak, studenci mają 10 % zniżki. - Yes, there is a special 10% off discount for students.

Czy wasza siłownia ma w ofercie treningi z trenerem personalnym? - Does your gym offer workouts with a personal trainer?

Tak, może Pan / Pani skorzystać z treningu z trenerem personalnym. - Yes, you can choose the workout with a personal trainer.

Ile kosztuje jedna godzina treningu z trenerem personalnym? - How much does one hour with a personal trainer cost?

Jedna godzina treningu z trenerem personalnym kosztuje 50 zł. - A one-hour workout with a personal trainer costs 50 zł.

Przepraszam, gdzie jest męska szatnia? - Excuse me, where is the men's changing room?

Szatnia męska jest na końcu korytarza po prawej stronie. - The men's changing room is at the end of the corridor on the right.

Going to the Park

Despite the season, Polish parks always look beautiful. They look especially amazing during early autumn (September, October) when the leaves start to turn red, yellow, and orange. The first weeks of autumn in Poland are called "the golden Polish autumn" since the colors of the trees and bushes look wonderful. If you decide to go on a trip to Poland in September or October, remember to go to the park for a long walk. These beautiful colors will make you feel delighted.

Park – park

Spacer – walk

Przechadzka – stroll

Spacerować – walk

Drzewo – tree

Staw – pond

Ławka – bench

Fontanna – fountain

Ścieżka / aleja – alley

Kwiaty – flowers

Liście – leaves

Krzewy – bushes

Krzewy różnane – rose bushes

Oranżeria – hothouse / orangery

Trawnik – lawn / grass

Miejsce piknikowe – picnic area

Kosz na śmieci – waste bin

Plac zabaw – playground

Huśtawka – swing

Karuzela – roundabout / carousel

Zjeżdżalnia – playground slide

Ptaki – birds

Kaczka – duck

Łabędź – swan

Wiewiórka - squirrel

Róża - rose

Dąb - oak tree

Klon - maple tree

Świerk - spruce

Sosna - pine tree

Kasztanowiec - chestnut tree

Żołędzie - acorns

Kasztany - chestnuts

Przepraszam, gdzie jest plac zabaw? - Excuse me, where is the playground?

Czy w tym parku są miejsca piknikowe? - Are there any picnic areas in this park?

Czy mogę rozpalić grilla w strefie piknikowej? - Can I have a barbecue in the picnic area?

Tak, grillowanie jest dozwolone w strefie piknikowej. - Yes, having a barbecue is allowed in the picnic area.

Tak, miejsce piknikowe jest obok placu zabaw. - Yes, the picnic area is next to the playground

Czy można tutaj przyjść z psem? - Are dogs allowed here?

Przepraszam, nie może Pan / Pani spacerować tutaj z psem. - I'm sorry, you can't walk your dog here.

Przepraszam, spacerowanie po tym trawniku jest zabronione. - I'm sorry, walking on this lawn is not allowed.

Przepraszam, wchodzenie do fontanny jest zabronione. - I am sorry, walking into the fountain is not allowed.

Going to the Church

Poland is a Catholic country; almost 90 percent of its citizens are Catholic, and at least one church can be found even in a small village. Surprisingly enough, there are around 10,000 churches in the whole country! If you decide to visit Poland, you should definitely see at least one church—whatever your religion might be. Churches that can be found in the old town areas are the most precious pieces of architecture because some of them were built during the Renaissance or even the Middle Ages! It is important to know that you don't have to take part in a mass to visit a church—you can just walk inside the building and admire the architecture. Some of the churches even have special tourist zones.

Kościół - church

Bazylika - basilica

Kościół katolicki - Catholic church

Parafia - parish

Ławka kościelna - pew

Ołtarza - altar

Ambona - pulpit

Msza święta - church service / mass

Organy - organ

Ksiądz - priest

Zakonnica - nun

Zakonnik - monk

Organista - organist

Rzeźba - sculpture

Ofiara - collection (collecting money)

Prezbiterium - chancel / presbytery

Dzwonnica - bell tower

Kaplica - chapel

Dzwon - bell

Wieża kościelna - church tower

Cmentarz - cemetery / churchyard

Przepraszam, o której godzinie jest kolejna msza święta? - Excuse me, what time does the next mass begin?

Czy mogę robić zdjęcia w środku kościoła? - Can I take pictures inside the church?

Czy mogę wejść na wieżę kościelną? - Can I climb up the church tower?

Przykro mi, wieża kościelna nie jest dostępna dla zwiedzających. - I'm sorry, the church tower is not available for tourists.

Robienie zdjęć w kościele jest dozwolone. - Taking pictures inside the church is allowed.

Czy mogę zwiedzić ten kościół z przewodnikiem? - Are there any guided tours around the church available?

Czy wejście na wieżę kościelną jest płatne? - Do I have to pay for going up the church tower?

Niestety, ten obszar nie jest dla turystów. - I am sorry, this area is not available for tourists.

Czy mogę zobaczyć przykościelny cmentarz? - Can I see the churchyard?

Oczywiście, cmentarz przykościelny jest udostępniony dla zwiedzających. - Of course, the churchyard is available for tourists.

Buying Souvenirs

Souvenirs are, of course, the inseparable part of each trip, especially when you decide to go abroad. T-shirts, fancy mugs, fridge magnets or postcards enable you to reminisce on the beautiful memories of the places you visited. When it comes to buying souvenirs in Poland, you can find a souvenir shop basically "just around the corner" with a lot of fancy stuff. Let's take a look at some useful vocabulary:

Pamiątka z podróży – souvenir

Pamiątki z podróży – souvenirs

Sklep z pamiątkami – souvenir shop

Na pamiątkę – as a souvenir

Koszulka – T-shirt

Kubek – mug

Pocztówka – postcard

Posążek / figurka – figurine

Zapalniczka – lighter

Brelok / breloczek – key fob

Długopis – pen

Magnes na lodówkę – fridge magnet

Zabawka – toy

Książka – book

Etui na okulary – spectacle case

Etui na telefon – phone case

Dzień dobry, chciałbym / chciałabym kupić pamiątki. – Hello, I would like to buy some souvenirs.

Oczywiście, czy szuka Pan / Pani czegoś szczególnego? – Of course, are you looking for something specific?

Niekoniecznie. Co Pan / Pani poleca? – Not really. What do you recommend?

Mamy bardzo ładne kubki i magnesy. – We have some nice mugs and fridge magnets.

Dobrze, wezmę jeden kubek i jednen magnes. - Okay, I will take one mug and one fridge magnet.

Który magnes chciałby Pan / chciałaby Pani kupić? - Which magnet would you like to buy?

Wezmę ten z górami. - I will take the one with the mountains.

Dobrze, czy coś jeszcze? - Okay, anything else?

Chciałbym / chciałabym kupić pocztówkę. - I would like to buy a postcard.

Oczywiście, którą pocztówkę chciałby Pan / chciałaby Pani kupić? - Of course, which postcard would you like to buy?

Poproszę tę z morzem. - The one with the sea, please.

Jeden kubek, jeden magnes i jedna pocztówka, to będzie razem 24 złote. - One mug, one fridge magnet, and one postcard, that will be 24 złotys.

Chciałbym / chciałabym zapłacić kartą. - I would like to pay with a credit card.

Niestety, nie może Pan / Pani zapłacić tutaj kartą. Przyjmujemy tylko gotówkę. - I'm sorry, you can't pay with a credit card here. We only accept cash.

Ok, w takm razie zapłacę gotówką. Proszę. - Okay, I will pay with cash then. Here you are.

Dziękuję bardzo. Miłego dnia. - Thank you very much. Have a nice day.

Geography

Countries – kraje:

Polska – Poland

Wielka Brytania – UK / Great Britain

Stany Zjednoczone / USA – the United States / the USA

Niemcy – Germany

Francja – France

Hiszpania – Spain

Czechy – the Czech Republic

Włochy – Italy

Portugalia – Portugal

Grecja – Grecce

Holandia – the Netherlands

Belgia – Belgium

Węgry – Hungary

Słowacja – Slovakia

Ukraina – Ukraine

Turcja - Turkey

Dania - Denmark

Norwegia - Norway

Szwecja - Sweden

Finlandia - Finland

Chorwacja - Croatia

Irlandia - Ireland

Islandia - Iceland

Rosja - Russia

Chiny - China

Japonia - Japan

Australia - Australia

Brazylia - Brazil

Argentyna - Argentina

Kolumbia - Colombia

Meksyk - Mexico

Kanada - Canada

Egipt - Egypt

Izrael - Israel

Continents – kontynenty:

Ziemia - the Earth

Europa - Europe

Azja - Asia

Australia - Australia

Afryka - Africa

Antarktyda - Antarctica

Ameryyka Północna – North America

Ameryka Południowa – South America

Ameryka Środkowa – Central America

Nazwy geograficzne – place names:

Ocean Spokojny – the Pacific Ocean

Ocean Indyjski – the Indian Ocean

Ocean Atlantycki – the Atlantic Ocean

Morze Bałtyckie – the Baltic Sea

Morze Śródziemne – the Mediterranean Sea

Morze Czarne – the Black Sea

Morze Czerwone – The Red Sea

Morze Martwe – the Dead Sea

Himalaje – the Himalayas

Alpy – the Alps

Andy – the Andes

Góry Skaliste – the Rocky Mountains

Tatry – the Tatra Mountains

Karpaty – the Carpathians

Sudety – Sudetes (the Sudeten)

Amazonka – the Amazon River

Nizina Europejska – the European Plain

Jezioro Wiktorii – Lake Victoria

Bajkał – Baikal

Rów Mariański – Mariana Trench

Krajobraz – Landscape:

Morze – sea

Ocean – ocean

Jezioro – lake

Rzeka – river

Staw – pond

Wodospad – waterfall

Strumień – stream

Plaża – beach

Las – forest / woods

Łąka – meadow

Góry – mountains

Góra – mountain

Łańcuch górski – mountain range

Wyspa – island

Pole – field

Niziny – lowlands

Wyżyny – highlands

Geography – Poland

If you decide to visit a different country, do a bit of research before you arrive. It is advisable to know the basic pieces of information about the area; for example, its surface features (mountains, plains, etc.), territorial units (parishes, counties, etc.) and the environment.

The country of Poland is divided into sixteen voivodeships. Each voivodeship consists of plenty of districts, and each district consists of smaller municipal districts and county boroughs. Also, each voivodeship has its own capital city with a local government.

Polish Voivodeships:

Dolnośląskie – Lower Silesian (capital: Wrocław)

Kujawsko-Pomorskie – Kuyavian-Pomeranian (capitals: Bydgoszcz, Toruń)

Lubelskie – Lublin (capital: Lublin)

Lubuskie – Lubusz (capitals: Gorzów Wielkopolski, Zielona Góra

Łódzkie – Łódź (capital: Łódź)

Małopolskie – Lesser Poland (capital: Kraków)

Mazowieckie – Masovian (capital: Warszawa)

Opolskie – Opole (capital: Opole)

Podkarpackie – Subcarpatian (capital: Rzeszów)

Podlaskie – Podlaskie (capital: Białystok)

Pomorskie – Pomeranian (capital: Gdańsk)

Śląskie – Silesian (capital: Katowice)

Świętokrzyskie – Holy Cross (capital: Kielce)

Warmińsko-Mazurskie – Warmian-Masurian (capital: Olsztyn)

Wielkopolskie – Greater-Poland (capital: Poznań)

Zachodniopomorskie – West Pomeranian (capital: Szczecin)

When it comes to the surface features, Poland has access to the Baltic sea on the north (the coastline is 440 km long), and to the mountains on the south (with the highest mountain being Rysy at 2,499 meters). The surface altitude becomes higher and higher as you move from north to south. In Northern and Central Poland, you will find lowlands and lake districts, whereas, in Southern Poland, you will find highlands and mountains. Here are some of the most beautiful pieces of landscape that you can see in Poland:

Baltic sea – as mentioned before, Poland has a quite long coastline (440 km). The Baltic sea is rather cold, yet it makes a good impression. There are a few beautiful resorts (for example Kołobrzeg, Trójmiasto, Świnoujście) and national parks (Łeba, Wolin) that you can visit.

Tatra mountains – one of the most beautiful places in Poland! The Tatra mountains offer many mountain trails with amazing views; however, some of them are only for advanced tourists with the proper equipment. If you decide to visit the Tatra mountains, you will probably stay in Zakopane—one of the most popular tourist destinations. Remember that the road to Zakopane is always crowded; sometimes you can be stuck in a traffic jam for long hours.

Karkonosze – this is a less popular mountain range, yet it is really beautiful. If you are looking for breathtaking landscapes without many tourists, you should go to Karkonosze. Its highest mountain is Śnieżka at 1,603 meters high.

Mazury – the most beautiful lake district in Poland. If you want your holiday to be peaceful and close to nature, go to Mazury. The lakes offer many opportunities for canoeists, sailors, windsurfers, and kitesurfers.

Hel – a really thin and long peninsula that is located on the Baltic Sea. In its thinnest place, Hel peninsula is only 100 meters wide! If you are into kitesurfing and windsurfing, it is the best destination. The windy gulf of Hel will give you the best opportunity to try these sports!

Sports

Even though Poland has not had the most successful football team, Polish people have always loved football. The Poles strongly support some local teams, and what is more, Poles love watching the Champions League. Besides, Polish people love ski jumping and speedway.

When it comes to doing sports, the Poles are quite active. You can see many people jogging, walking or riding a bike if you visit a Polish city.

Sports:

Igrzyska Olimpijskie – the Olympic Games

Liga Mistrzów – Champions League

Mecz – match

Piłka nożna – football

Piłka ręczna – handball

Siatkówka – volleyball

Koszykówka – basketball

Baseball – baseball

Futbol amerykański – American football

Skok w dal – long jump

Skok wzwyż – high jump

Skok o tyczce – pole vault

Rzut oszczepem – javelin throw

Rzut młotem – hammer throw

Sprint – sprint

Kolarstwo – cycling

Żużel – speedway

Formuła 1 – Formula One / F1

Tenis – tennis

Badminton – badminton

Golf – golf

Kręgle – bowling

Żeglarstwo – sailing

Tenis stołowy – table tennis

Gimnastyka – gymnastics

Siatkówka plażowa – beach volleyball

Sztuki walki – martial arts

Boks – boxing

Łucznictwo – archery

Strzelanie – shooting

Wyścigi konne – horse racing

Winter Sports:

Jazda na nartach – skiing

Skoki narciarskie – ski jumping

Turniej Czterech Skoczni – Four Hills Tournament

Łyżwiarstwo - ice-skating

Łyżwiarstwo figurowe - figure skating

Łyżwiarstwo szybkie - speed skating

Hokej na lodzie - ice hockey

Jazda na desce - snowboarding

Saneczkarstwo - tobogganing

Bobsleje - bobsleigh

Daily Sport Activities:

Bieganie - running / jogging

Spacer z kijkami / Nordic walking - Nordic walking

Spacerowanie - walking

Jazda na rowerze - bike riding

Jazda na rolkach - rollerblading

Jazda na wrotkach - roller skating

Jazda na deskorolce - skateboarding

Jazda na skuterze wodnym - jetskiing

Jazda na motocyklu - motorcycling

Taniec - dancing

Kalistenika - calisthenics

Wspinaczka górska - climbing

Wspinaczka ściankowa - indoor climbing

Siłownia na powietrzu - outdoor gym

Joga - yoga

Aerobik - aerobics

Aerobik wodny - aquarobics

Pływanie - swimming

Extreme Sports:

Skok na bungee - bungee jumping

Skok ze spadochronem - parachute

Spływ górski - white-water rafting

Windsurfing - windsurfing

Szybownictwo - gliding

Nurkowanie pod lodem - ice diving

Alpinizm jaskiniowy - caving

Narciarstwo ekstremalne - extreme skiing

Alpinizm - alpinism

Himalaizm - himalaism

Sports Equipment:

Narty - ski

Deskorolka - skateboard

Rolki - rollerblades

Wrotki - skates

Rower - bike

Łyżwy - skates (for ice skating)

Motocykl - motorbike

Mata do jogi - yoga mat

Ciężarki - weights

Lina - rope

Kask rowerowy - bicycle helmet

Ochraniacze - athletic support

Strój sportowy - leisurewear

Sanki – sled

Plecak – backpack

Buty wspinaczkowe – climbing shoes

Buty do biegania – running shoes

Kamizelka ratunkowa – life jacket

Rakieta tenisowa – tennis racket

Rakieta do badmintona – badminton racket

Bolid formuły 1 – formula 1 car

Spadochron – parachute

Żaglówka – sailing boat

The Weather

Polish climate is quite moderate. This means that there are four seasons (spring, summer, autumn, and winter) in Poland and each season is completely different. Spring in Poland starts in March and ends in May / June. The temperatures during the spring are totally diversified—in March, you may need a winter coat on one day, and a T-shirt and shorts on another. Summer in Poland is rather warm. Temperatures in June / July / August and even during the first weeks of September fluctuate between 68°F / 20°C and 89.6°F / 32°C. Autumn is similar to spring, as far as temperatures are concerned, yet during the autumn the temperatures drop gradually. The winter usually starts at the end of December and ends in February. It is important to know that winters in Poland are not that cold. The temperatures fluctuate somewhere between 30.2°F / -1°C and 32°F / 0°C. The last five winters in Poland were quite mild; the lowest temperatures were reported only during a few days in January.

As far as the weather forecast is concerned, you can watch it on Polish television every day. The main forecast is shown in the evening, but many others are shown throughout the day. You can, of course, check the forecast on the Internet, or even ask Google about the weather. Keep in mind that Polish forecasts display the temperature using only the Celsius system.

Prognoza pogody – weather forecast

Pogoda – weather

Słońce – sun

Temperatura – temperature

Świecić – shine

Słonecznie – sunny

Ciepło / ciepły – warm / hot

Zimno / zimny – cold

Chmura – cloud (chmury – clouds)

Zachmurzenie – cloudiness / overcast

Lekkie zachmurzenie – light overcast

Deszcz – rain

Padać – to rain

Przelotne opady – shower

Śnieg – snow

Opady deszczu – rainfall

Intensywne opady deszczu – heavy rainfall

Opady sniegu – snowfall

Intensywne opady śniegu – heavy snowfall

Grad – hail

Mgła – fog

Mglisty / mglisto – foggy

Ograniczona widoczność – limited visibility

Śliska nawierzchnia – slippery road

Ciśnienie atmosferyczne – air pressure

Wilgotność powietrza – air humidity

Niskie ciśnienie – low pressure

Wyskie ciśnienie – high pressure

Burza – storm

Błyskawica – lightning

Grzmot – thunder

Wiatr – wind

Porywy wiatru – wind blasts

Prędkość wiatru – wind speed

Silny wiatr – high wind / strong wind

Burza z piorunami – electrical storm

Wichura – windstorm

Nadciąga wichura – a windstorm is blowing up

Huragan – hurricane

Tornado – tornado

Pówódź / zalanie – flodding

Susza – drought

Przymrozek – freeze

Szron – frost

Szadź – hard rime frost

Witamy w prognozie pogody. – Welcome to the weather forecast.

Zobaczmy co nas czeka w dzisiejszej pogodzie. – Let's see what the weather is like today.

Na północy kraju będzie dzisiaj słonecznie i ciepło. – In the north of the country, it will be sunny and warm.

Na południu kraju mogą wystąpić przelotne opady deszczu. – In the south of the country, there is a chance of showers.

W centralnej części kraju mogą wystąpić silne porywy wiatru do 55.9 m/h / 90 km/h. - In the central part of the country, there is a chance of strong wind blasts up to 55.9 m/h / 90 km/h.

Ciśnienie atmosferyczne wynosi dzisiaj 1007 hPa. - The air pressure today is 1007 hPa.

Wilgotność powietrza wynosi dzisiaj 60 percent. - The air humidity today is 60 percent.

Dziś w całym kraju będzie ciepło i słonecznie. - Today we expect sunny and hot weather in the whole country.

Dziś po południu na północy kraju mogą wystąpić burze. - In the north of the country, there is a chance of a thunderstorm in the afternoon.

Dziś będzie padać w całym kraju. - Today it will be raining in the whole country.

Temperatura w północnej części kraju nie przekroczy 77 stopni. - The temperaturę in the northern part of the country will not be higher than 77°F.

W nocy temperatura spadnie poniżej zera. The temperaturę will drop below zero during the night.

Bądźcie ostrożni! W godzinach wieczornych spodziewamy się silnych wiatrów w całym kraju. - Be careful! We expect very strong winds in the whole country during the evening hours.

At School

Although the Polish system of education seems to be similar to the English one at first glance, there are certainly some major differences. Education of an individual starts at the age of six with one year of compulsory pre-school class (in Polish it is called *the 0 class*). Of course, a child can be sent to a playground at the age of three, four or five, yet going to a playground is not compulsory.

The actual education starts at the age of seven when a child goes to the first grade of a primary school (usually the 0 class takes place in the same school). The primary education comprises eight grades and ends with a standardized state exam. Next steps of education are not compulsory, yet nearly every student decides to get "secondary/high school" education.

After finishing primary school, a student can choose high school (*lyceum*—four years) that ends with a standardized state exam (matura), high school with vocational program (*technikum*—five years) that ends with *matura* and a vocational exam or only a vocational course (*szkoła zawodowa*) that ends with a vocational exam. It is important to know that *liceum* and *technikum* can provide a student with a high school degree, provided that he or she passes the *matura* exam. The vocational course can provide a student with the so-called vocational education but no official degree. In Poland, there are private high schools, yet they aren't popular at all. Polish students choose public high schools since they provide a really good education and they are completely free.

After passing the matura exam, a student can go to university. All public universities are for free—the education is state provided. Of course, there are private universities, yet the majority of students decide to go to a public university since they offer really good educational programs. Many students that already have a job choose a part-time program that involves going to classes on Saturdays and Sundays. Unfortunately, the part-time program is not for free, even for public universities.

School Subjects:

Edukacja – education

Język polski – Polish

Matematyka – mathematics / maths

Język obcy – foreign language

Język angielski – English

Język niemiecki – German

Język hiszpański – Spanish

Geografia – geography

Historia – history

Biologia – biology

Chemia – chemistry

Fizyka – physics

Religia – religion

Wychowanie fizyczne (WF) – physical education (PE)

Muzyka – music class

Plastyka - art class

Informatyka - IT class

Godzina wychowawcza - form period / homeroom period

Zajęcia dodatkowe - extracurricular activities

Kółko zainteresowań - special interest group

Zajęcia wyrównawcze - remedial class

Gimnastyka korekcyjna - remedial exercises

Zajęcia praktyczne - practical class

Zajęcia do wyboru - elective courses

Zajęcia wychowawcze - advisory class

Zajęcia wieczorowe - night class

At School:

Nauczyciel - teacher

Uczeń - student

Dyrektor szkoły - school head teacher / school principal

Sala lekcyjna - classroom

Lekcja - lesson

Zajęcia - class

Stołówka - cafeteria / canteen

Sklepik szkolny - tuck shop

Szatnia - changing room

Sala gimnastyczna - school gym

Boisko szkolne - school playground

Sekretariat szkolny - school's secretary office

Biblioteka szkolna - school library

Czytelnia - a reading room

Sala komputerowa – IT suite

Gabinet dyrektora – head teacher's office

Woźny – caretaker

Dzwonek szkolny – school bell

Przerwa – break

Przerwa śniadaniowa – lunch break

Świetlica szkolna – afterschool club

Autobus szkolny – school bus

Wycieczka szkolna – school trip

Sprawdzian / test – test

Ocena – grade (oceny – grades)

Kartkówka – short quiz

Kartkówka ze słówek – vocabulary quiz

Egzamin państwowy – state exam

Uczyć się – to learn / to study

Uczyć się na pamięć – to learn by heart

Czytać – read

Pisać – write

Słuchać – listen

Bawić się / grać – play

Wkuwać – swot / cram

Zaliczyć / zdać test – to pass a test

Oblać test / nie zaliczyć testu – to fail a test

Pisać egzamin – to take a test

Poprawiać test – to retake a test

Egzamin poprawkowy / poprawka – retake

Dziennik lekcyjny – register

Prezentacja – presentation

Egzamin ustny – oral exam

Egzamin pisemny – written exam

Zadanie domowe – homework

Projekt – project

Praca w grupach – group work

Praca w parach – pair work

Rozmowa – conversation

Dyskusja – discussion

Burza mózgów – brainstorm

School Objects:

Podręcznik szkolny – student book

Zeszyt ćwiczeń – workbook

Książka – book

Lektura szkolna – set book

Spis lektur – reading list

Słownik – dictionary

Zeszyt – notebook

Długopis – pen

Ołówek – pencil

Flamaster – marker pen

Kredki – colored pencils

Kredki świecowe – crayons

Farby plakatowe – poster colors / poster paints

Plastelina – plasticine / play dough

Pastele - dry pastels

Pędzel - brush

Blok rysunkowy - sketch pad

Ekierka - set square / triangle

Linijka - ruler

Kątomierz - protractor

Cyrkiel - compass

Gumka do mazania - rubber / eraser

Klej w sztyfcie - glue stick

Nożyczki - scissors

Piórnik - pencil case

Plecak - schoolbag

Ławka szkolna - desk

Tablica - blackboard

Biała tablica - whiteboard

Tablica interaktywna - interactive board

Marker do tablicy - whiteboard marker

Kosz na śmieci - dustbin

Gazetka ścienna - noticeboard / bulletin board

Dzień dobry, uczniowie! - Good morning, students!

Dzień dobry, Panie / Pani ... - Good morning, Mr./Mrs./Ms.

Siadajcie, proszę. - Sit down, please.

Otwórzcie podręczniki na stronie 46. - Please, open your books at page 46.

W pyszłym tygodniu odbędzie się kartkówka ze słówek. - Next week there will be a short vocabulary quiz.

Przepraszam, czy mogę wyjść do toalety? - Excuse me, can I go to the toilet?

Zadania 3, 4, 5 to zadanie domowe na przyszły tydzień. - Exercises 3, 4, 5 are homework for the next week.

Robert, czy mógłbyś wytrzeć tablicę? - Robert, could you clean the blackboard, please?

Dziś będziemy mówić o dzikich zwierzętach. - Today we will be talking about wild animals.

Czy mógłbyś to przeliterować? - Could you spell it out?

Przepraszam, gdzie jest stołówka? - Excuse me, where is the school canteen?

Przepraszam, jak dojdę do sali gimnastycznej? - Excuse me, how can I get to the gym?

O której kończy się lekcja? - What time does the lesson end?

Lekcja kończy się o godzinie 9:45. - The lesson ends at 9:45 AM.

Jakie przedmioty mamy dzisiaj? - Which classes do we have today?

Dzisiaj mamy matematykę, fizykę, informatykę, WF i geografię. - Today we have maths, physics, IT, PE, and geography.

O której godzinie odjeżdża autobus szkolny? - What time does the school bus leave?

Autobus szkolny odjeżdża o 15:00, zaraz po ostatniej lekcji. - The school bus leaves at 3:00 PM, right after the last lesson.

Dzisiejsze zajęcia są odwołane. - Today's classes have been canceled.

At the University:

Uniwersytet – University / college

Stopień naukowy – degree

Student – student

Wykładowca – lecturer

Wykład – lecture

Sala wykładowa – lecture room

Aula – lecture hall

Licencjat – bachelor's degree

Magister – master's degree

Dyplom / świadectwo – diploma

Zajęcia praktyczne – practicals

Praktykant – trainee

Praktykant w szkole – student teacher

Notatki – notes

Robić notatki – to take notes

Wygłaszać mowę – to give a speech

Przygotowywać prezentację – to prepare a presentation

Badanie – research / study

Przeprowadzać badanie – to conduct research

Wyniki badania – results of the study

Rektor uniwersytetu – college president / university president

Egzamin – exam

Sesja egzaminacyjna – exam session

Zaliczenie warunkowe – conditional promotion

Rok studiów - college level

Praca dyplomowa - thesis

Praca licencjacka - bachelor's thesis / BA thesis

Praca magisterska - master's thesis / MA thesis

Studia zaoczne - extramural studies

Studia dzienne - full-time studies

Kampus uniwersytecki - university campus

Dziekanat - deanery / dean's office

Doktorat - doctorate

Praca doktorancka - Ph.D. thesis

Absolwent - graduate

Absolutorium - graduation ceremony

Wydział - institute

Władze szkoły - school authorities

Rekrutacja - recruitment

Egzaminy wstępne - entrance exams

Wymiana studencka - student exchange program

Indeks - student book

Legtymacja studencka - student ID card

Kredyt studencki - student loan

Akademik - residence hall / dormitory

Europejski System Transferu Punktów (ECTS) - European Credit Transfer System (ECTS)

Przepraszam, gdzie znajduje się dziekanat? - Excuse me, where is the dean's office?

Dziekanat znajduje się na trzecim piętrze. - The dean's office is on the third floor.

Przepraszam, gdzie znajduje się aula C1? – Excuse me, where is the lecture hall C1?

Aula C1 jest na czwartym piętrze. – C1 is on the fourth floor.

Dzisiejsze wykłady są odwołane. – All of today's lectures have been cancelled.

Wyniki egzaminów zimowych są dostępne na stronie internetowej wydziału. – Winter exams results are available on the website of our institute.

Ten wykład jest nieobowiązkowy. – This lecture is non-mandatory.

Przepraszam, o której rozpoczyna się ostatni wykład? – Excuse me, what time does the last lecture start?

Ostati wykład zaczyna się o 17:00. – The last lecture starts at 5:00 PM.

Dzień dobry, chciałbym / chciałabym wypożyczyć książkę. – Hello, I would like to borrow a book.

Jaka książka Pana / Panią interesuje? – What book are you looking for?

Szukam ... – I am looking for ...

Proszę chwilkę poczekać. – Wait a moment, please.

Czy to jest książka, której Pan / Pani szuka? – Is that the book you are looking for?

Tak, to dokładnie ta. – Yes, exactly.

Czy mogę zobaczyć Pana / Pani legitymację studencką? – May I see your student ID card?

Oczywiście, proszę. – Of course, here you are.

Dzień dobry, chciałbym / chciałabym wziąć udział w wymianie studenckiej. – Hello, I would like to take part in a student exchange program.

Jaki kraj chciałby Pan / chciałaby Pan odwiedzić? – What country would you like to visit?

Jestem zainteresowany / zainteresowana studiowaniem w Polsce. – I am interested in studying in Poland.

Świetny wybór! Może Pan / Pani skorzystać z naszego nowego programu trwającego pół roku. – Great choice! You can take part in our new program that is a half year long.

Jakie uczelnie w Polsce mogę wybrać? – Which Polish universities can I choose?

Czy w Polsce będę musiał / musiała zdawać egzaminy? – Do I have to take all the exams in Poland?

Tak, wszystkie egzaminy będzie musiał Pan / musiała Pani napisać w Polsce. – Yes, you will have to take all the exams in Poland.

Czy mogą wziąć udział w programie na ostatnim roku studiów? – Can I take part in the exchange program on the last year of my studies?

Niestety, nie może Pan / Pani wziąć udziału w wymianie na ostatnim roku. – I'm sorry, you can't take part in the exchange on the last year.

Dlaczego? – Why?

Ponieważ musi Pan / Pani przeprowadzić badanie i napisać pracę tutaj. – Because you have to conduct the study and write your thesis here.

Professions and Jobs

Professions:

Zawód – profession

Lekarz – doctor

Nauczyciel – teacher

Biznesmen – businessman

Bizneswoman – businesswoman

Prawnik – lawyer

Pielęgniarka – nurse

Sprzedawca – shop assistant

Księgowy / księgowa – accountant

Strażak – firefighter

Żołnież – soldier

Policjant – policeman

Policjantka – policewoman

Szef kuchni – chef

Kucharz – cook

Kelner - waiter

Kelnerka - waitress

Pilot - pilot

Naukowiec - scientist

Listonosz - postman

Tłumacz - translator

Mechanik - mechanic

Hydraulik - plumber

Malarz - painter

Aktor - actor

Aktorka - actress

Kierowca - driver

Sprzątacz / sprzątaczka - cleaner

Dentysta - dentist

Rolnik - farmer

Inżynier - engineer

Kierownik / menedżer - manager

Fotograf - photographer

Muzyk - musician

Sekretarz / sekretarka - secretary

Kierowca taksówki - taxi driver

Pisarz - writer

Opiekun / opiekunka - babysitter

Piekarz - baker

Fryzjer - hairdresser

Filmowiec - filmmaker

Dziennikarz - journalist

Ksiądz – priest

Weterynarz – vet

Psycholog – psychologist

Badacz – researcher

At a Workplace:

Miejsce pracy – workplace

Biuro – office

Praca – job

Fabryka – factory

Firma – company

Siedziba firmy – headquarters

Korporacja – corporation

Pracownik – employee

Pracodawca – employer

Szef / szefowa – boss

Koledzy z pracy – colleagues / co-workers

Praca zdalna – remote working

Pracownik fizyczny – blue-collar worker

Pracować – work

Wypłata – salary

Zarobki – earnings / wages

Brutto – gross

Netto – post-tax

Podatek – tax

Awans – promotion

Dostać awans – to get a promotion

Dostać pracę - to get a job

Być zwolnionym - to be dismissed

Być zwolnionym natychmiastowo - to be fired

Zredukować personel - to make people redundant

Podwyżka - pay rise

Dostać podwyżkę - to get a pay rise

Praca na cały etat - full-time job

Praca na pół etatu - part-time job

Praca dodatkowa - side job

Praca zmianowa - shift job

Nocna zmiana / nocka - night shift

Rozmowa o pracę - job interview

Umowa o pracę - job agreement

Życiorys (CV) - curriculum vitae (CV)

Podanie o pracę - job application form

Stanowisko - position

Kwalifikacje - qualifications

Wymagania - requirements

Umiejętności - skills

Wykształcenie - education

Doświadczenie zawodowe - job experience

Dział kadr - personnel department / HR

Dział obsługi klienta - customer service department

Dział wsparcia technicznego - help desk

Wyjazd służbowy - business trip

Notatka służbowa - memo

Spotkanie - meeting

Urlop - leave

Urlop macierzyński - maternity leave

Urlop zdrowotny - sick leave

Urlop bezpłatny - unpaid leave

Płatny urlop wypoczynkowy - paid vacation leave

Przepraszam, gdzie jest dział kadr? - Excuse me, where is the personnel department?

Proszę przesłać CV oraz podanie o pracę. - Please, send your CV and a job application form.

Pracuję na pół etatu. - I have a part-time job.

Gdzie pracujesz? - Where do you work?

Pracuję w dużej firmie. - I work in a big company.

Co robisz zawodowo? - What do you do professionally?

Jestem prawnikiem. - I am a lawyer.

Jestem nauczycielem / nauczycielką. Pracuję w szkole średniej. - I am a teacher. I work at a high school.

Gdzie znajduje się firma w której pracujesz? - Where is the company you work at located?

Firma znajduje się w Warszawie. - The company headquarters is located in Warsaw.

Pracuję w systemie zmianowym. - I have a shift job.

O której godzinie kończysz pracę? - What time do you finish your work?

Dziś kończę o 17:00. - Today I'm finishing at 5:00 PM.

Dziś idę na nockę. - Today I'm working a night shift.

Jakie wykształcenie Pan / Pani posiada? - What educational background do you have?

Ukończyłem / ukończyłam uniwersytet. - I graduated / graduated university.

Jakie umiejętności Pan / Pani posiada? - What skills do you have?

Czy posiada Pan / Pani prawo jazdy? - Do you have a driving license?

Tak, posiadam prawo jazdy. - Yes, I have a driving license.

Jakie jest Pana / Pani doświadczenie zawodowe? - What is your job experience?

Pracowałem dla firmy ... od 2011 roku. - I worked for the company... since 2011.

Prosimy skontaktować się z naszym działem wsparcia technicznego. - Please, contact our help desk.

Proszę przesłać podanie o pracę do działu kadr. - Please, send your application form to the personnel department.

Dostałem / dostałam awans! - I got a promotion.

Czy mogę wziąć dzień wolnego? - Can I take a day off?

Jestem chory / chora. Jutro nie mogę przyjść do pracy. - I am sick. I can't go to work tomorrow.

Expressing Opinion

Lubić - like

Bardzo - very

Dobry- good

Zły- bad

Piękny - beautiful

Okropny - terrible

Obrzydliwy - horrible

Fantastyczny - awesome

Świetny - great

Fajny - fun / cool / super (informal)

Być zainteresowanym - to be interested in something

Bardzo lubić coś - to be keen on something

Szaleć na punkcie czegoś - to be crazy about something

Nie lubić - dislike

Nienawidzić - hate

Podobać się / lubić - to enjoy

Nie móc czegoś znieść – cannot stand something

Mieć mieszane uczucia – to have mixed feelings

Mieć czegoś dość – to be sick of something

Uwielbiać coś – to love something

Woleć / preferować – to prefer

Moim zdaniem... – In my opinion...

Myślę że / Uważam że... – I think that...

Powiedziałbym / Powiedziałabym że... – I would say that...

Według mnie... – To my mind

Uważam kogoś za ... – I consider somebody to be

Jestem przekonany / przekonana że... – I'm convinced that...

Dobry pomysł – a good idea

Zły pomysł – a bad idea

Wolałbym / wolałabym – I would rather

Wolelibyśmy – we would rather

Asking for Opinion

Co myślisz o...? – What do you think about...?

Lubisz..? – Do you like...?

Co sądzisz o...? – What do you think about...?

Czy lubi Pan / czy lubi Pani ...? – Do you like...? (formal)

Czy lubią Państwo..? – Do you like...? (formal plural)

Co Pan sądzi o... / Co Pani sądzi o...? – What do you think about...? (formal)

Co Państwo sądzą o.../ Co Państwo myślą o..? – What do you think about...? (formal plural)

Co o tym myślisz? – What do you think about that?

Myślę że to bardzo dobry pomysł. – I think it's a very good idea.

Lubisz owoce? – Do you like fruit?

Oczywiście, kocham owoce! – Of course, I love fruit!

Lubisz pierogi? – Do you like pierogi?

Tak, pierogi są smaczne. – Yes, pierogi are really tasty.

Lubisz czarną kawę? – Do you like black coffee?

Nienawidzę czarnej kawy. – I hate black coffee.

Mam dosyć jego gadania. – I am sick of his talking.

Podobał ci się film? – Did you enjoy the film?

Nie wiem. Mam mieszane uczucia. – I don't know. I have mixed feelings.

Bardzo lubię piłkę nożną. – I am really keen on football.

Co Pan sądzi o nowym komputerze w pańskim biurze? – What do you think of the new computer in your office?

Moim zdaniem jest całkiem dobry. – It is very good, in my opinion.

Szaleję na punkcie muzyki rockowej! – I am crazy about rock music!

Nie mogę znieść tej okropnej pogody. – I cannot stand this terrible weather.

Co myślisz o mojej nowej sukience? – What do you think of my new dress?

Jest piękna! Wyglądasz w niej bardzo bobrze. – It's beautiful! You look really pretty in it.

Jestem przekonany / przekonana, że on się spóźni. – I am convinced that he will be late.

Co Państwo sądzą o tym projekcie? – What do you think about the project?

Lubisz jeździć na rowerze? – Do you like riding a bike?

Wolę bieganie niż jazdę na rowerze. – I prefer jogging to riding a bike.

Podobają ci się moje nowe trampki? – Do you like my new sneakers?

Wow, wyglądają fantastycznie! – Wow, they look awesome.

Wolałbym pójść na spacer. – I would rather go for a walk.

Uważam go za świetnego pracownika. – I consider him to be a very good employee.

Family and Relationships

Family Members

Członkowie rodziny - family members

Rodzina - family

Bliska rodzina - nuclear family

Rodzice - parents

Rodzeństwo - siblings

Dzieci - children

Syn - son

Córka - daughter

Matka - mother (mama - mom)

Ojciec - father (tata - dad)

Ojczym - stepfather

Macocha - stepmother

Brat - brother

Brat przyrodni - stepbrother

Siostra - sister

Siostra przybrana – stepsister

Dziadkowie – grandparents

Babcia – grandmother / grandma

Dziadek – granddad / grandpa

Wnuk – grandson

Wnuczka – granddaughter

Ciocia – aunt

Wujek– uncle

Bratanek / siostrzeniec – nephew

Bratanica / siostrzenica – niece

Kuzyn / kuzynka – cousin

Teść – father-in-law

Teściowa – mother-in-law

Szwagier – brother-in-law

Szwagierka – sister-in-law

Relationships

Pokrewieństwo / relacja – relationship

W związku – in a relationship

Wyśjć za kogoś – to marry somebody

Żonaty (masculine) – zamężna (feminine) – married

Wziąć ślub – to get married

Ślub – wedding

Małżonkowie / małżeństwo – married couple

Mąż – husband

Żona – wife

Pan młody – groom

Panna młoda - bride

Państwo młodzi - bridal couple

Zaręczyć się - to get engaged

Oświadczyć się komuś - to propose to somebody

Zaręczyny - engagement

Pierścionek zaręczynowy - engagement ring

Narzeczony - fiancé

Narzeczona - **fiancée**

Chłopak - boyfriend

Dziewczyna - girlfriend

Chodzić z kimś - to go out with somebody

Randka - date

Randkować - to date

Zerwać z kimś - to break up with somebody

Rozwieść się - to get divorced / to get a divorce

Rozwiedziony / rozwiedziona - divorced

W stanie wolnym / singiel (m.) / singielka (f.) - single

Bezdzietny / bezdzietna - childless

Mieć dzieci - to have children

W ciąży - pregnant

Być w ciąży - to be pregnant

Cześć, to jest mój nowy chłopak, Tomek. - Hi, this is my new boyfriend, Tomek.

Jesteś żonaty / zamężna? - Are you married?

Nie, jestem wolny / wolna. - No, I am single.

Tak, wzięłam ślub / wziąłem ślub rok temu. - Yes, I got married last year.

Masz dzieci? – Do you have children?

Mam syna i córkę. – I have a son and a daughter.

Jak ma na imię twój brat? – What is your brother's name?

Mój brat ma na imię Karol. – My brother's name is Karol.

Ile lat mają twoi rodzice? – How old are your parents?

Moja mama ma 35 lat, a mój tata 37 lat. – My mom is 35, and my dad is 37.

Jesteś zaręczony / zaręczona? – Are you engaged?

Tak. Oświadczyłem się mojej dziewczynie dwa tygodnie temu. – Yes. I proposed to my girlfriend two weeks ago.

Tak. Mój chłopak oświadczył mi się dwa tygodnie temu. – Yes. My boyfriend proposed to me two weeks ago.

Masz chłopaka? – Do you have a boyfriend?

Nie, jestem wolna. – No, I am single.

Masz dziewczynę? – Do you have a girlfriend?

Tak, właśnie rozmawia przez telefon. – Yes, she is on the phone at the moment.

Wyjdziesz za mnie? – Will you marry me?

To jest mój syn Marcin. – This is my son Marcin.

Miło mi cię poznać. – Nice to meet you.

Gdzie mieszkają twoi rodzice? – Where do your parents live?

Moi rodzice mieszkają w Polsce, ale ja mieszkam w Niemczech. – My parents live in Poland, but I live in Germany.

Kiedy wyprowadziłeś / wyprowadziłaś się z domu? – When did you move out of your parents' house?

Wyprowadziłem / wyprowadziłam się od rodziców dwa lata temu. – I moved out of my parents' house two years ago.

At Home

Salon / pokój dzienny - living room

Kuchnia - kitchen

Łazienka - bathroom

Sypialnia - bedroom

Strych - attic

Garaż - garage

Dach - roof

Łazienka dla gości - guest bathroom

Ogród - garden

Jadalnia - dining room

Appliances:

Pralka - washing machine

Zmywarka - dishwasher

Mikrofalówka - microwave

Piekarnik - oven

Zlew - sink

Suszarka - hairdryer

Telewizor - TV

Żelazko - iron

Robot kuchenny - food processor

Odkurzacz - vacuum cleaner

Mop - mop

Sokowirówka - juicer

Mikser / blender - blender

Lodówka – fridge

Zamrażarka – freezer

Ładowarka do telefonu – phone charger

In the Kitchen:

Garnek – pot

Patelnia – frying pan

Talerz – plate

Szklanka – glass

Widelec – fork

Nóż – knife

Łyżka – spoon

Łyżeczka – teaspoon

Lada kuchenna – kitchen counter

Kran – tap

Ekspres do kawy – coffee machine

Szafka kuchenna – cupboard

Miska – bowl

Kubek – mug

Filiżanka – tea cup / coffee cup

Check out another book by Simple Language Learning

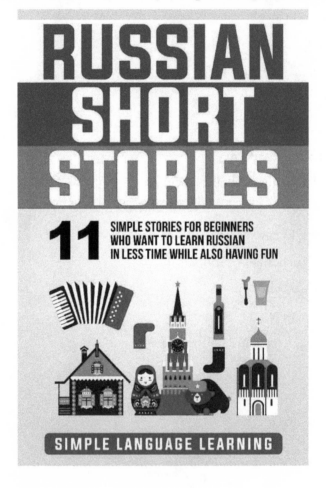